Praise for ENCOUNTERS:
A Lifetime Spent Crossing Cultural Frontiers

"What a story, told with verve, insight, and a sense of history! This account of growing up in the Philippines, internment during World War II, and a subsequent Foreign Service career in Asia and the Middle East against a background of international turbulence is brilliant testimony to all that is best in the American spirit. I suspect it of being a classic."

—Mark Peattie, Stanford University research scholar,
author of *Nan'Yo: The Rise and Fall of the Japanese
in Micronesia, 1885–1945*

"Nancy Forster has written a lucid, graceful, perceptive book that shows a deft grasp of the nuances of Japan and Asia. In particular, her book is a genuine tribute, and deservedly so, to her husband Cliff, who was interned as a prisoner of the Japanese during World War II yet rose above that searing experience to become a lifelong student of Japanese culture. Not everyone in our generation achieved such equilibrium, but it enabled Cliff to serve America and the cause of transpacific peace with dedication and skill."

—Richard Halloran, author of *Japan: Images and Realities,*
former foreign correspondent for the *New York Times*
and *Washington Post*

"Cliff and Nancy Forster, in their lifelong dedication to the U.S. Foreign Service, exemplified the best in American virtues: personal warmth, integrity, open-mindedness, and decency. They are the sterling personification of American 'can-do' spirit and idealism."

—Sue Yung Li, landscape architect and documentary filmmaker

"What a wonderful surprise to learn my wise and kind cousin, Cliff, was also a storyteller of remarkable talents. These fascinating accounts—of his youth in the Philippines and career in the Foreign Service—reflect a curiosity, insight and compassion that combine to produce a fascinating and illuminating read."

—Dan Rosenheim, vice president and news director
KPIX-TV San Francisco

"Cliff Forster's life and mine intersected many times over the last forty years. We shared interests and assignments in Burma, Japan, and Korea. Cliff was always a 'power for good' in his work, and this delightful memoir, written by his talented widow, is a clear reflection of what he did, and why he did what he did. America's relations with Asia benefited greatly from Cliff Forster's work, and his life is a clear argument for reconstituting an independent and well-endowed USIA."

—Donald Gregg, Chairman of the Korea Society,
former U.S. ambassador to Korea

"The reader will profit greatly from reading the memoirs of a true veteran. I appreciated the manner in which the author interwove her comments with Cliff Forster's account.

—Robert Scalapino, founder and former director,
Institute of East Asian Studies, University of California Berkeley

"This is one of the most fascinating and unusual memoirs I have ever read. Nancy Forster skillfully weaves her own insights with judicious selections from her late husband's writing, creating a seamlessly fluent and spellbinding narrative of an extraordinary life—a narrative that touches on seminal events of the twentieth century. A must read."

—Doug Merwin, publisher of MerwinAsia

ENCOUNTERS

A Lifetime Spent Crossing Cultural Frontiers

NANCY KEENEY FORSTER

Wind Shadow Press
Tiburon, California

Wind Shadow Press
Tiburon, California
www.windshadowpress.com

Library of Congress Control Number: 2009935951

Forster, Nancy Keeney

Encounters: a lifetime spent crossing cultural frontiers /Nancy Keeney Forster

ISBN-10: 0-615-31889-4
ISBN-13: 978-0-615-31889-9

CONTENTS

To Cliff, whose curiosity and zest for life transformed challenges into adventures...

And to all the friends and family members who cheerfully shared the journey...

And to the USIS colleagues at home and abroad who shared the public diplomacy mission...

And to those budding adventurers who will carry international dialogue forward in the twenty-first century.

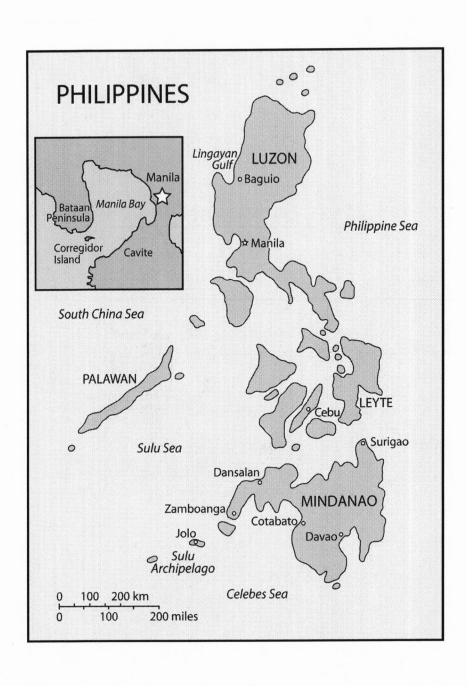

PHILIPPINES

Manila

Bataan
Peninsula

Manila Bay

Corregidor
Island

Cavite

*Lingayan
Gulf*

LUZON

○ Baguio

Philippine Sea

☆ Manila

South China Sea

PALAWAN

○

LEYTE

○ Cebu

Sulu Sea

○ Surigao

Dansalan ○

Zamboanga ○

MINDANAO

Cotabato ○

Davao ○

Jolo ○

*Sulu
Archipelago*

Celebes Sea

0	100	200 km
0	100	200 miles

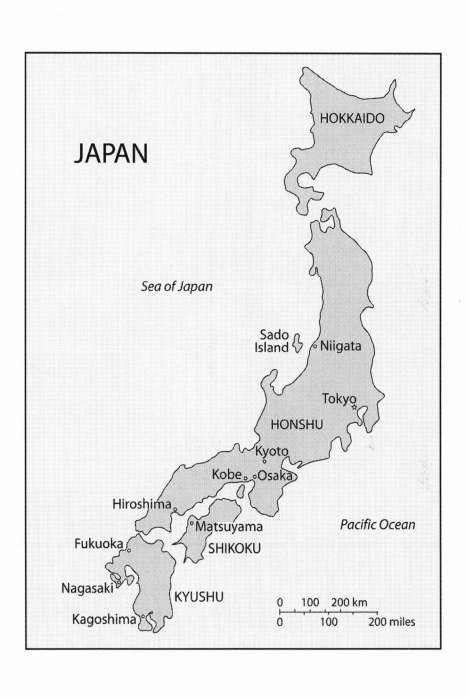

JAPAN

HOKKAIDO

Sea of Japan

Sado
Island ○ Niigata

Tokyo

HONSHU

Kyoto
Kobe ○ ○ Osaka

Hiroshima

○ Matsuyama

Pacific Ocean

Fukuoka

SHIKOKU

Nagasaki

KYUSHU

Kagoshima

| 0 | 100 | 200 km |
| 0 | 100 | 200 miles |

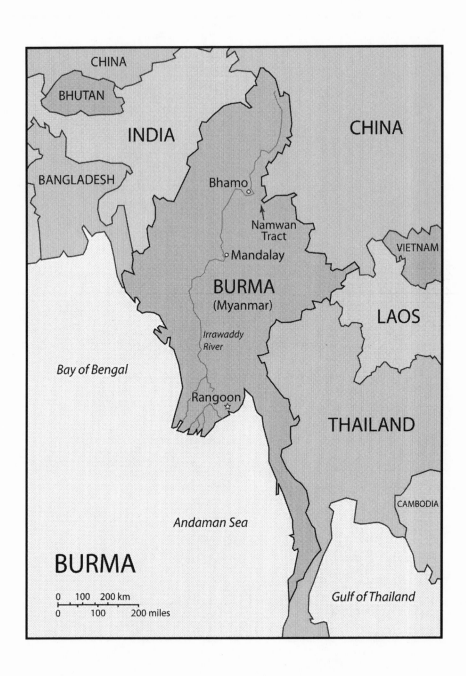

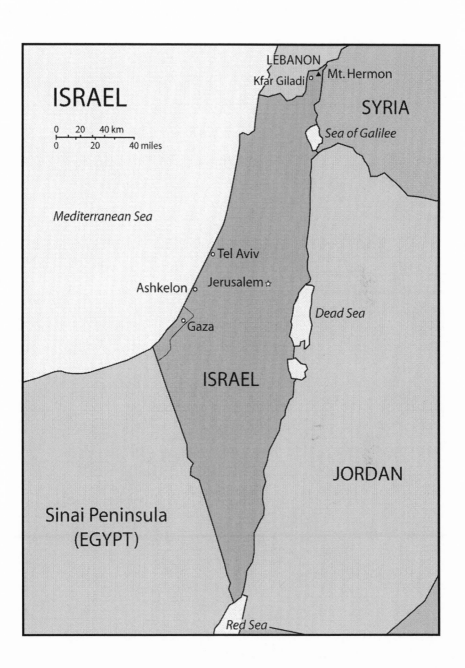

INTRODUCTION

IT TOOK ME TWO YEARS after the sudden death of my husband in September of 2006 to muster sufficient energy to inspect his collected papers. I knew that the Japanese tea chest in the hallway was full of manila envelopes stuffed with memorabilia, carefully labeled in his distinctive script "to be sorted later," and the two file drawers in the guest bedroom contained documents and draft chapters of a book about the Japanese general who had been responsible for Clifton Forster becoming a prisoner of war at age seventeen. I believed that prior to handing the latter over to a university library to be archived for scholarly research, I owed it to Cliff to read what he had collected and written.

Cliff was an internationalist by birth and projected that heritage into a lifetime of crossing cultural frontiers, nurturing an inborn sense of political and historic curiosity and following a career path that aimed to solve international differences by dialogue rather than by war. It was my gift and privilege to join him on that journey as a twenty-year-old bride in 1949, and to accompany him through the rest of his fascinating and productive life.

Born an American citizen in Manila in 1924, he grew up with friends of many nationalities, at a time and place where existing and impending conflicts were more than household conversations. Home-leave travels to Europe and China brought global unrest into even starker relief. Cliff was in his senior year of high school when the Japanese invaded and conquered the Philippines and he and his friends and family were interned.

After the war, Cliff chose to major in international relations at Stanford University. He then applied to the Department of State to work with a newly established arm of diplomacy, the United States Information Service. It was the perfect match for his convictions, and he brought enthusiasm and ready-made skills to his new job.

We returned to the land of his birth for his first tour with USIS, and went on to serve in countries as varied as Burma and Israel. Ironically, given the history of his youth, the majority of Cliff's Foreign Service years were spent in Japan. A year at Yale enrolled in Japanese language and area studies gave him additional tools to operate in Japan as it was pulling out of the ashes of war and defeat.

Retiring from the Agency to accompany me to Hawaii when I was offered a job there in 1983 ("You followed me around the world all these years and now I will gladly follow you to Honolulu"), he continued to promote learning about international affairs by working with local organizations dedicated to Asian and Pacific area scholarship and interaction, and continued to work on the book that would examine the nuances and contradictions of the life and demise of the man who conquered the Philippines in 1942, General Masaharu Homma. Cliff had secured original documents from the military trial and execution of the general; he had met and interviewed Homma's defense counsel in Baltimore and the general's daughter in Japan. Some chapters had been drafted, but the manuscript was incomplete at the time of Cliff's death.

When I went into those files and the tea chest envelopes, I found more than I had anticipated. Much of the Homma draft I had not read. A letter Cliff had written his sister on release from prison camp (which she carried with her from home to home until her death at age ninety-two) I had never seen before. I pored back over the transcript from a two-day oral interview by a Foreign Service colleague for the diplomatic archives in the Library of Congress, in which Cliff summarized his experiences as an officer in the field of public diplomacy, and I flipped through the pages of his family albums. I reread the four articles he published in the *Foreign Service Journal,* and the fourteen-page letter he wrote in 1995, at the time of the death of the girl who had lived next door during his schooldays, to her widower, describing their Manila childhood.

As I looked through these assorted documents and recalled other unwritten stories told by Cliff, as well as the adventures we had shared, I found echoes and sequels in the headlines and background stories of today's news and decided this material was too rich to be tucked away in archives. Cliff's stories and insights needed to be published. I have worked with the documents he saved, using excerpts and editing for clarity, and recounted some of those tales he told and adventures we shared to provide this record of a man with a mission and a zest for life.

The chapters of this book describe history lived, encounters enjoyed, some dreams fulfilled—and others still pending. It was a fascinating journey the first time; as I relived it while compiling this account, I gained deeper understanding and appreciation of my husband's life, my own life, and the multifaceted world we all inhabit.

1

ENCOUNTER ON SADO ISLAND

OUR FAMILY LIVED IN TOKYO from 1964 to 1970, and again from 1977 to 1981. Our second time in Tokyo, Cliff was Minister-Counselor for Public Affairs at the U.S. Embassy. Part of his job was to oversee American Cultural Centers in various cities and he frequently traveled to meet with government, media, and academic officials in prefectural outposts. I was with him on one of these trips in the early spring of 1978, to cities along the coast of the Sea of Japan which faced the Korean Peninsula. We scheduled a day for ourselves at the close of business, to visit an isolated island where we had not yet been and which could be reached by a ninety-minute ferry ride.

A few weeks earlier, Cliff had been injured in a traffic accident while attending a conference in the Philippines; he spent two weeks in a Manila hospital bed with a view of the site where he had been interned by the Japanese as a civilian prisoner of war. Our side trip to Sado was in part a celebration of his survival and return to good health. Cliff's account of that day and his encounter with the man who had turned his teenage world upside down was to be the first chapter of his book about General Homma. He wrote:

The spring snow was still on the mountains of Sado Island as we crossed the narrow strait from the port city of Niigata. A fleet of fishing vessels passed to starboard heading for the open sea, rugged wooden ships with their equally rugged crews busily working with their fishing nets. The main port on the island was like so many other small Japanese fishing ports with its strong smell of fish, the busy food stalls and shops along the waterfront, the colorful Japanese signs everywhere, and the recorded music blasting out from small restaurants and souvenir shops catering to the tourists who were being herded onto tour buses by their leaders who carried small yellow pennants. Female bus attendants in tight blue uniforms sang out destinations and departure times in high-pitched voices.

Sado was not a place visited very often in earlier times. Separated from the crowded eastern coastal plain by a mountainous region known as the *yukiguni,* or "snow country," it was a place apart from the mainstream. The island was buffeted by the frigid Siberian winds and its mountains and coastal areas were covered with snow during the long winter. Historically, it had been a place of exile for dissidents, the most famous being the nationalistic Buddhist priest Nichiren who antagonized the ruling Kamakura Shogunate in the thirteenth century with his political and religious reforms. Nancy and I had come to Sado to visit the site of his exile.

Since the buses were jammed with tourists and our time was limited, we decided to hire a taxi to cross the island. Both the taxi and the driver had seen their best years and we found ourselves traveling at great speed over narrow, twisting roads sending up clouds of dust. I was about to suggest that we slow down to have a better look at the scenery when he did this of his own accord. We were approaching a small town with picturesque thatched-roof houses surrounded by a mosaic of rice fields. School children returning home with their knapsacks loaded with books waved to us from the side of the road with shouts of "Gaijin!" (foreigner). They had obviously seen few of us in these parts.

In 1978, Cliff encountered a bronze likeness of his wartime captor General Masaharu Homma at a small village temple on Sado Island.

As we turned a corner in the road, the driver announced that we had come to an important town, the birthplace of a Japanese general who had fought the Americans in the Philippines during World War II. I leaned forward and inquired: "Who was this general?" He said he did not know for sure but he had heard that he defeated a famous American general who had been in Japan after the war.

"Was the American general Douglas MacArthur?" I asked.

He nodded vigorously, obviously relieved that the American general had been identified. The driver then inquired if I would like to visit a memorial to the Japanese general. I said I would and we continued down the road, stopping by a small Buddhist temple adjacent to a park. "The general is over there near the woods," he announced, pointing in the direction of a stone column with a bronze bust of a military figure.

The park was a peaceful place with tree-lined lanes on either side and a bamboo grove which stood close to the temple. Beyond the park were the rice fields and the Sado mountains, now cloud-covered in the late afternoon. Except for two or three school children and a hunched-over older woman sweeping leaves, the place was deserted.

The driver led us over to the memorial. As we approached it, followed by the curious children, I stopped in disbelief. The driver looked at me anxiously and Nancy could see that I was taken aback.

The bust was too lifelike and brought back too many memories of a time many of us had tried to forget. They were unpleasant memories for the most part and the encounter with our adversary on this distant island in the Japan Sea was entirely unexpected. I moved slowly towards the bust. There was the same large head I remembered from countless photographs, the strong features, thick eyebrows and the piercing eyes. An inscription carried only his name—Masaharu Homma—and the dates of his birth and death. Nothing more. No reference was made to his military campaigns in China and the Philippines or to his execution by an American military tribunal for war crimes.

I stood for several minutes before the memorial to the Japanese general who had planned and executed the invasion strategy in the Philippines which led to America's worst military defeat, followed by the surrender of American and Philippine forces on Bataan and Corregidor during the first six months of the war. It was a demoralizing defeat, a defeat which forged General Douglas MacArthur's resolve to return from Australia to liberate the Philippines in 1944.

I wondered how the memorial had been placed there, and when. Certainly it was not there during MacArthur's occupation of Japan as Supreme Allied Commander, since this would have been a violation of his policy forbidding any memorials to World War II Japanese military leaders. Having defeated MacArthur's forces, Homma would have been particularly taboo. Presumably, some interested party had erected the memorial in the General's hometown after the occupation.

A temple bell rang out. It was time to move on, to reach the west coast of Sado and return to the ferry that would take us back to Niigata. Before leaving, I turned back for a last look at the General. He had been portrayed well in bronze and I wondered what significance, if any, this memorial had for the local residents now, particularly those school children we had seen along the road or in the park. It apparently did not have too much significance for our driver who could not even remember Homma's name.

As we walked back to the car, the driver spoke up. He asked how I knew about General Homma and was curious about my interest in the memorial. I paused for a moment and then decided to give him a straight answer. "My parents knew him well, though we never encountered him face to face." I replied. "We were his prisoners in the Philippines." I did not mention that many Americans referred to Homma as "the butcher of Bataan" for the atrocities committed by his troops during the "Death March" following the surrender of our forces.

There was an embarrassed silence as the driver shook his head. He said he was very sorry about this and hoped I had not suffered too much. I said it had been a long time ago and that we had all suffered—Americans and Japanese alike—and survived to become good friends after the war.

The sun was beginning to set in the Japan Sea beyond the Sado mountains when we boarded the ferry for the return to

Niigata. Music was still blaring from the loudspeakers along the waterfront and Japanese tourists crowded the gangplank, toting their collection of souvenirs. The ship's loudspeaker blasted out a scratchy rendition of "Auld Lang Syne." Streamers were passed out to passengers and I tossed several to our taxi driver who was still standing on the pier below. He managed to catch two or three and followed the ship out to the end of the pier, holding onto the streamers while I held the other end—until they snapped in the wind. I waved to him as the vessel headed through the outer breakwater for the choppy open sea.

I saw how moved Cliff was by his meeting with the likeness of the general responsible for his internment. Encounters of this sort—echoes from the past—were very much a part of our fifty-seven-year marriage, and I always felt enlightened by the memories and reflections they inspired in Cliff. Our side trip to Sado in particular motivated him to learn more about General Homma as a fellow human being, and to reflect more deeply on the significance of circumstance and flow of history as it impacted his own life.

2

MADE IN ASIA

C HARLES FORSTER, accompanied by his pregnant wife Gladys and twelve-year-old daughter Gerry, first sailed into Manila Bay in 1923. Charles had been appointed Manager of the American colony's Red Cross chapter, an assignment he would embrace for the next eighteen years, until the Japanese Imperial Army occupied the Philippines and imprisoned "enemy aliens."

The Forster's son Clifton was born in March of 1924. At an early age, Cliff began his world travels. Before he was six weeks old, the family was on the winding road to Baguio, the hot-season capitol for those who worked for and with the Philippine Government. Throughout his childhood and youth, this mountain town had a special appeal for Cliff. He loved the old Pines Hotel with its giant fireplace, and the cottages where the family often stayed on the grounds of the Baguio Country Club. The marketplace swirled with activity as different mountain tribes came into town on the weekend. Walks in the woods and fireworks on July 4th were fond memories, and the mountain air was a welcome respite from the intense heat of Manila's tropical—and in those days un-air-conditioned—summer.

Identified by his first passport photo,
Cliff traveled with his parents to China and Japan in 1926.

At home in Manila, Cliff loved to visit his father's office, located on the Pasig River next to the American Governor General's residence at Malacañan Palace. He often sat on a stone embankment to watch the river barges go by. He soon was on the water himself, traveling with his parents on a Red Cross mission—taking teams of doctors, nurses, and dentists aboard a lighthouse tender, the M.S. *Bustamante*, to bring health services from Luzon to the outlying islands.

The first of many ocean voyages for the growing boy took place in 1926, when the family traveled from Manila to China and Japan, where Charles Forster attended an International Red Cross Conference in Tokyo. This was the first international conference of any kind for the newly enthroned Emperor Hirohito, who invited all the delegates and their wives to his Imperial Palace for tea on October 24th.

Decades later, when we were living in Japan and spent weekends at a beach cottage on the Miura Peninsula south of Tokyo, Cliff passed many winter afternoons organizing prewar Forster family photos. On each page he wrote lengthy narratives as he pasted pictures into a series of albums. Recalling the circumstances of that 1926 journey and recalling the impressions of the two-and-a-half-year-old, he wrote:

> The major adventure for me was exploring the Imperial Hotel in Tokyo which had been designed by Frank Lloyd Wright. It was love at first sight—a child's paradise with its floating balconies, patios, and hidden recesses.
>
> 1926 was the year our family discovered both Japan and China. En route to the International Red Cross Conference in Tokyo Father decided to establish contact with Red Cross Societies in China as well, moving from Hong Kong to Shanghai and Peking. China then was strife-ridden with warlords competing for power. A new revolutionary leader, Chiang Kai-shek, was preparing to march north to challenge the Peking warlord, Chang Tso-lin. Japan was reinforcing its position in Manchuria. In Hong Kong and Shanghai it was business as usual with the British, French, and Americans very much in evidence in Shanghai's International Settlement and French Concession. However, time was running out for all of them with the approach of the decades of the thirties and forties.
>
> The Peak Tramway and the rickshaws were a child's delight, and for some time my great ambition was to be either a Peak Tramway motorman or a rickshaw driver. Hong Kong harbor with all its ships had a very special aura and during the years since I have always been excited when approaching the Crown Colony. The Star Ferries and Peak Tramway are as much of a thrill to me today (1968) as they were over forty years ago.

Another forty years later, I delighted in revisiting the black-and-white photographs of the little boy who would become my husband. In one photo, he's in his mother's lap, riding a rickshaw in Hong Kong. In another, his father holds him high for a better view from the ship that is taking them north. I was struck by how fortunate Cliff was to be exposed to different cultures at so young an age, and how well these experiences served him throughout his life.

From Hong Kong north along the China coast to Tientsin via Shanghai aboard the British steamer *Lengtien,* the Forsters were the only passengers on board and I had the run of the ship. The coastal steamers were still protected from China's pirates with bars across the portholes. In Peking, Chang Tso-lin was still very much in control of the city. It was very windy and dusty while we were in North China that year and we had quite a problem with respiratory ailments.

Beihai Park or "Goat Hill" with its lovely Tibetan-like pagoda was another favorite place. Photos show Mother and Father before the Dragon Screen which made such a profound impression on me in 1926 and again in 1928 that I never forgot it. Fifty years later, visiting China for the first time as an adult, I insisted on seeing the screen again. This time it seemed smaller to me.

The walls around Peking were still standing then and were extensive. Most are gone now. Camels were very much in evidence within the city and near the Great Wall. Mother posed for a picture with young soldiers of Chang Tso-lin's warlord army. In a matter of months the new Nationalist forces under Chiang Kai-shek would be marching north and Chang Tso-lin would be the victim of an assassination plot by young Japanese officers while he was riding the Manchurian Railway.

In 1928, the Forsters returned to North China and remained for several weeks in Beijing, where Cliff, age four, was put in the care of a Chinese amah. Cliff later entertained his own children with tales of that childhood summer. The amah's prize possession was a wristwatch, which she took off for Cliff to examine. It slipped out of his hand into an open sewer and he recalled being held by his ankles, upside down, by that small lady who was determined that her ward would extract her treasure from the sewer. He recovered it. Later that day, she encouraged him to play dragon on the roof of their apartment building, sniffing the ground as he slithered along. The roof was paved with small pebbles and Cliff managed to get several lodged in his nose. He wondered—had she planned this as punishment? He wrote in the album, next to a photo of the amah: "She was an amazing character whose accounts of live dragons roaming the Peking streets resulted in some sleepless nights. I recall that she had very small feet. Mother told me that they had been bound at an early age."

When the Forsters left Beijing, the amah wept farewell tears and gave Cliff a small box containing a gift—a pair of her own tiny embroidered slippers. Cliff's sister Gerry, then age sixteen and an adventurous and independent-minded young woman, carried a souvenir of her own which she kept hidden inside her coat. Unbeknown to her family, she smuggled a live mongoose back to Manila to add to a growing home menagerie.

Cliff wrote in the album, "The political situation began to deteriorate very fast in 1928 with the emergence of Nationalist Chinese forces in the south and the sudden demise of Chang Tso-lin in Manchuria, where a new military command—the Kwangtung of the Japanese Imperial Army—was on the move."

In hindsight, Cliff recognized the significance of the tensions and conflicts leading to the massive war that would engulf all of East Asia in the coming decades. However, as a child growing up in one of Asia's comfortable Western enclaves, his present was delightful and the future looked bright.

3

A PHILIPPINE CHILDHOOD

MANILA WAS A MAGICAL PLACE for an American child during the colonial days. Amahs cared lovingly for the children and the housework was done by a cheerful team of houseboy, cook, and *lavandera.* This city, with its elegant Spanish architectural legacy (from four hundred years of Spanish governance) and American-designed public parks and broad avenues (following the Spanish American War in 1898 when the colony was ceded to the U.S.), was known as "the Pearl of the Orient." Its bay was the setting for year-round swimming, boating, and sunset strolls along the waterfront. School started early in the day but was dismissed by one-thirty, leaving long afternoons for childhood diversions.

Cliff shared many of those diversions with his next-door neighbor, Barbara Coleman. After the war, Cliff introduced her to his Stanford buddy, Dick Moore. Barbara and Dick were married at the University chapel in December of 1948, and the four of us became close friends that winter and spring before Cliff and I married and headed overseas to our first Foreign Service post. Our lives intersected frequently thereafter— on our early home leaves, during Dick's later assignment to Tokyo when he too became a USIS officer, and during our retirement years. Dick and

I, brought up in much less colorful environments, listened with awe to the reminiscences of our Asia-reared spouses. Following Barbara's death in 1995, Cliff wrote a fourteen-page letter to Dick, describing his and Barbara's Manila childhood.

> From 1932 to 1935, Barbara and her family were next door in a large and airy two-story home with a lovely garden and great view out over Manila Bay. Our home was basically a Philippine-designed house. It had a *nipa*-thatched roof (made of palm fronds) and *sawali* walls (made of woven split bamboo) and was only one story built up off the ground. Like the Colemans, we also had a magnificent view where we could watch the glorious sunsets over Mount Mariveles on Bataan and the island of Corregidor, a small dot at the entrance to the bay.

The Forsters lived in a Filipino-style home on the edge of Manila Bay.

To get to our respective homes we would leave the main
north-south road of F.B. Harrison and wind along a narrow
dirt street through the barrio of Baclaran with little children,
pigs, dogs, and chickens darting back and forth in front of us.
We were actually living right in the barrio and most of the
residents were fishermen. Their *bancas* (long fishing boats) were
pulled up on the beach close by. One of our great delights was
to watch the fishermen take off at sunset, returning early the
next morning when they would spread their nets along the
beach in front of our houses. Now and then they would share
some of their catch with us.

Soon after I met him, Barbara's brother Bill invited me
to join his crew in an upcoming "jellyfish war" using a sleek
Visayan outrigger canoe which his father had brought from
Cebu. Impressed by the craft, I immediately signed up, not
knowing what I was getting into. Barbara joined us on the
beach, a jar of vinegar in her hand, and said she would be
the nurse for the wounded. I asked her what this was for. "I
rub this on you if you get hit by jellyfish," she replied. Bill
explained what the war entailed. He had a pail of very live
jellyfish in his hand; we would attack the enemy in the Moro
vinta (sailing boat) owned by Don Cook's dad. Cook, a neighbor, had a team of three more boys, Bill had yours truly and
one other. The strategy was to maneuver broadsides as close
as possible to the enemy canoe and aim your jellyfish at the
opposing crew.

Fortunately, the war was short-lived with limited casualties due to parental intervention. We had attracted a crowd of
barrio dwellers and our parents, in addition to safety concerns,
sought to halt betting on the winners by the Filipino audience.

Barbara and I were avid movie goers and if we were not
swimming after school or playing around the neighborhood,
we would head downtown to take in a film. This inspired what
we thought was a very creative idea; I volunteered the family
garage as a movie theater for the barrio. I had received a small
Kodak film projector as a present from my folks, complete with

short reels of Charlie Chaplin, Harold Lloyd, Buster Keaton, Mickey Mouse, and Krazy Kat.

We timed our first showing for early evening when the folks were out for a reception or some other function. Our audience would be barrio residents and we would charge one peso for adults while small children could come free. Since they were silent films, Barbara and I would provide the voices and sound effects. To advertise our films, Barbara and I went around the barrio on my bike distributing announcements. We also went to the local *tienda* (neighborhood store) owner to post a special sign. While all the planning went well, opening night was a disaster. We had not counted on so many customers and there was a long line of mothers with their babies and small children, also a number of elderly people. I started the projector after Barbara made a short welcome speech. The garage was jammed and we could hear others outside shouting to get in.

The first film featured Charlie Chaplin and was a great hit. I don't remember the contents of the second film, but I do remember that the projector suddenly broke down and I had considerable difficulty starting it up again, while Barbara tried to sooth the audience. We managed to get through the show but were basket cases by the time it was over. To cap our problems, my folks returned early from their evening out to find a large crowd in their garage. They did not take kindly to our project, closed down the theater after its one-night stand, and forced us to tour the neighborhood and return their pesos to all the customers.

We were attending the American School, a small private school which had been established in 1920 for children in the foreign colony, primarily Americans with a sprinkling of British and other European nationals. Most of the parents were in private business although there were also some students from U.S. military families assigned to the Philippines. Another school, which both Barbara and I attended previously, was Central, a public school established in the early 1900s shortly after the United States annexed the Philippines. Its primary purpose was to educate the children of American civil servants although it expanded beyond this to include children of different nationalities whose parents wanted them exposed to an American public school education. When we were at Central there still were "Thomasites" as teachers. These men and women had come to the Philippines in 1902 on the U.S. Army transport *Thomas* as volunteer teachers who spread out into the countryside to introduce public education in the Philippines. The Thomasites were to become famous later as the inspiration for our Peace Corps.

The early thirties were not all fun and games. In January of 1932 the China conflict came that much closer to us with the sudden Japanese bombing attacks on the international port city of Shanghai. These attacks by the Japanese were in response to alleged violence against Japanese civilians living in Shanghai. Anti-Japanese sentiment had been rising steadily in China as Japanese naval units moved into Shanghai water. In late January, over 70,000 Japanese troops began their assault on Shanghai, resulting in heavy Chinese losses. The fighting ended in March with Japanese domination of the city.

In response to this Japanese aggression, the Manila-based U.S. 31st Infantry was ordered to Shanghai to protect American interests. British reinforcements also headed north from their colony in Hong Kong. My father left for Shanghai to work with the Chinese Red Cross providing medical relief to noncombatants and to assist in the evacuation of American residents if necessary. He brought back graphic accounts of the attacks, particularly the indiscriminate bombing of Chinese civilians in Chapei, a crowded working district of the city. The fighting had ended with a ceasefire arranged by the American and British consuls. It was not until May, however, that the Japanese completed their withdrawal from the city. Meanwhile, to the north, Manchuria was declared by the Japanese to be a Manchu-Mongolian State known as "Manchukuo," and "Henry" Puyi, the last emperor of China before the revolution of 1912, was installed as the puppet president.

Manila continued to be a very special environment for us and there was always an air of excitement—the barrio atmosphere, the friendliness of the Filipinos, our fishermen friends down the beach spreading their nets, the cock fights and local fiestas to which we were invited as kids, Mother Nature's fireworks at each sunset, and the exciting cloud effects over the Bataan and Cavite peninsulas across the Bay.

By the mid-thirties we became more concerned by the historical events taking place around us. In 1934 we were suddenly aware of a strong agrarian movement made up mostly of discontented farmers under alleged radical leaderships. They were called "Sakdals" and their movement was known as "Sakdalista" (to strike). We were told that they were anti-American and wanted immediate independence for the Philippines. There were suddenly reports that they were approaching Manila and Americans would be in serious danger. American families were advised to stay in their homes as Philippine Constabulary units took up their positions around the city and American military units were put on alert.

The first major encounter took place in Laguna Province, a small town called Cabuyao, where the Constabulary defeated Sakdals approaching the southern limits of the city. The fighting there was later referred to as a massacre, since some women and children were among the casualties in the Cabuyao churchyard.

The Sakdal uprising was of short duration and Manila was no longer threatened—if it ever really was. What did continue was the growing discontent among the farmers in Central Luzon who had suffered for many years, victims of land usury since Spanish time. This discontent would flare up again during the Pacific War with the birth of the "Hukbalahap" movement ("The People's Army to Fight the Japanese"), which was communist-led like so many postwar agrarian movements in Southeast Asia. The causes were legitimate enough and were easily exploited by radical leaders.

Final agreement was reached on independence for the Philippines, and in November of 1935 the Commonwealth Government was inaugurated with a dynamic Filipino leader, Manuel Luis Quezon, as its first President. The last American Governor

General, Frank Murphy, became the first U.S. High Commissioner to the Philippines as Quezon moved into Malacañan
Palace, the residence of Spanish colonial governors for three
centuries and American governors for just over three decades.
In ten years (1946) the Philippines would be granted full independence. Until then the U.S. would have responsibility for
the defense of the Philippines and foreign affairs, while the new
Commonwealth would handle its own domestic affairs.

On Inauguration Day, November 15, 1935, Barbara and I
joined in the celebration as American and Philippine flags flew
from all the government buildings and lamp posts. The big
event was the Commonwealth Parade with American and Filipino troops marching by President Quezon and visiting American dignitaries on the reviewing stand. That night the powerful
searchlights of the ships of the U.S. Asiatic Fleet crisscrossed in
the sky and magnificent fireworks displays exploded above the
Luneta Park as the Constabulary band played Souza marches.

The arrival of the first trans-Pacific flight of Pan American's
China Clipper from Alameda also took place that November.
Once again the city went wild as the "flying boat" appeared in
the distance over the eastern hills. Thousands lined the Manila
waterfront and ship whistles all over the harbor started blasting
away. My father had a small outboard boat which he named the
Alameda in honor of the California city where the flight started.
Motoring out into the Bay to watch the landing, we were part
of a problem. There were so many small craft that Captain Ed-
win Musick was unable to find space to land. He was forced to
circle several times while patrol boats signaled us to move away.

Another significant event just before the inauguration and
the China Clipper received very little publicity at the time. The
President Hoover pulled into Manila harbor in October bringing
a highly decorated American general back to the Philippines
with his aides. November events overshadowed the news of the
arrival of General Douglas MacArthur, who was to take over
the training of the new Commonwealth Army at President
Quezon's request. Long associated with the Philippines, Mac-

Arthur was delighted to be "home" again. All that Barbara and I remembered of the event was an inside page story carrying a photo of MacArthur in front of Pier Seven wearing a white sharkskin suit. Standing next to him, similarly attired, was one of his aides, Major Dwight Eisenhower, whose son joined us at the American school.

Our family was on home leave during the winter of 1936, accompanying my father to Washington and Geneva where he reported to officials at the American and International Red Cross headquarters in those cities on the Sino-Japanese conflict. This was the year of Hitler's Olympics in Berlin, Mussolini's attack on Abyssinia, and Franco's bombing of Madrid. The war fever in Europe was mounting and my father quickly booked passage from Genoa back to Manila by way of the Suez Canal and Indian Ocean on the first available ship, the German liner *Scharnhorst*. As we sailed south through the Canal, we passed a British naval vessel with a very dignified figure on the foredeck, shaded by a colorful umbrella. Emperor Haile Selassie was being evacuated from the Italian occupation of Ethiopia, looking every bit the monarch known as the "Lion of Judah" as he was being ferried into exile.

In 1937 the situation in China was heating up again. The Marco Polo Bridge shooting incident on the outskirts of Peking took place in July of that year, launching the full scale Sino-Japanese war. Japanese troops moved in to occupy Peking. Then came their second major attack on Shanghai in August, which turned out to be far more intensive than the one in 1932 as Japanese naval forces began to blockade China's port cities. Once again my father left suddenly for Shanghai, to evacuate women and children, bringing them down the Huangpu River on tenders to ships standing off shore. Back in Manila we read about their ordeal under heavy crossfire as the Japanese and Chinese aimed artillery at each other from opposite shores.

The *President Jefferson* pulled into Manila harbor with the refugees from Shanghai just as a major earthquake hit the city. Bill Coleman and I were with our Boy Scout troop on Pier 7 that night to assist the women and children as they came down the gangplank. All I can remember is total chaos as screaming mothers picked up their children and started running in different directions. One mother was convinced the Japanese had followed them and were bombing the city. Bill tried to calm her as plaster started falling from the ceiling.

Fortunately, members of my father's medical staff, which included a large number of Filipina Red Cross nurses, were on hand to work with the dependents and to get them on the buses waiting outside the pier. I found my father later that night visiting with the dependents, attempting to reassure them that they would all be cared for. He looked very tired and frail after the ordeal of the evacuation under fire and caring for the passengers en route to Manila. Needless to say, we were relieved to see him home again.

A number of the refugee Shanghai families stayed on in Manila, entering their children into our school. Many became our very close friends—and were to be uprooted again a few years later when we all were rounded up and taken into internment camp.

We became more conscious of European developments following Hitler's power moves in Austria and Czechoslovakia and Franco's increasing victories in Spain. Hitler had his supporters in Manila's German community and there were rallies at the local German Club. The large Spanish community in Manila was also united for the most part behind Franco; the opposition in Spain was viewed by local business and religious leaders as "communistic." Our German and Spanish schoolmates did not enter into discussions of these events, which had no effect on our long and friendly relationships with them. Spain's Civil War, however, did have a direct effect on our own family when the Spanish fiancé of my sister, who was by now a popular young member of the international social set, decided suddenly to leave for Spain to join the Loyalists against Franco. He was killed in the fighting at Alicante.

In Manila, the world's conflicts seemed far away and life went on in its same leisurely fashion. The presence of our

Asiatic Fleet in Manila Bay and the American flag flying over
MacArthur's headquarters at Fort Santiago in the Walled City
provided a strong sense of security. While there was some talk
of the Japanese pushing south, the general feeling was that it
would be most unlikely. They were too bogged down in China,
and the Allied colonial powers in Southeast Asia would be an
effective barrier to such aggression in any case.

Reading Cliff's account of those years, which are so full of the experience of history, I was reminded of stories he often told but didn't include
in his letter to Dick Moore. During the 1936 trip to Europe, at the age
of twelve, Cliff witnessed Mussolini speaking to crowds from a balcony
in Milan. Several years later, a German passenger ship anchored off the
Manila shore summoned German residents—his neighbors—to come
pledge allegiance to Hitler.

As the years unfolded, Cliff would be plunged even more fully into
history. In the meantime, his father was part of a force for the good in an
ever more troubled world.

4

CONSCIENCE OF A NATION

WHEN THE FORSTERS ARRIVED IN the Philippines in 1924 to serve in the Red Cross, the Governor General was Leonard Wood, who had formerly been with Teddy Roosevelt's Rough Riders in Puerto Rico. Wood directed the campaign to subdue Geronimo in the American Southwest before coming to the Philippines in the early 1900s with "Blackjack" Pershing to play an active role in the campaigns against the Moros (Muslims) in Zamboanga and Sulu.

Cliff took great pride in his father's commitment to making the Red Cross a revered institution in the life of the American Colony and the nascent Commonwealth. Representatives of the organization would heroically face the challenges of the Japanese invasion and occupation. The legacy left by the work of Charles Forster, with equal devotion to the Red Cross goals and activities by Gladys, provided a firm foundation for the war-torn country as it moved toward its July 1946 independence.

Cliff detailed the story of his father's work with the Red Cross in the photo albums he compiled in Japan. He wrote with particular pride about Charles Forsters' association with future President Manuel Luis Quezon, and his close ties with his Filipino staff.

It was with Governor General Wood's strong support that Father expanded on the work of the Philippine Red Cross. Manuel Luis Quezon, then President of the Philippine Senate, had a special interest in the Philippine Red Cross from the beginning. Born in the same year as my father, he had fought against Spanish domination of his country and later against us during the Philippine Insurrection. An active political leader who challenged Governor General Wood's desire to move more gradually to independent status, Quezon became the first President of the Philippine Commonwealth in November, 1935. Alfonso Aluit, in his 1972 history of the Red Cross in the Philippines, *The Conscience of the Nation,* writes of the "strong bond of respect and admiration" between Quezon and my father. "He would publicly declare his confidence in the Manager of the Philippine Red Cross. Ever a keen judge of men, Quezon saw in Forster a man of ability and character whose dedication to his duty was unswerving and unequivocal."

What impressed Quezon so much about the work of the Red Cross, as well as Leonard Wood and subsequent Governors General, was its wide regional effort to improve the nation's health with major education campaigns which went directly to the people. Disaster relief was also launched by Father as a major Red Cross responsibility—coming to the aid of typhoon-, flood-, and earthquake-ravaged areas. A strong volunteer program made it possible to establish links with the people in the provinces and the Red Cross symbol attained a new popularity by the early thirties.

My earliest memories of my father were of continual movement. He was always going somewhere on a relief mission or on a visit to a new provincial branch. We traveled again on the lighthouse tender *Bustamante,* this time with Red Cross doctors and nurses heading for a typhoon afflicted area. On some visits Mother and I would accompany him. The first domestic air transport to Baguio made it possible for Father to move into the Mountain Province more frequently to visit his doctors, nurses, and dentists working among the hill tribes.

I also remember his very special relationship with his Filipino staff, where there was mutual admiration and respect. One always sensed, even as a child, his strong sense of mission, involvement, and joy of work. Father always managed to have fun with his staff to relieve some of the great pressure during those pioneering days of an expanded Red Cross effort. Doctors and nurses in for a field conference helped launch our new sail-rigged *banca* (outrigger canoe) on Manila Bay before sharing in a picnic on our lawn.

Adventurous doctors and nurses enjoyed the Forsters'
new banca at a Red Cross staff party.

Throughout his professional life, Cliff followed the model of his father's dedication to his mission and the and warm relations with American and Filipino leaders and his own staff. The son, like the father, left his imprint on the distant soils where he trod; his vision and gentle but firm management skills set enduring programs in place, and long after he had left a posting overseas Cliff cherished the friendships he made there, keeping them alive with letters and—when the opportunity arose—visits.

On Armistice Day, November 11, 1937, the new headquarters of the Philippine Red Cross was dedicated on Isaac Peral Street in Manila. Father had worked on the design for months, inspired by California Mission architecture. He wanted the exterior to be rough-hewn and simple. Once, when the workers were trying to develop a pattern on the stucco, he jumped onto the scaffolding himself to get them to throw the mix on at random. He did not want it to be perfect. I recall the days and nights when I would roam the new construction with Mother and Father. It became a real labor of love and he wanted it to be a lasting symbol of the concept of service. The Hall of Mercy with its mosaic of a Red Cross mural in France had a special meaning for Father. It was inaugurated with dedication addresses by Commonwealth President Manuel Quezon and the then American Governor General, Theodore Roosevelt, and messages from the Red Cross Societies of Japan and China.

In the decades to come, this building, so beloved by Charles Forster, would figure prominently in both Philippine and Forster family history.

Charles Forster lovingly supervised construction of the new Red Cross building.
Cliff, holding the American flag, joined an international group of children
at a 1933 celebration in the "Hall of Mercy."

5

EVE OF CONFLICT

CHARLES FORSTER HAD BECOME INCREASINGLY CONCERNED about the spread of the Asian conflict. The Japanese acts of aggression in North and Central China had occupied much of his time in the decade of the thirties as he attempted to work out arrangements with the Japanese and Chinese Red Cross Societies on aid to noncombatants. A strong supporter of the Geneva Convention for the care of prisoners of war, he was greatly disappointed when the Japanese were not signatory to this agreement.

The Forster family was scheduled for home leave in early 1939, but with the tensions building in Asia and Europe, Cliff's father decided to postpone his and his wife's trip and send fourteen-year-old Cliff and twenty-six-year-old Gerry ahead of their parents to California. One goal was for Cliff to spend his tenth-grade year at Alameda High School while living with his grandmother. Except for a few months in an Oakland elementary school on an earlier home leave, this would be Cliff's only U.S.-based schooling until he entered university. His parents wanted him to have at least a degree of grounding in his national culture.

Cliff and Gerry's voyage to San Francisco was to be an adventure, and brother and sister were sent off with firm instructions from their father to avoid causing any international incidents as they stopped in Japanese ports. In Shanghai, they encountered Japanese guards who ordered them—at gunpoint—to bow. In Nagasaki, when Cliff took a photo of the harbor, his camera was confiscated and smashed.

In Kobe, Yokohama, and Tokyo they received a warmer welcome, as Cliff wrote in his manuscript about General Homma:

Lamp posts in the port cities of Kobe and Yokohama were decorated with Japanese and American flags and there were strong signs of friendliness everywhere we went. We had not expected such a feeling of goodwill at a time when there was growing opposition in the U.S. to Japanese aggression in China. At the Tokyo train station, a one-legged Japanese war veteran, dressed in the traditional white robe of the wounded, approached us on crutches and asked if we were Americans. When we told him we were, he bowed and in broken English thanked us for America's kind act to Japan.

Back on the ship we learned what had stimulated the good feeling. The American cruiser *Astoria* was returning the ashes of the Japanese ambassador, Hiroshi Sato, who had died in Washington. This gesture of goodwill had profoundly affected the Japanese. There was another outpouring of goodwill as our ship pulled away from the Yokohama pier. On the other side of the pier aboard the *Kamakura Maru* the "Takarazuka" women's theater troupe in their brightly colored kimonos did a lovely rendition for us of "Auld Lang Syne." They were headed for San Francisco to perform at the International Exposition on Treasure Island.

Once in California, Cliff settled into his year in an American high school. Among his American friends, he was viewed as an exotic outsider, with his tales of faraway places and people, his unfashionable clothes made by an Indian tailor in Hong Kong. A high point of his tenth-grade year was his discovery of the lure of amateur theater through student productions—a pastime that would lighten the atmosphere during those long days and nights of internment by the Japanese.

Cliff's parents finally returned to America in early 1940. Charles made an official visit to Washington to report on relief work and the China situation to Red Cross National Headquarters, and the family spent a very limited home leave together at their Oakland home base.

Charles Forster had purchased the house when he returned from Europe following service during World War I. A wooden bungalow, it served as a repository for treasures collected during the years living in the Philippines and traveling to China and Japan. Blue temple dogs and cloisonne vases from China, ornately carved furniture that once was in Manila's Malacañan Palace, Moro daggers and carved heads of Filipino tribesmen, Japanese scrolls and lacquer ware—all were exotic and bewildering to me when I first visited that house with Cliff. Most precious of all were boxes of post cards and photographs from those Asian years. These were the resources Cliff used for the annotated albums he put together later in Japan.

As we watched the sunset from our home in the Oakland hills overlooking San Francisco Bay, our conversation was generally upbeat as we discussed plans for our upcoming return voyage to Manila. My father pointed out that we would not be stopping at the usual ports. Our ship would bypass Honolulu and Yokohama, heading directly for Kobe. We would also bypass Shanghai and Hong Kong. My sister, who had decided to stay on in California, felt it was very risky for us to return and my father kept trying to reassure her that there was no immediate danger with the American military and naval presence in the Philippines. He also expressed a very high regard for General Douglas MacArthur and his efforts to build up and train the new Philippine Army for the Philippine Commonwealth Government.

During those few weeks in Oakland my father stayed close to the radio, listening to the latest news commentaries on war developments. Hitler's forces had invaded Denmark and Poland, ending the so-called period of the "phony war" when there had

been little movement since the outbreak of the European conflict the previous September. In China, the Japanese had mined
the Huangpu and Yangtze Rivers and by late April they were
preparing to launch a major offensive to control the Yangtze.

We waved a last farewell to my sister as the *President Taft*
edged away from the San Francisco pier, passing under the
Bay Bridge. My father and I stayed above decks to watch the
Northern California coastline recede into the distance. Later
that night in the cabin, which was creaking as we started to
roll, I entered the date of our departure in my diary—April 26,
1940—noting that this would be our sixth voyage westbound
to Manila.

Once at sea, we followed the ship radio news bulletins
and as we approached Japan there were reports of British and
French commando forces retreating before the Nazis in Norway,
after a bold but unsuccessful attempt to advance on Trondheim.
In China, the Japanese military were resuming their major
offensive to control the Yangtze and put greater pressure on
Chiang Kai-shek's Nationalist Government in Chungking.

Our first landfall was the rugged coastline of Japan's Izu
Peninsula with snow-capped Mount Fuji rising behind it to the
west. We had bypassed Yokoyama, proceeding directly to Kobe
where we arrived on the morning of May 9. The inner harbor
was crowded with military vessels and we noticed several Japanese troop ships. As we were docking, one of them was getting
underway, loaded down with soldiers singing martial songs. We
assumed they were China-bound and we watched as their families and friends lined the pier for a last farewell. The colorful
kimonos of many of the mothers, wives, and sisters were a vivid
contrast to the brown-uniformed infantrymen on the decks
with their knapsacks and rifles slung across their shoulders.

The mood in Kobe was quite different from our earlier
visits to Japan. For the first time we detected a distant and
unfriendly attitude. A store attendant near the harbor obviously resented my interest in Japanese political cartoon books
for children. While leafing through one of them, I came across

stridently anti-American cartoons depicting Roosevelt and Churchill as sinister leaders with evil intentions. Japanese soldiers were presented as the benefactors of the Chinese people fighting against the "Western capitalists and war mongers" with blood on their hands. The attendant ignored my request to purchase the book and made it clear that I was not welcome in his store.

On returning to the ship, my father was informed by the captain that the time for our departure would be advanced due to the "new conditions" in Europe. The Nazis had launched their blitzkrieg into the Low Countries on May 10. There was widespread apprehension among the passengers, many of whom assumed that Japan, as an Axis partner, would use this opportunity to move south into the Dutch East Indies. The fact that the ship was leaving ahead of schedule heightened their anxiety, as did the unexpected arrival of the American High Commissioner to the Philippines, Francis B. Sayre, and his wife. They boarded the ship to return to Manila following an official visit with American Ambassador Joseph Grew in Tokyo.

The *President Taft* was underway before sunset. Many of the passengers gathered in the forward lounge where they listened to BBC's shortwave news of the invasion. Chamberlain had just resigned and Winston Churchill was taking over as Prime Minister. There was also commentary on the evacuation of British forces from Norway several days earlier, following their defeat by the Germans.

Three days later we were entering Manila Bay, moving through the south channel close to the island fortress of Corregidor. The U.S. military barracks and our flag were clearly visible. Beyond Corregidor, cumulus clouds were already building up in the morning heat above the mountainous Bataan Peninsula. A destroyer of the U.S. Asiatic fleet, black smoke billowing from its four stacks, passed close to port, outward bound, as sailors waved to us from the fantail.

Shortly after we passed our naval base at Sangley Point on the Cavite Peninsula the Manila waterfront stretched before us with its palm trees and stately old residences, many of them dating back to Spanish colonial times. The U.S. Asiatic Fleet's flagship, the *USS Houston,* rode at anchor in the inner harbor with other ships of the fleet. On our starboard side were the gleaming white buildings of the new U.S. High Commissioner's office and the Army and Navy Club, while just ahead was the majestic Manila Hotel where General Douglas MacArthur, who was Military Adviser to President Manuel Luis Quezon of the five-year-old Philippine Commonwealth Government, had his residence. Just beyond the hotel and the port area, the towers of the old cathedrals came into view, rising above the walled city built by the Spaniards three centuries earlier.

As the *President Taft* moved in alongside Manila's majestic Pier Seven, then one of the world's largest and most impressive, we could hear the strains of "Mabuhay," the traditional song of welcome in the Philippines. Minutes later the gangplank was down and we were being greeted by friends with fragrant sampaguita leis.

It was May 12, 1940, and Hitler's blitzkrieg and Japanese advances in China seemed very far away. We were back in familiar surroundings with old friends, and the American flag flying over MacArthur's headquarters at Fort Santiago in the walled city inspired a renewed feeling of security and confidence. We were "home" again.

Back in Manila after the last Pacific voyage Cliff and his parents would take together, the winds of war would soon ruffle the placid existence of the colony's residents. Cliff's letter to Dick Moore described those final days of peaceful existence.

While the good life continued in Manila, we became more aware of events in Europe. In June of 1940 British schoolmates told us how their relatives had survived the Dunkirk evacuation and we joined French classmates in singing the "Marseillaise" with the fall of Paris. Then came the long period of Nazi aerial bombardment of England and the RAF pilots in their

Spitfires became our new heroes. I was now the editor of the school paper and I recall carrying the accounts of British students who had received letters from home.

In July of 1940 Japanese forces began moving into South China, pressing on the British Crown Colony of Hong Kong. Japan warned Britain at this time that it would have to stop shipments of war materiel to China through Hong Kong and Burma. Hong Kong decided to evacuate its dependents to Manila and my father was again asked to supervise an evacuation operation, which included the housing of British women and children in Manila and arrangements for their onward transportation.

New Year's Eve, 1940, was a very special night for some of us since we knew that this school year would be our last together. Barbara and I still had two years to go, but many of our friends would be graduating in the spring and going on to college back home. I remember sitting with Barbara and other schoolmates that night on the lawn of the Army and Navy Club, as we waited for the midnight hour to approach. Suddenly the sky exploded with fireworks from the Luneta Park and searchlight beams from our Asiatic Fleet. A cacophony of ship whistles added to the general excitement as we hugged and kissed each other and sang "Auld Lang Syne."

We would recall that New Year's Eve a year later as our forces pulled out of Manila for Bataan to avoid encirclement by the advancing Japanese troops. There would be no celebrating that night in 1941, with Manila about to be occupied by the Japanese. The fireworks would be of a different kind as our army engineers blew up the oil refineries of Pandacan and applied scorched-earth tactics to military installations to keep them from falling into Japanese hands.

The early months of 1941 seemed no different to us in Manila and the China war was still very remote. A false sense of security prevailed and the foreign community was assured repeatedly that there was no likelihood of a war coming to Philippine shores. General MacArthur maintained that the islands

could be defended in any event and that adequate preparations
were being made. And High Commissioner Sayre made similar
pronouncements, noting that the Philippines was well protected
and in no danger of attack. What we did not know at the time
was the pitiful state of our defenses there and the acrimony
building between MacArthur and Washington over his need
for increased budget support to build up those defenses. We
learned much later that the European theater was to be given
higher priority by Washington and this had been vigorously
opposed by MacArthur to no avail.

Two developments now took place which indicated that all
was not well. In May of 1941 the Navy ordered the evacuation
of their dependents. This was followed by a similar order for
Army dependents and we suddenly began to lose many of our
schoolmates. There were sad farewells and I remember standing with Barbara on Pier 7 late one afternoon as one of the last
military transports pulled out as the 31st Infantry band played
"California Here We Come."

While the civilian community became more apprehensive,
senior American officials in Manila continued to provide as-
surances that there was no need for concern. In early July, the
Japanese decided to advance into Indochina and Vichy France
subsequently agreed to provide the Japanese full use of Indochi-
nese bases. In late July we read the first reports of Washington's
decision to freeze all Japanese assets in the U.S. to prevent use
of American financial facilities which might be harmful to
American interests.

The Japanese were too close to Philippine shores for comfort
and the announcement in late July of President Roosevelt's decision to return MacArthur to active duty with the U.S. Army
and to take command of all Army forces in the Far East came
as great news to us, bolstering new confidence among the Manila community members. The inclusion of Philippine Commonwealth forces in his new command provided further reas-
surance that we would now be prepared for any eventuality. In
early fall troop reinforcements began to arrive. One afternoon

while walking along Dewey Boulevard, Barbara and I noticed large crates on U.S. Army flatbed trucks moving south in the direction of Nichols Air base. We subsequently learned they contained P-40 fighter plane parts for assembly and Barbara's brother Bill, boasting aeronautical knowledge, informed us that the new planes were superior to the old P-35 which had been the main force at Nichols. Also, the Navy was augmenting the Asiatic Fleet with a new submarine tender, additional subs, and a PT boat squadron. In October, nine new B-17 bombers arrived at Clark Field, followed by fifty pursuit planes. By November the general feeling was that we were in an excellent defensive position and that it was very unlikely the Japanese would risk any kind of invasion.

President Quezon was not so sure and his greatest concern, with the escalation of the crisis in Southeast Asia, was the welfare of his own people should the Philippines be invaded. Earlier in the year he had created the Civilian Emergency Administration whose members included General MacArthur. My father was appointed to this organization to handle the evacuation of civilian residents from Manila in the event of invasion. The president had known my father for many years and they had worked together during major disasters throughout the Philippines. Father wasted no time in establishing evacuation centers in surrounding provinces and staffing them with his disaster relief workers. By November the system was operational to move Filipino civilian noncombatants living close to military targets.

Quezon was also anxious to install an air-raid warning system to be supervised by the Manila municipal authorities. The first practice drill was treated like a big party. Our school friends went downtown that night to watch the drill from the roof of the University Club on Dewey Boulevard. Hundreds of Filipinos had gathered before sunset along the boulevard, bringing their picnic suppers. They spread their *patatis* (straw mats) on the grass while children played nearby on the seawall. Balloon and ice-cream-pie vendors did a thriving business. When

the new sirens went off there was a great cheer from the crowd.
Then the city lights went out as young Filipino males began
to serenade the ladies with their guitars. Disregarding drill
instructions, they also began to light up their cigarettes and
cigars, producing a firefly effect along the boulevard. Civilian
emergency officials were not pleased by this festive spirit and
called on the public to take future drills more seriously. As it
turned out, there were no more drills and when the sirens went
off the next time Manila was under attack.

For us, the most important event of that fall was the early
December annual basketball game with Brent School in Baguio.
In 1941 Brent would host the game and we would all travel
north by train through Central Luzon to Damortis on Lingayen
Gulf. There we would transfer to a bus for the zigzag ride up
the Kenyon Road to Baguio, the pine-forested capital of the
Mountain Province four thousand feet above the central Luzon
plain. It was an exciting prospect and many of us in senior high
signed up for the train ride and weekend activities in Baguio. It
was a terrific weekend, with our team winning the game and a
dance afterwards at the Baguio Country Club.

Just before the dance I ran into my father who was staying at the Club. He had been summoned north by President
Quezon for a special session with other members of the Civilian Emergency Administration, to review evacuation and other
civil defense planning. Colonel Richard Sutherland, MacArthur's Chief of Staff, represented the General at the meeting.
They had completed their meeting that afternoon. Father said
Quezon expressed his view that war was imminent, to which
Sutherland had replied that this was very unlikely. Quezon
did not agree and turned to my father, asking him how soon
he could begin evacuation of civilians from Manila. My father
replied that it could be implemented at any time. The President
said "Good. Start on Monday."

We left Baguio for Manila midmorning on Sunday, December 7th (Saturday the 6th, Hawaii time, on the other side of
the International Date Line), a tired but happy group. On the

return trip some of us watched the passing scene: the farmers
and carabaos (water buffalo) in the rice fields, the sugar cane
plantations—everything looked so green and peaceful. Others
read while still others lamented that we would have to return
to school in the morning. It had been a fun weekend and it
would be hard to get back to work.

As our train moved south along the Central Luzon plain
that Sunday afternoon, Japanese military transports were moving south from Takao, Formosa (Taiwan), with the 48th division of General Masaharu Homma's 14th Army while pilots of
the 11th Air Fleet prepared for their air strikes on Philippine
bases. And to the northwest of Hawaii, the Japanese carrier pilots of the Pearl Harbor Strike Force had been given their final
command to launch their surprise attack on Honolulu. By the
time our train reached Manila that evening, the Pearl Harbor
tragedy was only hours away.

About three o'clock in the morning my father came into my
room. He was always very calm, and his presence didn't register
at first. When he was sure I was awake, he said, "Cliff...son...
you should know...we're at war."

Boy, that was such a blow, but it really didn't dawn on us
how serious it was—it was so far away, and we never contem-
plated that we'd have conflict breaking out on our shores, in the
Philippines.

The next morning, Monday December 8th Manila time,
Japanese planes flew in over the Mountain Province to attack
Baguio's Camp John Hay. It was the first air attack on the Philippines and the building where we had played our basketball
match with Brent forty-eight hours earlier received a direct hit.

Most of us went to school that morning, which seems
strange in retrospect. The immensity of what was happening
only began to sink in later in the day with reports of a major
air attack on Clark Air Base and an invasion fleet coming from
the north. Meanwhile we cheered our pilots from Nichols Air
Base as several formations of the new P-40s flew over the school
headed in a northerly direction. There was an air of great

excitement as coast artillery units began to move into position with their antiaircraft guns a short distance from the school. Our school week ended abruptly shortly after noon when parents began to arrive to pick up their children and the principal announced that classes would be "postponed for a few days." We never went back.

6

DEATH OF A CITY

A MONG THE DOCUMENTS I FOUND in the tea chest was the July 1962 issue of the *Foreign Service Journal,* in which Cliff had published an account of the Japanese conquest of Manila. As I read the descriptions penned by the mature adult, it was easy to forget how young Cliff had been during those fateful days in December of 1941—the same age as our granddaughter, who in 2009 was studying her grandfathers' war in her senior year at a peaceful California high school.

In the afternoon of December 8th, I found my father at Red Cross headquarters busily preparing for the evacuation of civilians to points outside of Manila. Fleets of Manila buses and taxis were being chartered for the job. Around three in the afternoon reports began to filter in of the Japanese air attack on Clark Field seventy miles north of Manila. There were disturbing "rumors" that our planes had been caught on the ground.

The first attack in the Manila area came early Tuesday morning, December 9, and we had a front seat for this since our home was only a short distance from the air base at Nichols Field. My first impulse when the bombs started dropping was to run out into the garden and bring in the dog. My mother shouted at me to get back into the house. The bombers left almost as suddenly as they had come. There was a series of explosions as the flames shot skyward from the Nichols hangars. My father, who had returned home for a brief rest just an hour before, was on the phone with his office. He dressed quickly and told me to come along.

Filipino residents around Nichols Field were in a state of panic and heading out of the city along the road to Cavite, where my father felt they would be perfect targets for strafing attacks. As we approached the town of Paranaque we had to slow down. Hundreds of Filipinos were on the road, carrying or pulling their effects along in carts. At the plaza just across the bridge and in front of the old Spanish church we joined up with Red Cross staff members who had arrived a short time before with a loudspeaker system. Father climbed the stairs to the plaza bandstand and appealed to the refugees to turn back. They must not panic. There would be an orderly evacuation to prearranged points where there were stocks of food and doctors and nurses. The crowd began to pay attention and many did return that night. During the next several days it was possible to evacuate almost 100,000 Filipino civilians from such vulnerable areas as Nichols Field. But the attacks came so frequently from the air and the invasion forces moved so swiftly towards Manila in the next few weeks that most of the evacuation plans had to be shelved entirely.

The first major attack on our naval base at Cavite came on Wednesday, December 10, and started shortly before noon when a Zero fighter came roaring over the treetops, strafing as it went. There was a tremendous explosion close by and we discovered later that this first bomb in our vicinity had completely destroyed the antiaircraft position on the old polo field. In between Zero attacks and bomb explosions—the barrio of Ignacio, only a mile away had become an inferno of flame and smoke—we could get some idea of the Japanese bombing pattern, a pattern which became familiar to us as a daily event during the month of December. The Zeros, frequent visitors at first, did not make much of an appearance later. The silver bombers with the rising Sun, flying at great altitude and in perfect formation, would make a leisurely circle run around the Bay, dropping their bombs at Cavite, Nichols Field, the Port Area, the ships in the harbor, Neilson Field to the east. You could see our antiaircraft shells exploding far below the bombers. We simply did not have the range to reach them. And the few remaining P-40s which went up so courageously to take on the Zeros were outmaneuvered by the much faster Japanese aircraft.

The Wednesday raid, two days after the start of the war, left Manila completely defenseless. Right after that a number of us were assigned by the Red Cross to ambulance and relief work. My first assignment Wednesday afternoon took me to the Army and Navy Club landing where U.S. Navy small craft loaded with wounded and dying sailors and marines were arriving from the base at Cavite across the Bay. The lawn in front of the pool was lined with stretcher cases. The boats kept coming all afternoon and the ballroom of the club was converted into a temporary relief station.

As Christmas approached, many families became more apprehensive. Rumors began to spread of large invasion forces off northern Luzon. On Christmas day we learned that General MacArthur had decided to withdraw all troops from Manila in order to save it from further destruction. Manila was to be an "open city" and the Japanese had been so informed. All civilians were to stay in Manila, offering what assistance they could to the evacuation of military personnel. Trucks, buses, and cars were commandeered to transport remaining United States and Philippine forces to an "unknown destination."

Despite the "open city" declaration, the bombers came in on schedule the 27th and caught some of us by surprise near Fort Santiago in the Walled City. The bombs began to drop before the sirens even went off. We raced for the YMCA building and made it just in time. A third bomb exploded just down from the YMCA and shattered most of the glass in the windows. There were about a dozen American soldiers in the building, the remnants of a quartermaster unit waiting for transportation out of the city. A loudspeaker was hooked up at one end of the room and the voice of a lookout on the roof informed us that the bombers had passed over the Walled City and were now concentrating on the few ships remaining in the Bay. He gave us a running account: "a freighter's had it...now they are over Nichols...lots of smoke at Cavite...here they come again our way...take cover!"

A soldier standing at a pinball machine slammed his fist down on the glass cover: "He's ruining my game!" Another soldier, much younger, was sitting in a corner whistling "God Bless America." Around and around the bombers went while the lookout continued his running commentary for what seemed an eternity. The raid over, we emerged cautiously from the YMCA and it seemed to us as if the entire Walled City was on fire.

By Christmas the American civilians had been advised to move into the Bayview Hotel on Dewey Boulevard just across from our present embassy. The High Commissioner's office felt it would be best if we were not scattered around the city. We had heard by this time that Japanese forces were moving rapidly on Manila from the north and the south and that it would be only a matter of days before they were on the outskirts. Late in the evening of the 29th, I stopped by the office to see my father and found him in session with one of his field directors, Irving Williams, and his senior Filipino staff. I overheard my father saying that General MacArthur wanted to get the most severely wounded out of Manila immediately and that it would be necessary to locate a ship as soon as possible, any ship—just so it could float. Then they would have to find painters and a competent captain. Williams asked if the Japanese had agreed to safe passage to wherever they were going, and my father replied they would have to go ahead and hope for the best.

Not until later that night was I able to get a clear picture of what was going on. Over two hundred severely wounded American and Filipino officers and enlisted men from Lingayen were still lying in the military hospital at Sternberg in Manila. General MacArthur did not want them left behind with the Japanese about to enter the city. He had instructed my father to do everything possible to get the wounded out of Manila before it fell. My father cabled Washington headquarters, which in turn notified the International Red Cross in Geneva and they contacted the Japanese Red Cross in Tokyo.

The only ship available was of ancient vintage, a small interisland vessel called the *Mactan.* Her Filipino captain, Julian Tamayo, was a real veteran however, and he said he would do his best to get through to safety. Since the Japanese were only a short distance from Manila it was imperative to move fast. About a hundred painters, mostly students, were recruited and on the night of the 30th father met with them in the Hall of Mercy at the Philippine Red Cross. The *Mactan* with its rusty black hull would have to be transformed immediately into a Red Cross hospital ship. They would have to paint her sides white and a red band with Red Cross symbols would also be necessary.

Under Williams' able direction, the painters worked all that night and all the next day. The work was done in the inner harbor and Williams had spread large Red Cross flags over the hatches. The painters worked fast and well, looking anxiously skyward from time to time for possible enemy attackers. No attack came and by late afternoon Captain Tamayo was able to bring his ship alongside Pier One to take the wounded aboard. A long line of stretcher cases was on the pier and proceeded slowly up the gangplank. It was New Year's Eve. When I accompanied my father down to the *Mactan* shortly before midnight, lights were blazing along her white sides and Captain Tamayo greeted us warmly on the bridge. He said that he was a little concerned because he had no accurate up-to-date charts. The Coast and Geodetic Survey offices had been bombed out only a few days before. A naval officer aboard charged with getting the ship safely through the U. S. minefield off Corregidor assured Williams that he would be able to pick up charts from another ship, the *Don Esteban,* lying off Corregidor. Through all this discussion Captain Tamayo nodded his head and seemed very confident. Then Williams asked again about a reply from the Japanese to the Swiss message. Father shook his head. No reply had been received. He added that he was quite confident that one would soon come through. Later, he confided to me that he was not at all confident about this; but he knew that if his Japanese colleagues with whom he had worked in the Tokyo Red Cross since the days following the 1923 Tokyo Earthquake had any say about it, a reply would come through and full support would be granted.

When we went ashore and shortly after one a.m. we could hear the *Mactan's* old engines pounding and she began, laboriously, to edge away from the pier. The water around her reflected the flames shooting skyward from the Port Area. A ring of fires to the east silhouetted the old cathedral towers of the Walled City and you could hear the crackling of flames. Captain Tamayo waved to us from the bridge. We watched the *Mactan* until she was a small white speck on the horizon.

Since the Japanese occupied Manila some thirty-six hours after her sailing, we didn't learn until years later that the ship had made it safely to Australia.

New Year's Day found the streets of Manila deserted. There was a good deal of tension in the air now. The fire and smoke made the city oppressively warm and strangely silent. Night came and still there were silence and fires everywhere. Then, suddenly, late in the afternoon of January second, we heard it: a distant roar, steady but coming closer all the time. Coming up Dewey Boulevard from the south were thousands of Japanese troops. All on motor bicycles with small Japanese flags strapped to the handlebars. Rifles were slung into holsters along side the bicycles and each soldier had a knapsack and what seemed to us to be oversized helmets. I was reminded of Harold Lamb's accounts of the Mongol invasions—"the men on horseback." Now they were on bicycles. The occupying forces began to branch out on side streets all over the city. Several hundred turned left off the Boulevard into the entrance to the high commissioner's residence.

It was late that afternoon when we watched them, from our temporary quarters in the Bayview Hotel, haul our flag down and replace it with the Rising Sun. As they did so, they gave a victorious shout of "Banzai," repeated several times, raising their helmets over their heads. General Masaharu Homma was to make this his headquarters for the Bataan campaign. By nightfall machine guns and sentries surrounded our hotel. Tanks were the next to come up the boulevard, the deafening clatter of their treads going on late into the night as mechanized units followed the infantrymen into the city.

The Manila we had known died that night. With it died any illusions we had about our own invincibility and the naïve assumption that "it would never happen here."

What did not die on January 2nd and during the difficult years that followed was a faith in the future, strengthened during the occupation years by the magnificent support of the Filipinos who defied Japan's "New Order" for a way of life which had obviously meant as much to them as it had to us.

7

UNDER JAPAN'S
"BENEVOLENT CUSTODY"

THE AMERICANS WHO WERE ISOLATED in the Bayview Hotel waited through a long night of fear. The adults and teenagers recalled reports of the Japanese rampage against civilians when they conquered Nanking—"the Rape of Nanking"—and worried that there might be a repeat in Manila. All families, especially women and children, were advised to remain in their rooms behind closed doors that night. Marge Hoffman, a schoolmate of Cliff's whose family had been evacuated to Manila from China in 1937, recently sent me a letter recalling Cliff's support when, at the insistence of her father, she burned her prewar diary.

Cliff, my brother, and I walked across Dewey Boulevard to the bay one evening, as my father wanted me to dispose of a diary I'd kept since 1936. We'd been evacuated from Shanghai in '37, and I'd written some nasty things about the Japanese while in Japan in '39. Clifton lit the match to burn the diary and comforted me as I cried, watching it flame up.

In his letter to our friend Dick Moore, Cliff described the entry of the Japanese into the hotel the following morning, January 3rd, 1942. He had been assigned elevator duty that day, to manipulate the controls of the vintage "lift" for the benefit of passengers. A delegation of American businessmen, including some who spoke Japanese, was in the lobby to meet the Japanese soldiers.

Around midmorning, a Japanese major arrived in the hotel lobby accompanied by soldiers with fixed bayonets. Their khaki uniforms and puttees were still dust-covered and they kept glancing around the room furtively to detect any sudden moves on our part. The major was perspiring profusely as he removed his helmet and requested some tea. The next few minutes were devoted to remarks about Manila's heat: "Too hot—no good," he kept repeating, obviously pleased with his English. He then proceeded to tell us that we would be free again after Japan's victory. In the meantime, he said, we would be under the "benevolent custody" of the Japanese Imperial Army.

Some of the Japanese soldiers, it appeared, were ordered to inspect the hotel. Five of them entered Cliff's elevator, issuing guttural, barely decipherable orders to take them to the fifth floor. Cliff relived that harrowing elevator ride many times, telling the story to his children and grandchildren. The soldiers, armed with swords and bayoneted rifles, surrounded him. Nerves on edge, Cliff fumbled with the control lever, moved the elevator car by fits and starts, and arrived at the fifth floor— almost. Unable to maneuver level with the floor, he finally gave up and managed to open the door about a foot below the floor level. While Cliff muttered apologies, his passengers showered him with what he assumed were invectives and climbed out to begin their inspection of the rooms. When done, the Japanese returned to the lobby and left instructions that all prisoners were to pack their belongings since they would be leaving the next day, January 4th.

No mention was made of our destination and we were warned that any firearms found in our possession could result in the death penalty. The major then adjusted his sword, put on his oversized helmet, and bowed crisply before heading for the door, followed in single file by his soldiers.

The next morning we were jammed into buses and driven through familiar streets for the last time, passing many of our favorite hangouts—movie theaters, soda fountains, and shops—where we had spent so many delightful hours. Fires still blazed around the city and pillars of black smoke rose above the Walled City and along the Pasig River, where the remaining installations had been bombed the previous week. Japanese troops were in evidence everywhere and it seemed so unreal to have them in our familiar surroundings. Some soldiers were posting street signs in Japanese. Others were on sentry duty at the major intersections, checking out Filipino civilians. There were hostile looks from the sentries as our convoy of civilians moved through Japanese checkpoints. The few Filipinos who were on the streets waved and some even gave us the "V for victory" sign, which took courage under those circumstances.

Crossing the Pasig River, we proceeded up Calle España to Santo Tomas University, where our convoy turned into the grounds. We had arrived at our destination, a Dominican institution run mostly by Spanish priests. We noted that they were flying Franco's flag and the Rising Sun flag of Japan side by side over the main building. The university had been established during the Spanish regime and was alleged to have been the oldest educational institution under the American flag while the Philippines were still in our possession. Over 3,000 Allied civilians came that morning, mostly from the Bayview, and in subsequent days from outlying parts of the city and elsewhere in the Philippines. Roll call on February 3, 1942, accounted for 2,339 Americans, 875 British, twenty-seven Dutch, thirty-six Polish, four Belgians, nine of other nationalities—2,045 of these men—most of whom would spend the duration of the war behind the walls of this university, living under increasingly greater hardship with the passage of time.

The gates of Santo Tomas closed behind us and the Manila we had known from our childhood was gone.

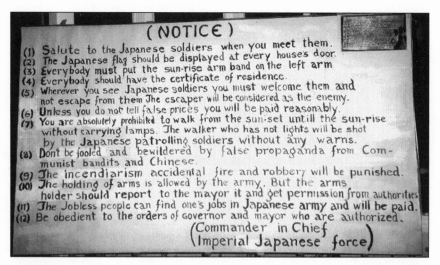

(NOTICE)
(1) Salute to the Japanese soldiers when you meet them.
(2) The Japanese flag should be displayed at every house's door.
(3) Everybody must put the sun-rise arm band on the left arm
(4) Everybody should have the certificate of residence.
(5) Wherever you see Japanese soldiers you must welcome them and
     not escape from them. The escaper will be considered as the enemy.
(6) Unless you do not tell false prices you will be paid reasonably.
(7) You are absolutely prohibited to walk from the sun-set untill the sun-rise
     without carrying lamps. The walker who has not lights will be shot
     by the Japanese patrolling soldiers without any warns.
(8) Don't be fooled and bewildered by false propaganda from Com-
     munist bandits and Chinese.
(9) The incendiarism accidental fire and robbery will be punished.
(10) The holding of arms is allowed by the army. But the arms
     holder should report to the mayor it and get permission from authorities
(11) The Jobless people can find one's jobs in Japanese army and will be paid.
(12) Be obedient to the orders of governor and mayor who are authorized.
                              (Commander in Chief   )
                              (Imperial Japanese force)

Japanese authorities promulgated strict rules for civilians in occupied Manila.

Cliff and his parents were now prisoners, as were their friends, business colleagues, and school teachers, along with missionaries from across the country and seamen who had been caught on commercial ships in Manila Harbor at the start of the war—a full-fledged international community. The Coleman family was also interned, minus Barbara's brother Bill. Shortly after the first attacks by the Japanese, without consulting his parents, he had enlisted with the U.S. army and was among those who were shipped out of Manila to the Bataan Peninsula to fight the forces of General Masaharu Homma.

Homma was the man in charge, the strategist, the commander. Those who became prisoners of war in the Philippines in January of 1942—the teenaged Cliff Forster among them—laid all blame for their fate on the shoulders of the Japanese general, and fanned their hatred for the horrors of Japan's war. It was only as a mature adult that Cliff would review those youthful events and weave them into a new look at the life and nature of the commander.

In the introduction to his manuscript about Homma, Cliff describes the harsh, disorganized conditions in the early days at Santo Tomas. Establishing order and providing basic needs for this international community was a huge challenge to the Japanese. The guards were military men, with no experience in managing civilians, little or no previous contact with foreigners, and no plans for this group other than to incarcerate them and maintain military discipline on this university campus. Their charges were to lead a monastic life.

No provision had been made for food, bedding or medical supplies, and conditions were chaotic. Japanese sentries lined us up in front of the building to check us for hidden weapons. We were then marched to our respective rooms. The sexes were divided and lived in separate classrooms in the main building.

About sixty men crowded into classroom 35 and we made out the best we could finding available sleeping space on the floor or improvising with classroom chairs and bookshelves, which we laid flat on the floor. The room was a mess with the furniture in disarray and a thick coat of dust. I managed to secure a bookcase for Father to stretch out on. He was very weak at this point and had lost considerable weight, having slept and eaten very little during the month of December.

Before turning in that night, I noticed a battered calendar on the opposite wall, which still showed the date of December 8, presumably the last day of classes. A painting of Christ hung askew next to the calendar and a blackboard along the west wall still had chalked poetry in Spanish, probably the writing of a Dominican instructor or one of the students.

Fortunately, the Americans and British who were the majority of internees were by nature organizers and, as Cliff wrote, they soon created their own domestic infrastructure.

Men who had been executives in their Manila banks and businesses began to organize committees to meet the basic needs of the internees. An executive committee was selected to serve as a governing body and operate as liaison between the prisoners and the Japanese overlords. Cliff noted that these men "faced difficult problems and challenges in the months to come. This committee was often on a razor's edge, protecting camp interests while attempting to satisfy Japanese demands—no mean task."

Other committees were created to provide food and medical care and to institute safety and sanitation measures. Professional talent was on hand; doctors and teachers who had served the international community in Manila were now fellow internees. An education committee organized outdoor classrooms and Cliff and his International School classmates found themselves resuming the lessons that had been interrupted in December. An entertainment committee was challenged to boost camp morale. The Americans organized baseball teams and a British couple who had performed on the Manila stage prewar began to plan evening variety shows and drama productions. Cliff was an enthusiastic participant in several plays, nourishing the appetite for amateur theater he had developed during his one school year in California. Professional journalists in camp located a mimeograph machine and limited supply of paper and began publishing a camp journal, *Internews*. Cartoons by camp artists and sly innuendo in articles by the reporters sought humor in the degradations of daily life and subtly poked fun at the Japanese. Bound copies of issues that survived the internment and liberation were among Cliff's treasured files, and I pored over them with awe and fascination when I found them more than fifty years later.

Every able-bodied person had a job to do. "Volunteers" were assigned to handle kitchen chores, garbage disposal, and general cleanup. An old dump was turned into a garden that produced greens, beans, and yams for the camp kitchen. Cliff was part of the garden team and specialized in growing talinum, a substitute for spinach that his friends said was horrible to eat, but it provided needed nourishment. Getting the garden into shape, Cliff wrote to Dick Moore, "was tough work since old automobile parts, castaway hospital equipment, tin cans, and metal and glass had to be dug out before seeding and planting."

The big problem at first was to get hold of food before starvation set in, since the Japanese had assumed no responsibility for supplying the camp with staples. On January 7, my father met with members of the newly organized Executive Committee and it was agreed that the Red Cross should resolve the problem by taking over the feeding of the camp and handling the payment for all supplies. He organized a central purchasing committee and was able to contact one of his most able Red Cross workers, Mrs. Patricia Intengan, to supervise outside market purchases. Pat, as we all knew her, soon became known as the "Angel of Santo Tomas," a small feisty lady who fearlessly walked through the front gate by the sentries, wearing her Red Cross arm band.

Our first commandant, Lieutenant Hitoshi Tomoyasu, agreed to Red Cross initiatives and even authorized the Red Cross to establish field kitchens in the camp, bringing in the necessary equipment. Realizing that there were Red Cross food supplies in Manila warehouses when the Japanese occupied the city, Father was able to contact one of his senior staff members, Dr. Joaquin Canuto, to arrange for a limited transfer of these supplies to Santo Tomas. Much of the food consisted of cracked wheat which had been destined for China when the war started. Canuto, through skillful negotiating, was able to get the cracked wheat and a large shipment of army cots out of the warehouses that had been sealed by the Japanese, sending them into Santo Tomas in Red Cross trucks.

The amazing part of this operation was that my father and other American Red Cross personnel had not been recognized by the Japanese military authorities whose internment of the civilians was a violation of the Geneva Convention. Whatever was achieved during those early weeks in Santo Tomas had to be accomplished through high-risk contacts with the Filipino Red Cross staff outside the camp who acted with great courage under difficult circumstances. Without their help we would have all faced starvation. Mention should also be made of the hundreds of Filipino friends, neighbors, servants, and former business staff and colleagues who flocked to the front Santo Tomas fence to pass food, clothing, bedding, and other necessities through the bars to their former employers and their families. The Japanese attempted to turn the crowds away and were profoundly disturbed by this strong expression of loyalty to the internees. The fence was subsequently screened with sawali matting to control the flow and prevent the entry of any contraband.

*Civilian internees adjusted to a new lifestyle under the "benevolent custody"
of the Japanese—preparing food, doing laundry, and whiling
away the hours communally.*

Among the food items passed through the fence by the Filipinos were peanuts. These were turned into peanut butter, which was eaten with bananas—a nourishing snack! To his dying day Cliff would eat bananas with peanut butter spread on each bite, a culinary treat passed on to his family.

One evening after they had been in camp for a few weeks, while Cliff was chatting with his friends after the distribution of cracked wheat, one of the men from his room sought him out.

He seemed anxious and asked where my father was. I told him he was meeting with the Executive Committee.

"Then, get him fast. Three Japanese want to see him right away." He added, "I think they're Kempeitai."

The Kempeitai were the dreaded secret police. I found my father in the Executive Committee office and we walked back together. He said little, but seemed relaxed given the circumstances. What followed was an intensive interrogation outside our room as the Kempeitai sought to identify his position with the Red Cross, determine how long he had been with the organization, and ascertain what kind of association he had with the Japanese Red Cross Society in the prewar years. One of the Japanese referred to a thick file, obviously a dossier on my father, who proceeded to reply to their specific questions.

He described his activities with the Red Cross since World War I, when he had been assigned to France to assist refugees and other noncombatants from the war zone. He then said that he had first come to the Philippines in 1923 as manager of the American Red Cross to set up a program of disaster relief and to provide public health services to the people of the Philippines. As to his prewar association with Japanese Red Cross officials, he described it as very close, having worked with them to supervise American Red Cross relief assistance to the victims of the Great Earthquake in Tokyo of 1923.

"Who did you work with?" asked one of the interrogators.

"Mostly with Prince Shimadzu, Director of the Japanese Red Cross Society," he replied, adding that they had established a close working relationship since the Tokyo Earthquake.

"Did your association continue?"

"Yes, for many years." Father then explained how he had attended the regional conference of Red Cross Societies in 1926, hosted by the Japanese Red Cross Society in Tokyo, and the strong Japanese interest in disaster relief activities in the Philippines. He went on to say that the next conference was to have been in the Philippines in 1933 but was cancelled due to the China conflict.

The Japanese interrogators suddenly went on the offensive. "Why did you supply the Chinese Nationalist Government with food and medical supplies after 1937?"

"Because that was my mission," he responded, looking directly at them before continuing. I could see that they were agitated and I began to worry about Father's situation, although he remained calm and collected. He then noted that both the Japanese and Chinese Red Cross Societies had agreed to work with the American Red Cross to assist noncombatants in the event of conflict in China, but that the Japanese had subsequently cancelled such assistance.

"Because you refused us access through China ports you occupied, we had no alternative." Father was in good form, holding his own, but they didn't seem to be listening and had obviously already made up their minds.

The exchange became very tense and Father was flatly accused of partisanship, of favoring the Chinese over the Japanese in the China conflict. His status as a Red Cross official therefore could not be recognized. They then indicated he could be released from camp, at which point he said he only would do this if his Red Cross status was recognized and he could continue with relief efforts under the Geneva Convention. This request was ignored and when he asked if he could communicate directly with Prince Shimadzu in Tokyo, he was firmly told that this would not be possible.

Several days later, Father suffered a severe heart attack in camp, and the camp doctors strongly recommended he accept a medical release to an outside hospital. The pressures of the first weeks of the war and the long nights without sleep had caught up with him. Once again he refused to be released until leaders within the camp convinced him that he would be in a much better position to function outside the camp, where he could maintain closer contact with his Filipino staff. Mother, who had been staying in another room with women and children, would be allowed to accompany him.

In early February I helped my father and mother pack up their few belongings and we walked slowly down to the front gate together for a last farewell. The guard lowered his rifle and motioned me back from the gate. As my parents drove off, my father gave me a final thumbs-up signal.

8

"CHEER UP, EVERYTHING'S GOING TO BE LOUSY"

FIVE WEEKS BEFORE HIS EIGHTEENTH BIRTHDAY, Cliff was on his own, with his father ill in Manila in the care of his mother and their devoted Filipino Red Cross staff. The senior Forsters would be under house arrest, still in "benevolent custody," until they were able to leave the Philippines. Although separated from his family, Cliff was in the company of his best friends—they were even attending classes for their final year of high school—and enjoying the mentorship of his friends' parents and the adult men of room 35. All would share the trials and cherish the triumphs which they could achieve within their constrained society.

During the first weeks in camp, we found we were too busy to worry excessively about our living conditions and what the future might hold. It was only later that the mood changed with the realization that no help would be coming and that the Japanese were advancing steadily into the South Pacific. Internees became more introspective. Why was this happening to us and what had gone wrong? There was growing criticism of Washington leadership as well as our military leaders in the field. Why weren't we better prepared in the Philippines and how had the Japanese achieved such quick supremacy over our forces? MacArthur himself even came under attack for destruction of our B-17s on the ground and for his continually optimistic communiqués when his defense lines were falling apart. There was a general feeling that we had been misled and deserted.

We attempted to follow the progress of the war as best we could but it was depressing to do so with the constant barrage of Japanese propaganda about their victories. We did manage to get hold of BBC, Radio Australia, and other Allied news reports which were occasionally slipped into camp by Filipino friends coming through the package line. The reports were usually hidden under food labels or sewed into clothing and we became increasingly concerned that our good friends were taking too many chances.

MacArthur had set up a "Voice of Freedom" on Corregidor and it was from this source that we could learn from time to time about the fighting on Bataan. For the first few weeks these reports indicated we were holding successfully against formidable attacks by Homma's forces. The rumor mill in camp also went to work during this early period to offset some of the depression, and there were wild stories about "100-mile convoys" en route to the Philippines with reinforcements. MacArthur, it was rumored, would soon begin his counteroffensive to liberate Manila.

Some of the elderly internees, many of them survivors of the Spanish American War in the Philippines, would sit around in the corridors trying to top each other's rumor. One night I came across one of them in the men's shower room peering through the window. "Did you see it?" he asked excitedly. "See what?" I asked. "Macarthur's big guns," he replied. "You can see the flashes in the north. And you can hear our artillery." I looked through the window and saw and heard nothing but did not have the heart to tell him.

There was no counteroffensive and the convoys never came and the days and nights began to drag on interminably. The mood was rapidly shifting from relative optimism resulting largely from much wishful thinking to pessimism, frustration and, with some, deep anger over their plight.

Not long after my parents left, Dave Harvey, a musical actor by profession and head of our Entertainment Committee, pulled some of us together to put on a vaudeville show to cheer everyone up. We had some exceptional professional and amateur talent in camp, including Dave. He changed the lyrics of an old song to create a new one, "Cheer Up, Everything's Going to Be Lousy," and had the entire camp audience join in singing:

> *Cheer up, everything's going to be lousy.*
> *You'll still be eating cracked wheat every day.*
> *You can eat your mush without any milk in the morning.*
> *But the prune juice works in the same old fashioned way.*
> *You may have been the president of Manila's leading store,*
> *But you've still gotta haul the garbage from the third and*
> *   highest floor.*
> *You may grumble now at beans and peas,*
> *But wait till you start on the bark of the trees.*
> *You think the Flit is decreasing mosquitoes' sway,*
> *But they're going into mass production any day.*
> *The lines are getting longer—just like the ones on your face,*
> *But wait till you're five years older and still in the same old*
> *   place.*
> *The rumors may be all that you need,*
> *But soon you'll begin to believe what you read.*
> *So, cheer up, everything's going to be lousy...*

The show attracted several of the Japanese guards. The words meant nothing to them, but they seemed to like the melody and began to clap in unison with the audience.

An attempted escape from camp took place the day we heard of the fall of Singapore, and it had a devastating effect on all of us. We heard screaming from the first floor. I can still remember the empty feeling in my stomach. The escapees were well known to us as they lived in nearby rooms. One of them, an engaging young Englishman, worked on the same camp garden detail I did. He had a great sense of humor and always seemed to be in high spirits. Internees had been warned from the outset that anyone attempting to escape would receive the death sentence. Their scheming had gone on regardless, as the future seemed more and more hopeless. The two Englishmen, Thomas Fletcher and Henry Weeks, and an Australian, Blakey Laycock, made their escape at night. They were captured the next day north of the city and returned to the camp where they were beaten unmercifully by their captors.

We headed for the main floor to get a better handle on what was happening. When we reached there a large crowd was already beginning to gather, including many of the shipmates of the escapees, whose merchant ship had been bombed only two days before the fall of Manila. Tension was building fast and I could overhear several of their mates threatening to rush the Japanese guards to free them. Calmer heads prevailed, however, cautioning them to keep their cool since the Japanese had the guns and we did not. All were warned that a real bloodbath could result with the loss of many innocent lives should we give the Japanese guards the excuse to open fire.

The three men were taken from the camp with their hands tied behind their backs. We could see that they had been badly beaten and their faces were puffed up and bleeding.

Our executive committee immediately petitioned for clemency but this was ignored and on Sunday afternoon, February 15, the escapees were transported to the Chinese Cemetery a short distance from the camp. Forced to sit with their legs hanging over open graves that had been dug for them, they were blindfolded and shot at close range with 25-caliber automatics.

An Anglican priest who had been allowed to attend the execution described it to the executive committee. One of the Englishmen, Harry

Weeks, had been married only a month before he left for the Philippines. Weeks gave the priest his wife's address, said he might now be a father, and asked the priest to send her a message

Lt. Tomoyasu, the camp commandant, told Earl Carroll, the chairman of the executive committee, that he regretted the execution. He felt corporal punishment would have sufficed; however, the orders for execution had come from higher authorities and he could not intervene. Right after this, the commandant was transferred from Santo Tomas, but before leaving he expressed his friendship for the internees in an interview with the editor of *Internews*. I found the article in the February 7, 1942 edition of the camp newspaper.

JAPANESE OFFICER VOICES FRIENDSHIP

A personal feeling of friendship for Americans and British has developed during his service as commandant of the Santo Tomas internment camp, Lt. Hitoshi Tomoyasu, of the Japanese gendarmerie, said today.

In an interview with the INTERNEWS editor, the retiring commandant said his friendship is much greater than he previously believed possible under the circumstances.

The interview was conducted in the commandant's office, through Ernest Stanley, official interpreter.

"When I first came to this camp," he said, "I did not know what my feeling was toward the internees, because you were enemy nationals. My previous contact with foreigners was in Kobe and Shanghai. I thought them proud and lacking in understanding of the Japanese.

But since I have been here, our cooperation and understanding have brought to me a feeling of friendship that I did not expect was possible under the existing circumstances. I have found that at heart you are just the same as Japanese. My feeling of friendship for you has grown deeper as time goes on.

In the discharge of my duties here, I always have had to work under orders from above. I appreciate your understanding of this situation.

If the cooperation that has existed in this camp were possible on an international basis, there would be no cause for international dispute.

I hope this friendship will continue. I want to work for the good of the internees as long as possible. Wherever we are, we can work on this same basis.

In the past months other nations have misunderstood us, and we have misunderstood them. I never expected the affairs of this camp to go as smoothly as they have, under the circumstances.

I have never had a chance for this close contact with Americans and British. I find now that I have to tear myself away from my job here.

I wish to express my appreciation to Mr. Carroll and members of the executive committee for their efforts. I wish them continued success in their work, and I pray for the well-being of the whole camp."

Lt. Tomoyasu had visited Vancouver and Seattle when he was nineteen years old. He said at that time he was favorably impressed by both Canadians and Americans, but this feeling tended to disappear during subsequent international tension, until he came to this camp.

Another story in this edition of *Internews* told about the entertainment program scheduled for that evening. It was to be a *despedida* (farewell party) for Lt. Tomoyasu. It was noted that he had attended the variety show the previous week and "demonstrated considerable appreciation of musical numbers."

It was interesting for me to read between the lines of the mimeographed paper. Clearly, these words were written during the very difficult time following the executions, and distress in the camp was no doubt high. Still, the camp leaders understood that Tomoyasu had acted on orders, and were trying to keep the peace the best they could.

Their leadership impacted the young Cliff Forster. Ironically, his experience as a prisoner of the Japanese made him realize how important it was for people with conflicting cultural views and aspirations to interact with each other. Those difficult times opened the door to his later work in diplomacy—including many years in postwar Japan.

Subsequent commandants would be less gregarious than Tomoyasu, and their rule progressively harsher. As internees, the civilians were at the mercy of their guards and the commandant of the camp who was their leader. Those Japanese were members of a generation, many from the hinterlands, that had grown up having little contact with foreigners. What they learned about the outside world was information fed to them by an omnipotent government with an efficient propaganda machine. Past injustices, real and imagined, were emphasized. Japan's glorious history and righteous ambitions were stressed. Outsiders (the Japanese word for foreigner, *gaijin,* means "outsider") were stereotyped as evil in the case of the Western allies or, in the case of Asian neighbors, in need of Japanese beneficence and leadership.

Cliff's account continues, describing further events that impacted morale inside the camp.

At the end of February, only two weeks after the prisoners' execution, the Japanese-controlled media in Manila reported that the combined U.S., British, and Dutch fleets had been destroyed in the Battle of the Java Sea by Japan's "invincible navy." This was followed by reports of the Japanese invasion of the Netherlands East Indies and the Dutch surrender of Java on March 9. Meanwhile, in the Philippines, the Japanese propaganda machine told of increasing Filipino troop defections on Bataan and some of the Filipino columnists sympathetic to the Japanese began to attack American troops for their anti-Filipino sentiments and the abuse of Filipinos in the front lines.

The only opposition now to Japan's southward thrust was in the Philippines, where MacArthur's forces continued to hold out on Bataan and Corregidor against Homma's 14th Army. As long as MacArthur held Bataan we remained hopeful in Manila. Those hopes were badly shaken in March with the first Japanese news reports that MacArthur had "deserted" his troops "to escape" to Australia. The Japanese depicted this as a recognition by MacArthur that Japan was victorious and as an example of American cowardice, alleging that no Japanese commander would leave his forces in the face of defeat.

We subsequently learned from our outside sources that MacArthur had been ordered by President Roosevelt to proceed to Australia to take command of Allied Forces in the Southwest Pacific; still, his departure left us with a deep feeling of loss. The details of MacArthur's remarkable journey from Corregidor by PT boat through Japanese-held waters to Mindanao and then by plane to Australia did not reach us until much later.

While there was some satisfaction in knowing that MacArthur had eluded Homma for a second time, this soon gave way to frustration and intensifying anxiety as reports reached us that Homma had launched a massive offensive against our forces on the Bataan front.

Inside the camp, daily routines kept everyone busy. The school year was coming to an end in March, as was customary before the intense heat of Manila's summer. One of the mentors for the young men was Professor Robert ("Doc") Kleinpell, a micropaleontologist from Berkeley who was caught by the war while on an assignment seeking gold in Baguio's mountain area. His interests and knowledge ranged far and wide. Doc presided over sessions that burst the boundaries of high-school curriculum, inspiring his pupils to think about world history as a global pageant, a story that echoed the past and in the long run would move far beyond the current world conflict to feature new forces equally challenging to the men and women of their generation. He foresaw the Cold War.

So the class of '42 was ready to graduate, and its members would finish their high school education with heightened wisdom, if not traditional content or style. At the ceremony, Cliff presented the class gift to Mrs. Croft, the principal—a roll of toilet paper. In this community where a lavatory monitor handed out one sheet at a time, it was a gift to be treasured.

There were moments of levity, yes, but the trials were never far from thought. As I read Cliff's manuscript, I was struck by how quickly he'd been forced to transition from a lighthearted teenager to a serious observer of the world.

During February and March, Homma began to receive fresh reinforcements to break through the American defenses on Bataan. The final offensive began on April 3 and we read the distressing reports in the Japanese press of increasing air and artillery bombardment of both Bataan and Corregidor. While we refused to accept the Japanese version of their military successes, we also knew that we had no reinforcements and that disease and malnutrition had taken their toll on our troops after three months of jungle warfare. The fate of our men hung in the balance and on April 9 General Edward King, commander on Bataan, decided with great reluctance that he had no alternative but to surrender in order to prevent the complete annihilation of his troops.

Those who had surrendered on Bataan were malnourished, sleep-deprived, and assembled without food or water. Many were ill or wounded. Homma had anticipated there would be 40,000 men, but the numbers were closer to 75,000: 64,000 Filipinos and 11,500 Americans. In the following week, the prisoners were force-marched sixty-five grueling miles from Mariveles across from Cavite to San Fernando in central Luzon. Those who fell were executed or left to die. The survivors were then packed into sweltering boxcars for a twenty-five-mile slow ride to Capas and marched another eight miles to Camp O'Donnell where they were interned. Between five and ten thousand Filipinos died on the journey, and about 1,100 Americans. This was the "Bataan Death March," when more soldiers died than were killed during the entire Bataan campaign.

The prisoners in Santo Tomas would not know the full extent of this disaster until after they were liberated. They did hear of the defeat at Corregidor.

We knew it would only be a matter of time before our forces on Corregidor met the same fate as those on Bataan. Once again, the Japanese-controlled press extolled their "ever-victorious" warriors with daily coverage of their aerial assaults and heavy coastal bombardment of the island-fortress. Then came the reports of the Japanese landings on the island and the close-quarter fighting which followed.

Once again there were banner headlines—CORREGIDOR SURRENDERS—and our hearts sank. News photos showed a war-weary General Wainwright and his senior officers sitting across the table from General Homma and his commanders in the small town of Cabcaben on Bataan. Wainwright, the veteran cavalryman who had taken over MacArthur's command, looked worn and thin in his rumpled khakis after months of combat while Homma sat, impassive, wearing an immaculately starched uniform and open-collar shirt, his ceremonial sword at his side. The Manila media described the final surrender of Corregidor in great detail, publishing General Wainwright's radio message on May 7 calling on all American and Filipino troops in the Philippines to lay down their arms. There were many teary-eyed faces in camp as we read and reread his surrender message. The realization that America had suffered its worst military disaster with the capture of tens of thousands of American and Filipino troops began to sink in, deepening the mood of despair in camp.

Though the Santo Tomas internees did not know the details of the Bataan march, they did know that the Japanese in Manila were celebrating their victory with the forced march of many of the Corregidor defenders from the harbor front through the streets of Manila to a prison a short distance from their own camp.

The Japanese had planned this march in conjunction with their victory celebrations, but it backfired on them as Filipino bystanders tossed food parcels to the American prisoners, waved and gave the "V for victory" sign.

General Homma made his triumphal entry into Manila on May 9 and there were banner headlines and photos of the victory celebrations around the city. We later learned that Filipino officials were forced to march in the parade and that the Japanese were dissatisfied by the low turnout and lack of public response. Our camp guard detachment even had their own celebration over sake down at the front gate and we could hear their shouts of "Banzai" late into the evening.

While the doctors from Corregidor were treated as military prisoners, the nurses who had worked in the military hospital on the island were spared the horrors of the death march and military camps. They were sent to Santo Tomas to join the civilians interned there.

According to the Japanese media, the Philippines had now become part of Japan's "Greater East Asia Co-Prosperity Sphere" and in early June Homma announced that Filipino war prisoners would be released to help rebuild the country. The release was described in the media as an example of Japan's benevolence. Little mention was made of the fact that the prisoners would first have to sign an oath of loyalty to Japan. There were also promises of independence for the Philippines and a puppet regime, made up of officials who formerly served in the prewar Commonwealth Government, was established to work with the Japanese Military Administration on domestic affairs. These Filipino officials were highly praised in the Japanese media for staying on to cooperate "in restoring peace and order" unlike President Manuel Quezon, "the American lackey" who had "fled" to Australia with MacArthur, thus "deserting his people."

It would be more than a year before Cliff learned about a very personal tragedy from that difficult time. Bill Coleman, Barbara's brother, had been among the forces captured on Bataan and marched north in the infamous Death March. He survived that march and was put on a ship with a number of other prisoners, headed for Japan to serve there as forced labor. There was no indication that the ship carried Allied prisoners of war, and it was spotted as a legitimate target by American bombers. Crippled by a direct hit, it sank, killing all aboard including Cliff's outrigger canoe captain from the "jellyfish war."

9

A BRIEF REUNION

NEARLY FOUR MONTHS AFTER THE family said farewell in camp, Cliff was able to secure a pass to visit his parents. His mother sent a note via a Red Cross nurse that Charles Forster was not well and she was anxious that Cliff see him. Former applications for permission to visit had been denied, but Cliff now had a forty-eight-hour pass in hand and instructions to avoid any contacts with Filipino civilians and to keep away from public places.

Any such contact could be punishable by death along with any attempt to engage in "espionage or propaganda" activities. I was given a red arm band which I was to wear at all times. The Japanese character "bei" on the band would identify me as an American. The Japanese guard checked me out carefully at the gate, gave me a look of contempt, and forced me to bow.

Once outside the gate, I took a deep breath and looked around for some kind of transportation, realizing immediately that it would be difficult to avoid contact with Filipino nationals if I were to get around town. I hailed a *carromata* (horse-drawn vehicle which I had used often before the war) from across the street. The *cochero* or driver was a portly Filipino with a jolly face who introduced himself as José. He was smoking a large cigar and insisted that I sit on the front seat with him. I hesitated, recalling the Japanese warning about fraternization, but he waved his hand and told me not to worry.

"How long you in there?" he asked, pointing to the Santo Tomas tower. "Almost six months," I replied. He shook his head and asked me if I wanted to take a puff on his cigar. I declined. "It will make you strong again," he said with a hearty laugh. Then he lowered his voice. "I have good news. Listen carefully." I could hardly hear him so I moved closer. "MacArthur is coming back soon." "How do you know?" I asked. "Radio broadcasts from Australia and America" he replied. "He said he will return." This was the first indication I had of the general's famous "I shall return" speech.

For the remainder of the ride across town José regaled me with accounts of Japanese defeats in the Pacific and particularly the number of ships that had been sunk and planes shot down. At one point we passed a large billboard with a map of Asia and the Pacific. Small Japanese paper flags depicted the extent of Japanese victories and I noticed they were all the way down to the Solomons and up into the Aleutians. He turned to me with a mischievous smile. "At night we change their flags. In the morning they find American flags or we push back their flags to Japan. Now they have extra guards for the big map."

As we moved along the city streets I noticed that Japanese flags were flying over the official buildings and the hotels. The old street names had been changed to Japanese names. Taft Avenue had become "Daitoa" or "Greater East Asia," the Jones bridge across the Pasig River had been renamed "Banzai" and MacArthur's old headquarters at Fort Santiago was now known as "Fuji-heiei" for Japan's famous mountain.

The driver took special pleasure in pointing out geisha establishments and cabarets which occupied many of the old residences as well as familiar restaurants and hostelries. "They bring many girls from Japan and Korea." He said. As we passed one restaurant we could hear Japanese singing and the high-pitched voices of what we assumed were geishas. When we reached our destination I thanked José for the ride and the good news he had shared with me. He emphatically refused to accept any payment. "Mickey Mouse money," he said. "We will celebrate when MacArthur returns and you can buy me a San Miguel beer." He gave me a "V" sign, wished me well, and started down the street.

Father was located in a small emergency hospital established by the Red Cross just before the war and it was still staffed by several of his doctors and nurses. The chief physician, Dr. German de Venecia, was an impressive doctor who was greatly admired by his patients, many of them casualties of Japanese brutality in and around Manila. The Filipinos frequently challenged Japanese guards, refusing to obey their orders. Some had been shot. Others had sword and bayonet wounds. They expressed strong contempt and hatred for the Japanese occupiers. "They're not winning any support for their Co-Prosperity Sphere," Dr. de Venecia said, pointing to a young boy who had lost his leg to a Japanese sword. "He refused to bow to a sentry."

I found my father hard at work in his room, drafting a letter. He looked very thin and wan and seemed to be shocked by my appearance as well. "So good to see you son," he said. "It's been much too long." I asked him how he was doing and he said "the old ticker" was not what it used to be. "But I'm with friends and that makes it tolerable. Your mother is also taking good care of me."

He then asked me about conditions in camp, condemning the executions in February. I didn't want to worry him unduly and said conditions could be a lot worse. "They're pretty bad up north," he commented. "Many of our prisoners were killed after the Bataan surrender on the forced march to Camp O'Donnell." He had received reports from his doctors and nurses and was trying to get additional information on the condition of the surrenderees. "This is an absolute violation of the convention on treatment of prisoners of war and I intend to do something about it."

I noticed that he had a copy of the Geneva Convention which he had underlined and there were extensive notes in the margins. "What can you do about it?" I asked. He said he was writing General Homma directly with a strong protest and would provide him with a copy of the Convention. He picked up his draft of the letter he was working on and passed it to me. The letter was concise and to the point, referring to specific passages in the Convention on treatment of prisoners. Father called particular attention to the importance of Red Cross access to the camps under the Convention in order to provide assistance to the POWs. Earlier attempts at lower levels to obtain access had been unsuccessful. Now he was going to the top.

"How do you plan to do that?" I asked.

"By going through the newly organized Philippine Red Cross," he replied. He was quite optimistic about getting through because of his earlier work with the Japanese Red Cross in Tokyo. "They will still remember me and I'll send them copies."

I admired father's determination but had strong doubts that he would succeed, although it was certainly worth a try. His own status as a Red Cross official had been ignored by the Japanese but he wasn't about to give up. I recalled his earlier determination to evacuate MacArthur's wounded troops from Manila to Australia hours before the occupation of Manila. The odds were against him then as they were now, but his concern for the victims of war, both military and civilian, drove him on. He still had hope that there would be some kind of humanitarian solution to this problem. In any event, an effort had to be made to get Homma and his senior officers to respect these principles in order to prevent further mistreatment of helpless prisoners.

Time had run out on Cliff's forty-eight-hour pass and he would not see his parents again for sixteen months. As he bid them farewell, he grieved over his father's despair that all his years spent in humanitarian work and the principles that he cherished were being undermined. His father's letter to General Homma, Cliff wrote, was his final effort. "It turned out to be a futile one."

10

MEMORIZED CODE

L IFE IN CAMP SETTLED INTO a dreary routine, punctuated by
the hard work of meeting the basic needs of the community and
an increasing sense of hopelessness among the prisoners. Cliff left
camp to see his parents on only the one occasion, but a few other times
he and fellow internees were sent out on work details to unload ships.
While escorted through the streets of Manila to the harbor, they paid
careful attention to what they noticed, what the Japanese were doing.

As the months passed—and then a year—individuals as well as their
representative committees tried to boost morale and retain some semblance of normalcy. Doc Kleinpell started offering regular college classes
to the young internees. Husbands and wives, although still separated in
assigned sleeping rooms, scavenged materials to build family "shanties,"
where they could meet in the daytime and occasionally cook a family
meal out of the few hoarded bits of food that remained in their possession. The teenagers found an unsupervised nook in one of the stairwells
and met there in the evenings to chat, reminisce, fantasize about the
future, and celebrate each other's birthdays. Then—as Cliff wrote in his
letter to Dick Moore—some of the boys and men were taken away.

Early in the spring of 1943, Japanese Premier Tojo came to Manila and reportedly was highly displeased over guerrilla raids on Japanese troops and continued Filipino support of the Americans. The existence of a large civilian internment camp in Manila was particularly annoying to Tojo and shortly after his departure the commandant's office notified us that a new camp would be built forty miles southwest of Manila. Eight hundred supposedly healthy males, accompanied by the Corregidor nurses, were selected to move south to build the new camp on an agricultural college campus, Los Baños, where ultimately all Santo Tomas internees would be held.

I was among the chosen and in May our eight hundred were lined up outside the front entrance to Santo Tomas to be picked up by Japanese army trucks. The night before there was a farewell party with our classmates, out of the Japanese guards' sight. We didn't know when we would meet again and it was an emotional farewell. The next day the entertainment committee rigged up some speakers and played a few recordings as we assembled for departure—"God Bless America" and "It's a Long way to Tipperary"—which they blasted at high volume until they were ordered by the guards to turn off the system.

For the trip we were crowded into old railroad box cars with corrugated tin roofs. Japanese soldiers insisted on closing the doors and the heat became very intense. By the time we reached Los Baños many of us were dehydrated and there was very little water available at the camp site. No preparations for our welfare had been made and we had to fend for ourselves. The commandant at the new camp made it clear that our main function was to start building barracks for the rest of the internees at Santo Tomas, who would follow in a few months. It was tough work and we would be on very limited rations.

Mail from Santo Tomas was infrequent and it was a special treat when a letter came from Barbara. Her letters were always upbeat and fun to read and did much to raise my morale during that early period at Los Baños. The days dragged on interminably with a small dish of rice and now and then a banana

or some leftover cracked wheat for breakfast and more rice and
beans with occasional carabao meat for dinner. Later we found
a source for additional fruit through clandestine contacts with
Filipino farmers when the Japanese guards were out of sight.
But this became increasingly risky. Meanwhile, we worked on
the new structures with whatever materials the Japanese could
give us. The whole business was very frustrating and our guard
detachment did not make things any easier. The materials provided were inadequate and we warned the commandant that
the first typhoon would decimate the barracks. It did. And we
had to start over.

Cliff did not write or speak much about the five months he spent at
Los Baños. In a letter he wrote to his sister after repatriation, he mentioned that he suffered a severe case of dysentery at the camp and lost a
great deal of weight. Mostly, when sharing his experiences in later years
with family and friends, he recalled the moments of levity, though they
were few and far between.

After the first barracks collapsed, the commandant called a meeting
of all the internees. Seated on a makeshift stage were the senior Japanese
officers plus an unidentified soldier who sat to one side with his head
lowered to his chest. The commandant derided the poor construction
that had caused the collapse of their buildings, pointed to the soldier,
and said it was his fault. He had been in charge of the project and was
incompetent because "he is a Korean." Much to the annoyance of the
commandant, the prisoners burst out laughing.

Even under these newly harsh circumstances, internees found ways
to keep up their spirits. Their shows continued. Cliff had the role of the
zany brother who thought he was Teddy Roosevelt in the play *Arsenic
and Old Lace*. His one line was "Charge!" as his character fantasized leading the battle of San Juan Hill in Puerto Rico, and with an effective
loudspeaker system in place it reverberated through the camp. Japanese
solders rushed out of their quarters, ready to repel invaders. They surrounded actors and audience, accused the group of signaling guerrillas
who were hiding in the hills, and demanded custody of the person who
had given the order. The internees refused to identify the perpetrator,

showed the commandant the script for the play and, through an interpreter, explained the plot. The play was not allowed to continue, but the guards' guns were lowered and Cliff's stage identity remained secret.

In his letter to Dick, Cliff wrote about the unexpected reprise for him and his family.

The Coleman family was among those internees who were later moved south to Los Baños from Santo Tomas once the barracks were completed. But I was unable to welcome Barbara since I was among those selected for repatriation in September of 1943—as a dependent of a Red Cross official, one of several exchange categories determined by the international negotiators.

Before Cliff left Los Baños, Doc Kleinpell gave him a "report card." This was the only document Cliff carried with him to America to indicate that he was qualified to handle university-level work. He had no high school diploma certifying that he had graduated as a member of the class of 1942 in Santo Tomas, no evidence that he'd even attended high school.

LOS BAÑOS INTERNMENT CAMP
LAGUNA PROVINCE, PHILIPPINES
SEPTEMBER 20, 1943

STATEMENT OF ACADEMIC RECORD
L.B.I.C. EDUCATION DEPT., COLLEGE DIVISION

To Whom It May Concern:
At the time of repatriation, Mr. CLIFTON FORSTER had completed approximately the first half of the work in the first-semester course (sixty lectures in Morphology and Taxonomy of Plants and Animals) of the internment camp's two-semester college freshman course in General Biology. Subjects covered up to date Included General Biologic Principles (Cell morphology, physiology, growth and reproduction, Genetics, comparative morphology, Embryology, Ecology and geographic distribution,

Paleobiology and organic evolution, and Taxonomy), Plant Morphology (General plant morphology, physiology, and reproduction, tissues and tissue systems, leaves, roots, stems, flowers, and fruits) and Systematics through the Thallophytes. Thus left uncompleted were the systematics of the higher plants and of the animal kingdom.

Mr. Forster's class record up to date has been <u>Excellent</u> <u>(grade A)</u>.

> Robert M. Kleinpell INSTRUCTOR
> (Ph.D. in Paleontology at Stanford 1934,
> Assist. Prof. in Micropaleontology at
> Calif. Instit. of Technology, 1939)

From Los Baños, Cliff was sent back to Santo Tomas for a short time and was able to reconnect with those classmates who had not gone with the original group of eight hundred to the new camp. Not wanting to leave Manila while his buddies remained interned, he tried to arrange for someone go in his place. This was not an option, since the three Forsters were on the Red Cross-generated list for repatriation.

So Cliff set out to do what he could to serve those he would leave behind. He gathered names, addresses, and phone numbers from a large number of internees, memorized as many as he could, and hid the rest where he hoped Japanese officials wouldn't find them when they searched the departing passengers. Additionally, a committee of camp elders gave him a special code to remember, with no details of when or why he might need it.

On September 26th, Cliff rejoined his parents after almost a year and a half, and 127 repatriates traveled by train to Lingayen Gulf, along the same route Cliff and his high-school friends had traveled two years before, on the eve of Pearl Harbor. When they reached the gulf, the prisoners found the Japanese ship *Teia Maru*—formerly the French liner *Aramis*—anchored offshore, already carrying hundreds of repatriates from Japan and China.

The first stop on their journey to freedom was Saigon, where they picked up French citizens. Then they sailed through the Strait of Malacca between Singapore and Indonesia, on towards the southwest coast of India. Their destination was Mormugao in Goa, a colony of the neutral nation of Portugal.

Waiting in port was the Swedish ship the *Gripsholm,* which had left New York with a passenger load of Japanese citizens who had been held in the United States since the war began. The *Teia Maru* docked alongside and the passengers of the two ships passed each other in two lines and were checked off, one by one, Allied national against Japanese, as they exchanged vessels and destinations.

With over 1,400 repatriates aboard, the *Gripsholm* departed for the long voyage home via the Cape of Good Hope and Rio de Janeiro. As Cliff described it, "Full-course dinner meals awaited us and a two-year collection of *Life* magazines—to sate our hunger for food and news." Additionally, the Forsters received a telegram from Manuel Quezon, via the American Consulate in Bombay, India. The ailing Philippine president—who had accompanied General MacArthur from Corregidor to Australia, and had since continued on to Washington D.C.—extended his "cordial greeting and best wishes for a safe and early arrival in the United States."

As soon as they were transferred to the *Gripsholm,* Cliff began to reconstruct all the information he had memorized, and started writing letters to the families back home. His reports by mail and by phone would be the first solid information those families had received since December, 1941.

Throughout his internment, Cliff had been fascinated by the Japanese use of propaganda. Always hungry for news, even unwelcome and perhaps distorted news, he read the official Japanese newspapers avidly and made notes in a journal, in which he also described Japanese activities and recorded summaries of daily life in the camp. In reading the Japanese view of events, he learned a great deal about the perceptions that had become principles for Japan's military.

While waiting at Santo Tomas to be repatriated, Cliff made cryptic notes from his journal and took along some of the edicts, figuring that if the Japanese found them it wouldn't matter since "I was just taking their material back." He entrusted the journal to a friend to save for him, and later learned it had been lost in the internees' rush to safety when Los Baños was liberated.

During the long voyage home, Cliff reconstructed what he could recall from his notes and his memory of the Japanese newspaper coverage, their propaganda, their version of what was going on, not only in the Philippines but elsewhere in the Pacific. He also wrote about how the Japanese had taken over the Philippine government and created a puppet regime with a former government official, José Laurel, at the helm.

When the *Gripsholm* docked in Rio, a U.S. intelligence agent boarded, sought Cliff out, and asked him to repeat the code given to him by the camp elders at Santo Tomas. What Cliff did not know until later was that an internee at Los Baños was maintaining a hidden radio transmitter that could be used to communicate with guerrillas hiding in the mountains. This code would be useful in planning a risky operation behind Japanese lines to rescue the internees at that camp during the final days of the war

11

"WE CHERISH LIFE MORE
THAN EVER BEFORE"

F ROM RIO DE JANEIRO, THE *Gripsholm* sailed to New York, docking
on December 1, 1943. Her arrival was a joyful public celebration—
saluting fireboats shot cascades of water, and crowds of well-wishers lined up along the shore.

Naval Intelligence representatives came on board the *Gripsholm* after
her arrival, requesting any information from the passengers that might
shed light on the wartime activities and capabilities of the Japanese. Cliff
spoke with them about his reconstructed journal notes. Some days later, he
was called to Washington to share those notes and answer more questions.

The U.S. Navy officials in Washington were particularly interested in
learning about the layout of the camps. Where was Santo Tomas located
in Manila, and how was the camp situated at Los Baños? Which buildings
at each were occupied by the internees? This information would be kept
on record to inform the military in the case of rescue attempts later on.

Cliff's father had been asked to come to Washington as well, to
report on his experiences with the Japanese to his colleagues in the
American Red Cross Headquarters. The elder Forster also met with Paul
McNutt, who had been high commissioner in the Philippines after it was

declared a commonwealth, and father and son took this opportunity to call on the president of the Philippines, who lay in his bed at Washington's Shoreham Hotel, terminally ill with tuberculosis. Charles Forster highly respected Manuel Quezon, with whom he had worked so closely in those days before the outbreak of war to provide for civilian needs. It was unfortunate that this statesman did not survive to lead his nation into independence.

While they were in Washington, Cliff wrote to his sister, who had remained in California when the Forster family returned to Manila in 1940. She had since married and had a baby, and worried constantly about her captive family.

I had never seen Cliff's letter to his sister before I delved into that tea chest containing old documents. Gerry had saved it, and Cliff had found it among her treasured belongings after her death.

> Roger Smith Hotel
> Washington, D.C.
> Dec. 7th, 1943
> 10:30 P.M.

Dear Gerry and Dick—

We have just received your letter of the 4th December. This'll make the second letter I have mailed to you from the east coast. I sent a long letter from Rio airmail, leaving nothing untold. I expected that I had reached you long ago. There must be a terrific hold up somewhere!

We can hardly wait until we see you!!! We have been going around in a daze. I guess we're built for just so much and no more. To suddenly have thrust upon you skyscrapers, surging masses of white faces, good food, taxis, uniforms, bright lights, and at the same time to be literally swamped with mail and telephone calls—meeting mothers of prisoners of war and old friends—well you can imagine!

Gosh! If only you knew how we *felt*, or could have seen us on that ship where the Statue of Liberty came into sight. Many began to sing "God Bless America." I couldn't. I had a strange choking sensation in my throat and I guess I was all bleary eyed because Bill (a pal from China) turned to me and said "Wipe your eyes, Cliff. They're wet."

Even now it's hard to believe that soon we'll all be together. It's great to know that also very soon I'll be with little Charlie! Boy! Aren't we the lucky ones though! Look—I feel as though I'm going to get very gushy so I'll check it now. Words simply can't describe the emotions I feel knowing that we'll soon be in Los Angeles together. To tell you the truth—it's still a dream world.

What struck me most powerfully when I first read Cliff's letter to Gerry was the *voice*. Here was the authentic voice of the nineteen-year-old, so different from the voice of Cliff's other writings—unmitigated by time.

The revealing letter penned by an extraordinary young man continued for several more pages.

Your letter of Dec. 4th worried us somewhat. I still can't understand why that Rio letter didn't reach you. The three of us wanted to clear ourselves of letters and phone calls (we're still at it) that is why we have not written before this. Naturally we know how you must feel since the Rio letters did not reach you.

You say Dad acted dumb over the phone. That made us laugh. It's a natural reaction with all of us. I kick myself for not being there and yet I know I might have been dumber than Dad. It's simply IMPOSSIBLE to actually realize we're home in America, that there's such a thing as freedom. Incidentally we called you again later but made no contact. The first sensations of homecoming had more or less subsided and we thought we'd sound saner.

We didn't write a letter on the boat to mail when we disembarked because the State Dept. informed us that it would take at least a month to reach you. Gripsholm mail was to be strictly censored. Therefore we thought we'd wait. The way you talked in your letter you seemed to think life has no meaning for us

any more. Don't kid yourself! It's just the opposite—after what
we've been through we're in love with it. We cherish life more
than ever before. You'll find me raring to go and do things and
wild about every little thing I see—probably too enthusiastic.
This is a natural reaction. Being close to death several times
and seeing so much of it in December and then lying prostrate
with dysentery and thinking I'd never see the U.S. again you'll
find that my conception of the value of life—intrinsic and
otherwise—has made a very radical and to me wonderful
change! That goes for Mom and Pop too.

Your questions were great! I'll answer them for you. No
Mom and Dad were not in Sto. Tomas. Due to illness (he's
picked up wonderfully now) Dad was luckily released with
Mom to live outside in a little apartment on Isaac Peral. Being
of military age I was kept in Sto Tomas until May 14, '43. At
that time 800 young men were hauled off by the Jap military
to Los Baños where we were to build a new camp on the side of
Mount Makiling. Crowded into boxcars we made the five hour
trip under the blazing sun. We were practically isolated which
was not so hot! There I had dysentery, lost weight and sometimes wondered if I'd see the folks again. Yes—it was pretty
bad. On Sept 20 the 29 of us to be repatriated left for Sto
Tomas where I joined the folks after nearly a year of separation.
Of course I looked like a skeleton then. We weathered the train
trip to Lingayen Gulf where we boarded the Jap ship. We have
oodles to tell you about that 18,000 mile journey which took
us over the equator four times. However that can wait. It would
take at least ten more pages to describe Rio alone!

We received your $17.50 telegram. At least the folks did.
Being in Los Baños I never knew about it. The Intl Red Cross
didn't come to the P.I. simply because the Japs didn't want it
there! Probably guilty of what it might see in war prisoners'
camps.

Yes—I did see Helen Butenko several times before I left for
Los Baños. She looks fine and sends her regards. Martin never
did return to the P.I.

The food was fair. Mom and Dad did alright. At Los Baños it was pretty fierce—basically *rice*.

No Gerry—we were not *doped* or treated brutally. Most Americans were respected. The Japs stayed on their side of the fence and we stayed on ours. Once three of our men were shot for an attempted escape. Twice I had to work under Jap soldiers by force—but outside of these instances nothing happened. Of course we always lived in a state of anxiety and expectation. I never did like that "musical chairs" game—more so when you were next.

Dad was completely ousted from his work. All Americans, Britons were. Mom and Dad occupied much of their time cooking, reading—all in all a very dull, seemingly endless life.

The Japs are cruel, yes—but to Filipinos. This does not mean, however, that all of them are cruel. I've witnessed horrible scenes that I had not thought humans capable of. But let's forget that aspect of the whole thing.

No—Wolfe is not running the Red Cross. The Japs have taken it over lock, stock, and barrel.

We have never been slapped. As far as I know no white female has been raped. In Los Baños we were forced to bow to Jap officers. I'll tell you more about that later.

Considering your visit to the spiritualist: Mom and Dad did live in a little house. Pop was stewing and pacing the floor (he usually does this when he gets sore). We did go single file to get on the ship at Lingayen Gulf but not across a rice field— we had to stagger across sand dunes. Maybe the bowing you're talking about in connection with Dad and Italy might be of some interest. The day we got the news about Italy capitulating the camp at Los Baños went wild. I was so excited I raced past a Jap officer without bowing. I hadn't even noticed him. The next minute he let out a terrific howl and reached for his sword. I bowed low and beat it. There's nothing you can do about it while they have the guns but there were times when I felt awfully stubborn.

This morning was historic for me. I went in with Dad to meet President Quezon at the Shoreham Hotel. Bedridden and

emaciated and unable to speak—his eyes still had a remarkable luster to them. He and Dad embraced each other and tears
actually flooded into his (Quezon's) eyes and streaked down
his cheeks. I'll never forget the way Dad and he looked at each
other. If ever I have seen the love of fellow man in the eyes of
two men—that was it. They were silent for several minutes
and simply held on to each other's hands firmly. For me it was
one of the most dramatic moments I have ever witnessed. Then
Quezon looked up at me, smiled and extended his hand. I took
it in both of mine and said slowly, "This is a great privilege,
Mr. President." My voice cracked before I was halfway through
and then a picture of the three of us was taken.

If you only knew how queer it made me feel—shaking
hands with that frail man, an exile from the country I had been
in only three months before.

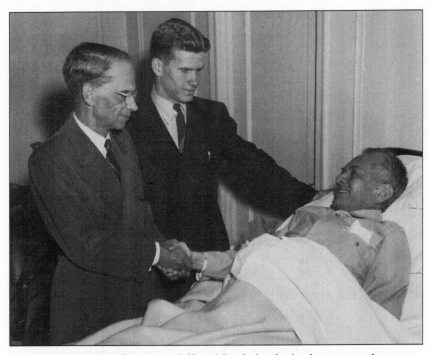

*Repatriated to the U.S., Cliff and his father had a heart-wrenching
visit with the bedridden President Quezon.*

Then I accompanied Dad to see McNutt. I left soon after and went to the Lincoln Memorial.

You can see now how we're constantly on the go. Maybe you can realize also how it might be possible to make allowances for our dazed condition. Dad was an hour and a half with Quezon, two hours with McNutt at luncheon. Mother and I have been writing to prisoners of war relatives at Red Cross headquarters. Everyone there has been grand to us.

Mother says she mailed a letter on the ship. As I said before it'll be tough getting that stuff through! She also wants you to call us by phone whenever you feel the urge (Minneapolis, etc). All calls are on us!!!!

And now I'm going to close with this last note: Buck up, Gerry, and cast all those fears aside for we're nearly home. Last night dining with a Lieutenant Commander at the Mayflower Hotel (the Navy Dept. treated me royally after I submitted information) I heard one of your new songs—"I'm Dreaming of a White Christmas." The song fit my mood exactly—that's just about what I was doing.

Remember that I'm writing for the folks too who, after a full day's work, dropped off to sleep two hours ago. It's now midnight and this is still Dec 7th, the second anniversary of the day the Japs blasted our peaceful lives to hell and separated us and thousands of others.

> Crateloads of Love
> See You Soon!
> Clifton

Attached with a paperclip to Gerry's letter was a snippet of paper with the following jotted notes. Could this be part of the missing letter that the Forsters had sent from Rio?

12 PM—Have just rc'd batches and batches of letters—from friends, relatives. Noticed in your letter emphasis laid on working for those still back there. That's least of your worries. Am

personally carrying over 500 addresses. State Dept on board
has kept us working on card system to list everything we know
about anyone we know. This has taken weeks—a thorough
job. When I arrive in New York I will take some time to write
and mail countless letters. I intend to devote my whole time
to it at first. Because of stories told by repatriates on last ship
it seems Japs got sore and didn't like the idea of so much unfavorable propaganda getting out about them—so—no more exchange. However, as Pop says "You can't stop the people from
talking" and—of course—the truth *sure* exists! So much for now.
NEW YORK NEXT!!

The "last ship" Cliff referred to was the first prisoner exchange from
Asia, in early 1942, when senior diplomats were repatriated from Asia

The U.S. Department of State billed each of the repatriated prisoners for the cost of their *Gripsholm* voyage. The Red Cross paid for the
Forsters.

12

SEAMAN FIRST CLASS FORSTER

AFTER THEIR INTERVIEWS IN WASHINGTON, Cliff and his parents traveled across the United States, visiting relatives in Minnesota en route. They were reunited in Los Angeles with Gerry, who introduced her husband Dick and baby son Charles to the returnees. Finally, the family found refuge in their house in the Oakland hills, from which they could look across San Francisco Bay to the Golden Gate Bridge and the waters which led to the "Pearl of the Orient."

Back in familiar surroundings, Cliff continued writing letters to families of the internees who remained in Manila. One of these went to the grandparents of Margaret Hoffman, the friend Cliff had comforted when she'd burned her diary before internment, and whom I later met when Cliff and I returned together to the Philippines. Marge remained with her family at Santa Tomas until the liberation of the camp in February of 1945. A few years before Cliff's death, Marge returned the letter, which had been saved by her family. Although he painted a rosier picture than the realities experienced by the internees during the remaining months of their internment, once again I felt the young Cliff Forster jumping off the page.

5963 Manchester Drive
Oakland, California
February 2nd, 1944

Dear Mr. Hoffman:

I have recently returned from the Philippines with my parents aboard the exchange ship Gripsholm. I was interned by the Japanese in Santo Tomas with Mr. and Mrs. Hoffman and their two children, Margaret and Bill. Just before my departure from the islands on September 26th, the Hoffmans gave me your address and told me to be sure and contact you.

I knew the Hoffmans before the war; we were next-door neighbors. Margaret, Bill and I attended the same school. We used to have grand times together. During December, the first month of the war, when we were being bombed constantly by the Japanese, the Hoffmans left for one of the Provinces to the north of Manila. When it came too "hot" for them up north they returned to Manila and lived at the Bayview Hotel. I was also staying there with my family. Our homes had been very close to a military objective and were nearly bombed time and again.

On Jan. 5th, after the Japanese had occupied Manila, we were removed to the internment camp at Santo Tomas. Conditions at first were far from favorable. The food and sanitation setup was very bad. However, as time dragged on, the conditions improved. We were allowed to build shacks on the camp grounds. Mr. Hoffman had lumber and, selecting a nice location, built himself and the family a little home. It means the world to them. Fortunately, they have access to outside funds and can procure additional food from the Filipinos. This really helps as the food line is certainly not much to talk about!

Margaret and Bill attend classes. Margaret is now enrolled in a college course. Bill is in his last year of high school I believe. Both are doing very well by themselves. Mr. Hoffman keeps himself busy as does Mrs. Hoffman. She is quite a cook.

The Japs have more or less turned the camp over to the internees. They have their guards down at the front gate. We have had very few unpleasant circumstances to contend with—certainly not like our soldiers after the fall of Bataan. I believe this is largely due to the fact that we are civilians.

Margaret is now a very attractive girl—I should say young lady. Bill Jr. is six feet tall I believe. You would certainly be very proud of them. Margaret has a boyfriend who has been one of the camp's topnotch athletes. Margaret, Bill and I usually met each other in the hall after the 9 p.m. roll call and proceeded to the cookie counter and then sat on a bench outside until about ten p.m.

On May 14, 1943, I was transferred with eight hundred men to another camp south of Manila. I did not see the Hoffmans again for four months. On Sept. 20th, 1943, twenty-seven of us were returned to Santo Tomas to be repatriated. Just before I left Santo Tomas for the exchange ship, on Sept. 25th, the Hoffmans gave me a farewell dinner in their shack. We had wonderful sausages, peanut butter and cookies. It was one of the best meals I had in internment.

Margaret and Bill were down in front to say goodbye to me before dawn. We were then transported north to the embarkation point on a train.

I hope that the little I have told you will help. The Hoffmans will always remain very close friends of mine. I have missed them time and again. Do not worry too much over their welfare. The Japs, for some strange reason, have been rather decent to the civilians and will undoubtedly remain so.

If you have any particular questions you want answered please contact me.

There is a good chance for their repatriation. However, they bank more on the return of the U.S. Marines. Whatever the case they will then come through the experience with flying colors.

Only too glad to be of further assistance to you, I remain

Sincerely yours,
Clifton Forster

The California refuge was only temporary. Charles was summoned back to Washington D.C. by the Red Cross, to head up an agency being established for Philippine war relief. Cliff, who wanted nothing more than to cross that beckoning ocean to release his friends who were still interned, signed up for a two-year stint in the U.S. Navy in May of 1944. He completed boot camp in Idaho and applied for the submarine corps. Only after all of his perfectly healthy wisdom teeth were extracted (a requirement for submariners, since no dentists traveled on those vessels) was he told he did not qualify. Next he sought to fly to Manila as an aerial gunner in a bomber. But a discovery that he had inadequate peripheral vision nixed that option. The third choice was to join the crew of a landing craft for the projected reconquest of the Philippines.

After months of basic training and a stint at a naval base in Algiers, Louisiana, Cliff was sent to Treasure Island to await shipment from San Francisco Bay to the war zone. His dream of rescuing his interned buddies, however, was not to be fulfilled; his records had reached Naval Intelligence, and he received orders to proceed directly to Washington. (Cliff's nephew Charles recalls him telling the family that the sailor who delivered the new orders assumed he was an officer due to the request from on high, and was surprised to find him scrubbing out garbage pails). The familiarity of the young recruit with the geography and culture of the Philippines was just what the office needed to supplement its planning for coming engagements.

Seaman First Class Forster, at age twenty, found himself in the company of high-ranking officers, working with the Chief of Operations for Naval Intelligence. The value of his work was later recognized by a commendation signed by the Secretary of the Navy, James Forrestal.

For exceptionally meritorious achievement in the Office of Naval Intelligence from 1 October 1944 to 1 April 1946 as an assistant for the Philippines to the Head of the Far Eastern

August 20/1944 / Naval Base, Algiers—New Orleans

Youth Held by Japs Seeks Manila Assignment

While on leave, Seaman First Class Forster visited his family in Oakland. Instead of rescuing his interned schoolmates in the Philippines, he was recruited by Navy Intelligence.

Section. His unusual knowledge and background of Philippine affairs and personalities, combined with tireless and loyal devotion to his assigned tasks, contributed materially to the success of Naval Intelligence. His complete and accurate monograph on the North Coast of Luzon and the Cagayan River Valley, prepared from personal knowledge and supplemented by exhaustive and tedious research, represented a substantial contribution to operational planning in the Philippine Islands. The data he compiled on Philippine personalities materially aided in the reestablishment of civil government and in ferreting out of collaborators and enemy agents. Forster's performance of duty reflected high credit upon himself and upon the United States Naval Service.

Cliff, who had longed to return as a liberator to his homeland, was to be a spectator from afar of the historic events that took place in the Philippines shortly after he arrived in Washington. General MacArthur was able to fulfill his pledge of "I shall return" to the Filipinos—and to those prisoners growing thinner and frailer day by day in the internment camps. On October 20, 1944, MacArthur waded ashore on the island of Leyte in the central Philippines. While one of the largest naval battles in modern history was fought against the Japanese offshore, the MacArthur's Allied forces on shore were to encounter ferocious resistance until their final victory in the summer of 1945.

Not long after the Leyte landing, an officer in Naval Intelligence handed Cliff a pack of photos that had been developed from a roll found on the body of a Japanese soldier killed during the fighting in the Philippines.

"Can you tell us anything about these?" the officer asked Cliff. Indeed, he could! The shots had been taken in Santo Tomas, and included a rear view of him in the communal shower and one where he was resting on a hoe in the camp garden. The dead solder had been part of a team that was dispatched to record for the world's admiration the idyllic life that the civilians in Japanese custody were enjoying on their university campus. An "idyll" that would find little verification in the view of the internees!

Cliff settled into his work in Washington, becoming reconciled to wearing his sailor suit and remaining Stateside for the duration of the war. He even began to dream of what he would do when the war ended. He hoped to take advantage of the G.I. Bill of Rights and attend Stanford University, then learned that with no high-school diploma he would be ineligible for admission as a freshman. As a fallback plan he began taking courses in the evening at George Washington University, which had less stringent requirements and was within walking distance of the room he rented on H Street. He hoped that he later might be able to transfer to Stanford as a sophomore.

Two years down the line, his dreams would converge with my own.

13

THE FINAL BATTLE FOR MANILA

WHILE FATHER AND SON BOTH were working in Washington, Charles at the Red Cross headquarters and Cliff with Naval Intelligence, they were closely following the news from the Philippines. Much of it was heartrending, building up to a crescendo of horror at the Red Cross building in early 1945.

The battle for Manila in February was one of the bloodiest of the entire Second World War. As American forces moved in to liberate the city, the trapped Japanese troops fought every inch of the way, while American artillery pounded the Japanese-held neighborhoods, ravaging much of the city in the process. American forces sent a column of tanks through enemy lines to reach and take command of the Santo Tomas camp on February 4th. There were casualties among the internees, but most were saved. Cliff regretted not being part of that rescue mission, but he rejoiced that some of his friends were now in truly benevolent custody, in American care, receiving food and medical attention. And they were coming home.

However, terrible news was received regarding the Red Cross Headquarters. Cliff remembered his father's constant attention to detail

"You are guest in protective custody of the Japanese Imperial Army."

Internment took a terrible toll on once robust men. This display was part of an exhibit for a reunion of internees in California.

during the months that building was being constructed; for Charles Forster it had been "a real labor of love." The building symbolized the humanitarian mission and unstinted devotion to Red Cross principles by the Filipino staff and their American director. It was intended to be an oasis of succor to victims of war and of peacetime disasters, a beacon for the health and welfare of residents throughout the island nation.

The head of the Red Cross, José Paes, who was a member José Laurel's puppet cabinet, was told on December 22nd to accompany that group to Baguio. The Japanese military commanders had ordered them to evacuate under guard to the Japanese rear line command post in the mountains. Before leaving, Paes held an urgent meeting with the chairman of the Red Cross Board, Vicente Madrigal, and they appointed Modesto Paraclan acting manager. The following day he assumed the position. On February 10th, the Red Cross building was the site of a deadly rampage.

Acting manager Paraclan wrote an eyewitness report, "Massacre in the Red Cross Headquarters," for the records of the Philippine Red Cross and the American Red Cross. When Cliff and I moved to Manila after the war as young newlyweds and met with the survivors of his father's Red Cross staff, Charles Forster's longtime personal assistant, Faustino Alfilar, presented his own file copy of this report to Cliff so he would always be reminded of the war's final days in his birthplace and the tragedy that occurred in the Hall of Mercy.

That copy was among Cliff's papers in the tea chest. Many times during the years we were together, Cliff would refer to the dreadful events that took place in the Hall of Mercy, but he never described them in detail. It wasn't until I read Paraclan's report in 2008 that I understood the extent of that massacre and how devastated Charles, Gladys, and Cliff must have been when they learned of it.

Paraclan described how the Red Cross, defying the Japanese orders to have nothing to do with Santo Tomas or "enemy aliens," provided medical aid for the internees following their rescue. Three Red Cross workers were arrested by the military police for violating those orders. As the artillery battle intensified and the Japanese began setting fire to buildings in the center of Manila during early February, Paraclan organized other staff members to establish the Red Cross building as a refuge and an emergency hospital. He wrote:

> While we intended to keep our building merely as emergency first aid and hospital, our location made us the natural and only refuge place for all the people all around us whose homes were then being burned or destroyed, and we became a refuge center from this day on.
>
> From Sunday, February 4, to February 10, my staff of doctors and nurses worked continuously day and night, without letup,

hardly without sleep, food, etc. and barricaded by the Japanese. Even during fire, anybody seen in the streets were shot. On Saturday, February 10, the massacre in the Red Cross, of which the following is the complete story, came and from that day the Red Cross building was abandoned by us with the dead and dying and bedridden patients in it...

Suddenly Saturday afternoon, a squad of Japanese entered the Red Cross building and began to shoot and bayonet everybody they found in the building. That day, we had four cases of major operation and several other bedridden patients. In the late afternoon, Dr. German de Venecia, on duty with us as volunteer surgeon since last Monday, was preparing with an attendant two cases for operation. Miss Rosario Andaya, a nurse on volunteer duty, was out at the main corridor keeping order among the large crowd that filled the building to overflowing. As we heard the noise of rifle fire in every section of the building, Miss Andaya screamed for mercy to spare the lives of a mother and a child beside her. Before we knew what happened a soldier with drawn bayonet came into the temporary combined office/operating room/ward, where I was, and all of us—Dr. de Venecia who had just walked over to my corner, Misses Lobarisa and Pas, both nurses and an attendant—ducked into our respective corners for safety. First Dr. de Venecia was shot twice while he was seated at his corner. The soldier next aimed at the refugee-attendant beside him, but missed her. The attendant threw herself over to where the two nurses had covered themselves up with mattresses beside my desk. The solder overturned the two cots in front of my desk and saw two patients crouching underneath. One bayonet thrust finished each one of them. Another bayonet thrust at the girl that had escaped the first shot aimed at her caught Miss Pas underneath. Looking underneath my desk, the soldier fired two shots at me but the bullets passed between my feet, scraping the bottom rim of my Red Cross steel helmet. After me, he shot a young mother with her ten-day-old baby along with her mother, the baby's grandmother. That, for all the Japanese knew, finished all of us in the room without exception.

More shootings went on around the rest of the building. From
where we were we could hear victims in their death agony, the
shrill cries of children and the sobs of dying mothers and girls.
We did not dare move. When the job was done, to the apparent satisfaction of the murderers, we heard the pharmacy being
ransacked, then some soldiers eating the major noon meal that
had been spread on our table but we did not have any time to eat.
About ten o'clock, we dared to whisper to inquire of each other
who among us about my desk were hurt. It was then I found that
Miss Lobarisa was safe, completely unhurt while Miss Pas had a
bayonet thrust and she was bleeding.

Eluding a sentry, Paraclan managed to escape from the building once
most of the soldiers—believing all were dead—had left. Reluctantly, fearing retribution, the owner of a neighboring house allowed him to hide in
the garden. Unable to leave the neighborhood because Japanese sentries
had sealed off all streets, he met a few survivors among the Red Cross
Staff and they found shelter where they waited while the battle raged on.
When they were finally able to survey the damage, they estimated that
"about thirty of some sixty refugees and patients had been killed." In his
report, Paraclan tried to understand what had motivated this rampage.

What could be the explanation for this beastly murder of
innocent victims? None that I know of except that the following
incidents may throw much light into the case:
On Friday morning, a squad of Japanese marines came to the
building and asked us why we were taking in so many people.
We explained that the people whose houses around us were being demolished by fire had no home to go to and we could not
refuse them as the Red Cross building was the only building
intact in the entire neighborhood. The fact that only three shells
out of hundreds of thousands fired into that part of the city for
an entire week every minute of the day and night had hit the
Red Cross building testified to the accuracy of the American fire.
Thus it was the only safe place for refuge. The soldiers told us not
to take any more people, particularly if they were not Filipinos

or Germans and that nobody should be allowed to go upstairs. Not contented, they examined all the baggage of the refugees, but apparently did not find anything they did not like and they left. In the afternoon another squad came and wanted to use the back yard for a place in which to make those infernal mechanical noises that are undoubtedly intended and do serve to confuse the American artillery about the number of places they (the Japanese) had and also about the accuracy of American fire. All around us, such devices were being used extensively and systematically and, to the uninitiated—even to me until I had finally observed what they are and what they were for—they sounded like artillery volleys. To prevent them from using our place without directly telling them of my objections, I stayed where the soldiers were. As evening came, they ordered me to get out of the yard and to close the doors and windows leading to it. I obeyed but still kept watching them somehow. That night they did not do anything except sleep.

The following morning, they went about the rooms, on my invitation, to see what was going on—operations every minute of the day, patients suffering in bed, children and women lying down, pasted to the walls during a barrage. They did not seem to see anything wrong, at least they did not say anything until they saw me ordering Marcelino, our boy, and a volunteer attendant to replace two Red Cross flags that had just then been blown down, and they told me not to replace them, saying in broken English: "No good, American very bad, no like Red Cross. Japanese okay." They also saw on my desk a temporary cardboard sign I had just finished writing with the text, PHILIPPINE RED CROSS EMERGENCY HOSPITAL—OPERATIONS GOING ON—REFUGE HOUSE—WOMEN AND CHILDREN. They told me not to hang it, one soldier throwing it off my desk at the point of his bayonet.

When they came back at six in the evening what had been behind all their interest became clear: They did not like the Red Cross; they did not want us there, hence the cold-blooded murder, without warning of any kind and without asking any explanations as to who was who.

Paraclan began writing his report on February 13th, after Filipino Scouts in the advance columns of the American forces reached the Red Cross building and told everyone in the area to clear it for street fighting. They ran for their lives through Japanese machine-gun fire, and, on instructions from a lone American soldier whom they met while running, followed a newly placed phone line on the ground to a concentration of American soldiers and safety.

The Americans took control of the Red Cross building on February 14th. By then the structure was a tragic remnant of the once impressive labor of love.

The prisoners at Los Baños were rescued on February 23rd. With split-second timing, Filipino guerilla forces, American paratroopers (who landed as the Japanese guards were doing morning calisthenics, having left their weapons outside the building), an artillery diversion, and an amphibious battalion executed a coordinated attack and the Japanese were caught by surprise. This provided a window of time before nearby Japanese troops could arrive, in which the prisoners were ferried across a lake at the camp's edge to safety and freedom. Here, at last, was the longed-for good news.

14

VICTORY!

THE BATTLE OF MANILA WOULD rage for another ten days before the city, now a smoldering ruins, was liberated. Three and a half months later, World War II was over.

In his Homma manuscript, Cliff described the jubilation in Washington D.C. at the news of Japan's surrender.

Washington, like the rest of the nation, went wild with the news of Japan's surrender on August 15, 1945, and the crowds surged up Pennsylvania Avenue to the White House. A bemedaled paratrooper with the "Screaming Eagles" patch of the 82nd Airborne was kissing and hugging every girl he could find. He picked up an elderly lady who had given him a big hug and spun her around. "Grandma," he shouted, "your boys are coming home!" A black sailor shared his whiskey flask with him and they did a little jig together on the sidewalk. The crowd cheered as the paratrooper scaled a lamp post near the Willard Hotel on F Street, toasting the end of the war with the flask as he reached the top.

In front of the White House several Marines mounted Andrew Jackson's horse in the middle of Lafayette Park and one managed to climb up on Jackson's shoulders, tossing his Marine hat into the humid night air. An Air Force group along with some sailors and soldiers meanwhile scaled Lafayette's statue nearby. One shouted "Lafayette, we are home!" Someone shouted "Let's go see Harry" and this time the crowd started moving towards the White House. President Truman appeared on the front portico and the crowd began singing "For He's a Jolly Good Fellow." The President was all smiles and raised both hands giving the "V for Victory" greeting.

Back at the Navy Department, we followed the government cables with great interest—the arrival of a Japanese delegation in Manila to receive instructions on the plans for the occupation of Japan, Admiral "Bull" Halsey leading his mighty naval armada into Tokyo Bay, MacArthur's flight to Atsugi Air Base south of Tokyo to assume his new duties as occupation commander and, finally, the great climax—the signing on September 2nd of the surrender documents aboard the U.S.S. Missouri.

We welcomed General Dwight Eisenhower, Supreme Commander of the Allied Expeditionary Force, as he led the Victory March of his troops down Pennsylvania and Constitution Avenues past the Washington and Lincoln Monuments. The Washington crowds were out again jamming the sidewalks to welcome Admiral Chester Nimitz, commander of U.S. Pacific forces, as he rode standing in an open sedan followed by his Navy and Marine officers and men.

In the nondescript Chevrolet Stuart Building on 5th and K Streets across from the old market near Chinatown, Captain Ellis Zacharias was closing down his special operation known as Op-16-W of Naval Intelligence. During the last months of the war he had attempted valiantly with his small staff to reach moderate pro-Western Japanese leaders around the Emperor to bring about an early surrender. Fluent in Japanese, Zacharias had been a naval attaché in Tokyo before the war and had established many contacts among the more moderate elements. He felt strongly that a personalized effort talking directly over shortwave to these leaders could have succeeded, and the captured documents we'd processed for him made it clear that Japan's military resolve had been weakening.

Cliff said that Zacharias had not been informed about the decision to use the atomic bombs in Hiroshima and Nagasaki. The Captain felt more time should have been given to allow the Japanese to consider the Potsdam Declaration and the terms of surrender. Cliff had great admiration for this officer, his grasp of Japanese psychology, and his dedication to using radio transmissions to reach the more moderate leaders in that country. Zacharias would serve as a role model for the professional diplomat Cliff would become.

In later years I thought often of Captain (later Admiral) Zacharias holed up in his small office adjacent to ours as he worked long hours. He was one of the few who made the important distinction between the pro-Western moderates and the anti-Western militarists in attempting to bring the conflict to a speedier conclusion. Had there been more time he might have succeeded. But time had run out and the decision had been made to drop the bomb on Hiroshima.

One afternoon in early January of 1946 I was summoned by my commanding officer in the Stuart Building. A Marine colonel who had served with the Fourth Marines in China before the war, he was a man of few words with a gruff manner. I found him smoking his pipe while examining some papers on his desk. He looked up. "I understand you were in the Philippines when the Japs invaded in 1941." I replied affirmatively. "How much do you know about the general in command of the invasion force, a fellow called Homma?" I said I knew very little about him, commenting that he had returned to Japan soon after the fall of Corregidor in May of 1941.

"We never saw him in our camp in Manila," I added.

"But you were his prisoners?" he shot back. I replied affirmatively.

There was a long and somewhat difficult silence. The Colonel looked up again from his desk with those piercing eyes. "The Jap general is going to be tried for atrocities by MacArthur," he said. "Do you think he is guilty?" The Colonel had a reputation for fast, probing questions and wanted quick, direct, but reflective answers. I replied, "Many atrocities were committed by his soldiers following our surrender on Bataan."

"You are referring to the Death March?"

"Yes sir," I replied. "The Death March took place under his command."

"So you feel he is guilty?"

"Yes, sir."

"Did he give orders to do that?"

I told the Colonel I didn't know for sure but that the killings had been widespread along the route of the march. He rose from his chair and went over to the window.

"I want you to give me summary reports on the trial. Try to be objective and look for evidence of guilt."

Late one afternoon I stopped off at my favorite coffee shop on the way back to my quarters. It was getting dark and a winter storm was approaching. Judy Garland was singing her "Trolley Song" on the radio. The proprietor, a cigar hanging from one side of his mouth, came over to my side of the counter. "How many more days until discharge?"

"Exactly one hundred and twenty," I said.

"What will you do then?" His cigar smoke was all over the place and I moved my coffee to avoid his ashes.

"Probably college" I told him.

He removed the cigar from his mouth and pointed it at me. "Big mistake. How old are you?"

"About to turn twenty-two."

"Good," he said, "start off right." Go into the restaurant business. Make money before there's another depression."

I went back to my coffee as the bell on Judy's trolley went "clang-clang" just as one of those old Washington street cars was going by the window. A light snow was beginning to fall.

Someone had left the evening paper on the counter so I began to leaf through it. I was suddenly riveted to an article on one of the inside pages. The headline read "Homma Takes Blame for Bataan Death March Fatal to 17,000—Moral Responsibility for Ordering Journey is Accepted in Trial." The substance of the AP story was that the Japanese general had indicated during the cross-examination that he was morally responsible for anything that happened under his command.

"Who's guilty?" The proprietor with his smelly cigar was hovering over me, trying to read the article.

"A Japanese general being tried in the Philippines," I said.

"Those Japs are all guilty, particularly the generals!"

An older, slightly inebriated gentleman at the other end of the counter overheard this and agreed emphatically. "Damn right," he said. "All bastards."

I decided to move on and asked if I could take the article along.

"Take the whole paper," he said, "and tell me more about this general the next time you are in here."

I was anxious to show the paper to my father who had been called to Washington from retirement to manage a Philippine war relief organization founded by private citizens. I knew he would be interested in General Homma's admission of guilt and we could celebrate together. This was assuredly the end of Homma and I could also now wrap up my report for the colonel.

Entering the old Claridge where my father and mother resided at the time, I raced up the stairs to their room where I found my father sitting near the window looking out across Lafayette Park. The same evening paper was on the table by his side. "Have you seen the news about Homma?" I asked. "He's admitted his guilt!" My father nodded slowly, then suggested I sit down on the sofa and join him for a cup of tea. I said I just had some coffee and should be getting back to my own flat before the snow got any worse. He then said he had read the article with interest and some concern. I assumed he would share the view that justice had been done at last. General Yamashita, defeated by

MacArthur on his return to the Philippines, had received his due. Now it was Homma's turn.

Father remained silent for a few moments before commenting. Then he looked straight at me. "What makes you think he's guilty?" he asked.

"The evidence submitted against him," I replied. "All those atrocities committed by his troops during the Death March." I also mentioned that the general had accepted moral responsibility for what had happened.

I was perplexed by what my father was trying to tell me. "You should make a distinction," my father continued, "between his acceptance of moral responsibility and any actual admission of guilt by him for what happened." My father noticed my confused expression. "Give this one a lot of thought," he advised, "before you reach any final decisions of your own."

It was his view that night that whatever action was taken on the Homma case could establish important precedents for the future and that we should proceed with great deliberation on any final verdict. "We are still too close to the events themselves to make any intelligent and objective assessment of real guilt," he concluded.

I found his response disturbing and said so. How could he possibly raise any question about the general's guilt considering that his own staff in the Philippines had been victims of atrocities? I even recalled my father's unsuccessful efforts to get through to Homma in 1942 while he was under house arrest in Manila. He had tried desperately to reach the General on the subject of the Geneva Convention in respect to the treatment of prisoners of war. I also recalled his deep anguish and despair when he did not receive any replies to his appeals.

I remained puzzled, dismayed, and a little angry. As I started home through the snow that evening I knew I would have to part company with my father on the question of Homma's guilt. I had always had great admiration and respect for my father's objectivity and humanitarian instincts but his reasoning now was very confusing and difficult for me to understand. Homma, like

Yamashita, was obviously guilty of war crimes. The evidence was quite clear. Why would there be any question or doubt about this?

The streets were empty and silent as I headed back to my flat on 21st Street. Washington during a snowfall at night is always a lovely sight, but I was too involved with my own thoughts about the conversation with my father to enjoy it.

I decided to take my usual shortcut past the old State Department Building next to the White House, cutting over diagonally to the Department of the Interior. I found myself in front of the National Headquarters of the American Red Cross. The tall white columns in front of the building were illuminated by spotlights on the front lawn. I stood across from the building looking up at the Red Cross symbol above the entrance. The bright red was such a vivid contrast to the snow on the ground and I was struck again by the beauty and grace of the structure. This had been my father's headquarters from the time he went to France with the Red Cross to work with refugees during the First World War. Now another World War had ended with great loss of life and within two months Homma would be executed.

A few months after Homma's death, Charles Forster would be gone as well.

Cliff received an honorable discharge from the U.S. Navy on April first, 1946. His parents' Philippine war-relief work was over, and they had headed home to California. Cliff was anxious to go get on a cross-country train and join them as quickly as possible.

Just before leaving Washington, Cliff received news that his father had suffered a heart attack while on a trip to visit the Humboldt County redwoods and was in a hospital in a Northern California lumber town. By the time Cliff reached Scotia, his father was dead.

For the remainder of his journey home, Cliff traveled with his mother on a train with a coffin in the baggage car behind them, accompanying Charles Forster to his final resting place at the Oakland cemetery.

We buried my father in the East Bay hills overlooking San Francisco and the Golden Gate with the Pacific beyond. We knew he was fond of that view and we placed on his grave a simple bronze plaque carrying the Red Cross symbol which had meant so much to him.

15

TWO LIVES CONVERGE

THE SUMMER AFTER HIS FATHER'S DEATH, Cliff helped his mother and sister spruce up the family house and grounds. Gerry moved with her family into the lower level of the Oakland bungalow, which had been converted into a pine-paneled basement refuge by Cliff and his father during one of their home leaves from Manila.

Cliff still had visions of studying at Stanford University. With a transcript showing a year of satisfactory undergraduate work at George Washington, he applied and was accepted as a sophomore transfer student to Stanford in September 1946.

I too had been accepted to Stanford, as a seventeen-year-old freshman.

At the time I left home for California, the farthest west I had ever been was to the shores of Lake Michigan, and I'd never left America. I'd lived in Grand Rapids until age ten, when my parents divorced. They both remarried; my sister and I lived with our mother and stepfather in Rye, New York, and my brother stayed in Michigan with our father and stepmother. As the oldest sibling— Vail was seven years younger, Roddy nine years younger—I was sent to visit in Michigan during school holidays. At the age of twelve I thought I was pretty sophisticated, traveling solo on Capitol Airlines between the two homes.

In my tenth-grade year my mother felt I was not being sufficiently challenged at Rye High School and shipped me off to the Baldwin School for girls in Bryn Mawr. That school was a huge challenge! Latin and chemistry, long papers in English and substantial ones in French, and a requirement to preside over morning chapel every few weeks nearly submerged me my first year. But I survived, graduated, and was thankful in years to come—both as a university student and a Foreign Service wife—for the research and public-speaking skills I learned there.

Stanford was my father's suggestion, much to my mother's annoyance. She wanted me to do the proper Westchester County thing and attend a New England school. Also, she lamented, "You'll go to California and meet an attractive man, get married there, and I'll only see you once or twice a year." But my father was paying the college bills, and the headmistress at Baldwin told Mother that "Nancy needs to spread her wings; she's ready for a coeducational university."

It was a great leap for me, from the cloistered halls of a girls' boarding school near Philadelphia to the Palo Alto farm campus that welcomed demobilized war veterans, most of them older in worldly experiences as well as years. A professor who became a close friend and visited Cliff and me in Tokyo decades later said those were the most stimulating classes he ever taught. The ex-soldiers, sailors, and airmen were ready to soak up learning and had wisdom of their own to add to class discussions. For me, the gatherings over coffee in the student union were often as eye-opening as the lectures of the professors. And we Stanford women had to pay close attention in class and work hard to keep up with the pace set by the men.

My father had, with strong parental persuasion, joined his father's law firm as soon as he received his Harvard Law School degree in the 1920s. He broke out of that mold during the war. Although he was well beyond draft age he was sufficiently outraged by the attack on Pearl Harbor that he signed up the following day with the Army Air Force. His war was in the same theater as Cliff's, as Cliff and I would discover early in our acquaintance. My father served on General MacArthur's legal staff in Australia and was in the grueling campaigns up through New Guinea and on to Leyte in the General's wake. Returning home from the Philippines, he stopped at Stanford University to do some military business and was smitten by the ambiance of the campus. Hence, his recommendation to me.

Cliff and I met in the fall of 1947 as fellow workers at the Institute for International Relations, Stanford's student gathering place for those interested in global affairs. He was the IIR president and I was the secretary. He and fellow war-veteran members organized and ran a conference—the Western College Congress—that would bring together students and speakers from colleges and universities throughout the American West to contemplate challenges and solutions for the postwar world order.

Cliff presided. My job was to record the activities of the day, find a pay phone when the session ended, and telephone a report to Paul Smith, the editor of the *San Francisco Chronicle*. A Stanford graduate, Smith wrote up the phoned-in stories and published them in his paper. I don't remember now what I reported or what he published, but I do recall vividly the anger voiced by some of the delegates during the sessions. Students from India and Indonesia lashed out at the colonial rule still imposed by Western powers on their people, the British still in India and the Dutch in Indonesia.

This was a perspective new to me. It startled Cliff, who believed American colonialism in the Philippines (which had ended with full independence in July of 1946) had been benign, beneficial, and appreciated by the Filipinos. He recalled the close working relationships between his father and Filipino citizens, the easy friendships with residents of his neighborhood barrio, the devoted support of those Filipinos who risked Japanese wrath to bring food and news to the prisoners in Santo Tomas, the guerilla fighters and Filipino soldiers who suffered hardships and death to resist the Japanese and fight alongside the Americans.

International politics were evolving into a very different confrontation—and conceivably just as lethal—from the one Cliff had grown up knowing. The challenges of the first half of the century came from totalitarian dictatorships seeking to expand their control. This new world order featured political ideologies spawned by a combination of Marxism and struggles for agricultural and labor reform by peasants and workers. Former seekers of empire were replaced by new actors on the stage, colliding with established power structures. There was a lot to study, to discuss, and to ponder in our classes in political science and history.

When the Western College Congress was over, confident that we had found solutions to all the problems of the postwar world, the planners celebrated with a dinner at Fisherman's Wharf in San Francisco. My date was another student, but Cliff and I took note of each other when we discovered what each was eating. At one end of the table, he was eating a hamburger. At the other end I was also eating a hamburger. Both of us, we learned, were allergic to shellfish.

That winter Cliff invited me to his fraternity's formal dance. Other dates followed. We had seen a lot of each other by the time we each left campus for the summer, but when Cliff suggested I accept his fraternity pin as a token of commitment, I was not ready to commit.

He headed for Humboldt County with Dick Moore and another fellow student, Hal Mason, looking for summer work that would net them spending money for the following year. The three had met as fellow inhabitants of temporary university housing for veterans at a former military hospital. Celebrating the previous New Year together, they had traveled to Pasadena to see the Rose Bowl parade and found free lodging with their sleeping bags on the floor of Barbara Coleman's apartment. Her family had moved to Los Angeles after repatriation and Cliff had been anxious to see her again and, incidentally, introduce her to his new friends.

I went to Europe to study in a summer program at the University of Zurich. "It will be good value for the money," I told my father over the phone as I requested funding for the program. "I'll earn eight college credits, and with the extra course load I've taken each term I can graduate early and save you money in the long run." He agreed to fund the summer adventure.

Cliff wrote me regularly in care of the American Express office in Zurich. The three buddies had secured jobs at the lumber mill of George Sauers, a Stanford alumnus who had a soft spot in his heart for his university's students. They were each given an initial task to toughen them up for the hard labor of transforming redwoods from forest dwellers to building materials. Cliff's task was to cut down, by himself using an axe, a small redwood that stood next to a warehouse. When he reached the point where the tree would fall (hopefully in the open space and not on the roof of the warehouse), Cliff knew there was something he should call out but in his moment of excitement forgot about *"Timber!"* and instead shouted *"Fore!"* The redwood fell safely, at which point Cliff rushed to the tip of the felled tree, cut off a few inches of foliage, and included this sample of his prowess in the next letter he mailed to me in Zurich.

With a pocket full of money from his summer employment, Cliff bought season tickets to all Stanford's football games, at home and away, one for him and one for me. That pretty well sewed up my social calendar for the fall! I was introduced to Cliff's family and when Stanford played the University of California at Berkeley, we stayed over Saturday night at the Forster home in Oakland. I very much enjoyed his lovely mother, who took it upon herself to fatten me up by filling my plate with enough food to feed three people (or sustain a prisoner of war for a week), his lively and adventurous sister, and the "baby" Charles who was now seven and re-vered Cliff and his friends as a gang of special big brothers and sisters.

Three Stanford buddies worked in a lumber mill the summer of 1948. Cliff's visiting sister Gerry snuck into the picture; Dick Moore is on the right.

Cliff majored in international relations; I ventured into a range of studies entirely new to me, including Asian history. His choice was a natural outgrowth of his passions and experiences. Mine was inspired by the freedom to sample exotic courses plus curiosity aroused by the accounts of those returned veterans over coffee.

One of the professors on the Stanford faculty was Claude Buss, who in the twenties and thirties had followed an early career teaching college history by serving as a U.S. diplomat in China. In 1941, he became deputy to the last High Commissioner in the Philippines, Francis B. Sayre, and when Sayre retreated with General MacArthur from Manila to Corregidor and then Australia Buss was left in charge. He was on the *Gripsholm* prisoner-exchange voyage with the Forsters, and knew Cliff's parents.

After my first class on Southeast Asia, taught by Professor Buss, I was ready to take a course from him each term. He was an inspiring, generous teacher. His lectures presented complex political situation from both sides and left his students to evaluate the evidence and draw our own conclusions. At the end of each term, he invited us to an evening at his Palo Alto home.

Cliff, too, took every class he could from Claude Buss, and it was Buss who encouraged him to apply for the Foreign Service once he graduated in 1949, recommending him to the woman who was recruiting young officers to establish American Cultural Centers in outlying cities of the Philippines. Cliff was thrilled at this prospect; he later confessed that one reason he joined the Foreign Service was to secure free transportation back to the land of his birth.

In the fall of 1948, Cliff again offered me his pin, and this time I accepted. The commitment led to plans for getting married, but first it was Cliff's turn to meet my family. We decided to travel together to Michigan and then New York over the Christmas holidays.

My father invited Cliff into his downtown law office in Grand Rapids for a man-to-man talk. "Young man," he wanted to know, "just how do you plan to support my daughter in style and comfort?"

Cliff replied, "Sir, I believe I'll have a job with the U.S. State Department."

"State Department?" exclaimed my father. "Can't you get a job with someone *reliable* like Standard Oil or National City Bank?"

The visit was not off to a good start. When Cliff went on to explain that the job might well be on the island of Mindanao in the southern Philippines, my father, who was already suspicious of this stranger being brought into his home as a possible mate for his daughter, had his displeasure compounded. His view of the Philippines was a combination of the total discomfort he had experienced quartered in a military tent on the island of Leyte and the stories of expatriates' moral depravity written by Somerset Maugham. Cliff had not come with the credentials Dad would have preferred—a proud American heritage and aristocratic schooling like his at The Hill School, Princeton, and Harvard. But the young man did have credentials, which had been researched and were detailed in a folder on the lawyer's desk. The Forsters' distinctive service and high standing in Manila and Cliff's own distinctive service in the Navy were noted and tipped the balance towards tentative approval. My father and stepmother proposed to publish an engagement announcement in the *Grand Rapids Herald* and to host a formal engagement party at the Kent Country Club when we stopped by for a return visit after seeing my mother.

The East Coast interlude also had its confrontational moments, especially with my Wall Street-broker stepfather who instinctively mistrusted anyone remotely connected with the government. "They all live off the fat of the land, the taxpayers' hard-earned money," he intoned. But Cliff's charm and maturity melted my mother's initial hostility. My grandfather, a respected New York lawyer who was distinctive among his neighbors in Greenwich, Connecticut, for being an ardent Democrat, had his heart-to-heart talk with Cliff. Roger Baldwin came out of his library, arm around Cliff's shoulders, and announced in the presence of the family that had assembled for Christmas dinner, "Nancy, I *like* your young man and wish you both every happiness." He and my grandmother offered to host a July wedding at the Round Hill Chapel nearby to be followed by a reception in their lovely garden. But my grandfather extracted a promise from me. If I was going to marry and go abroad after only three years of college, I had to find a way to complete my college degree. I had already laid the groundwork to do just that and happily made my promise. Cliff and I returned to California formally engaged.

Dick and Barbara Moore had been married in early December. Dick continued his Stanford studies while Barbara worked as secretary in a

College sweethearts looked west across the Pacific toward their future.

local office, and they lived in a small apartment near campus. We often double dated on weekends. A number of the internees who had returned from the Philippines lived in the San Francisco Bay area, a few of them attending Stanford, and I had my first introductions to some of those who had shared Cliff's childhood and teenage experiences. Doc Kleinpell, who created Cliff's "report card" for undergraduate studies in the internment camp, had moved into a house a block downhill from the Forster home in Oakland and those whom he had mentored in Santo Tomas would gather, with girlfriends and wives, to dine on his wife's delicious tamale pie and to continue their lively political discussions with him.

Cliff, in the meantime, had submitted his formal application to the Foreign Service. During their discussions, the recruiter for the American Cultural Centers had advised that officers headed for the hinterlands would fare better if they were married and had the companionship of wives to embark as teams for a new adventure. It so happened that he would indeed be married.

Cliff graduated in March and I was to continue classes until mid June. He used the intervening months, while his application to the State Department was processed, to begin graduate study and do research on agrarian movements in China. I learned that by taking extension courses from the University of California while on our first foreign assignment I could gain the needed credits for graduation. However, in order to meet Stanford's graduation requirements, I needed to complete my major while still on campus. In the middle of my junior year I had not even selected a major but was happily attending courses that struck my fancy, à la carte, after I had fulfilled the general education requirements. When I added up my credits I found I was close to a degree in history, but even taking more history spring term I would be three credits short.

Professor Buss, who by this time had taken the young Forster and Forster-to-be under his wing, came to the rescue. "You can do a special research project for me to earn those missing credits. And it should relate to the part of the Philippines where Cliff will be assigned." My special independent study paper was on the Moros (Moslem Filipinos) of Mindanao and Sulu, which gave me knowledge and understanding that were to come in very handy.

Cliff was officially accepted into the Foreign Service, and our plans for the future took shape. After our July wedding and a training interlude for

Cliff in Washington, we would start our journey together—in marriage and diplomacy—with a Pacific voyage to Manila in August.

As soon as classes ended I headed for New York to help with wedding preparations and to put together a basic wardrobe for a two-year stint in the tropics. Cliff proceeded directly to Washington to receive briefings on current events in East Asia and begin training in the field that would shape the rest of his life.

"Public diplomacy"—extending foreign policy initiatives beyond the halls of embassies and foreign offices—was a new policy overseen by the U.S. Department of State following the end of the most destructive war in history. It was believed that by reaching out to people, ordinary citizens who would meet Americans and learn about American culture, the U.S. could strengthen ties between nations and lessen the danger of future hostilities. Deemed successful enough to rate an agency of its own, the venture was to spin off as the separate United States Information Service (USIS), within a few years. (Later, the name changed to U.S. Information Agency, USIA, but continued to be known as USIS overseas.) At the time of Cliff's initial training in Washington, American Centers were already being opened in outlying cities around the Philippines.

Cliff took off four days over the weekend of July 9th so we could get married and have an overnight honeymoon before returning together to Washington. It was a beautiful wedding in the historic New England chapel on Round Hill Road in Greenwich, a few miles from my grandparents' home, where the reception was held in the sunken garden in which I had played as a child on summer visits. A momentous event, but much of our attention was directed to what lay ahead in the Philippines.

When we, duly married, attended the daily briefings at the State Department, pins were regularly being pulled out of the China map behind our informant's desk. They represented U.S. consular offices in China that were being abandoned as the Communist forces of Mao Tse-tung advanced steadily southward, moving ever closer to achieving the People's Republic of China, which they would proclaim in Beijing on October 1st, 1949.

We sailed in late August from San Francisco on the *President Wilson* for a delayed three-week honeymoon, courtesy of Uncle Sam, carrying a lot of new learning in our intellectual baggage.

Cliff took four days off from his diplomatic training in Washington for our wedding in Connecticut.

16

MABUHAY

BOARD THE *PRESIDENT WILSON*, I was already being introduced to a whole new world. My summer studying in Zurich and traveling around Europe had been my first time abroad and, while an eye-opening experience, it didn't begin to prepare me for the different people, landscapes, and cultures I would meet—and come to love—in Asia. Fortunately, in Cliff I had a first-class instructor whose enthusiasm was contagious.

Traveling by ocean voyage to a our first post allowed us the luxury of time—time to relax, to reflect, to read, and to shed what was left behind in preparation for what was ahead. During our three weeks at sea, we ate meals with foreign expatriates who were old Asia hands and a Filipino judge who had been a prewar member of the Red Cross board of directors and remembered Cliff as a youngster. They had much wisdom to share with us. Our port calls in Honolulu, Yokohama, and Hong Kong also provided memorable experiences.

Honolulu, whose tropical beauty Cliff had been extolling since we first met, was off limits—a longshoremen's strike kept us from docking. The U.S. mail was taken ashore, food brought aboard, and Hawaii passengers were allowed to embark and disembark. That was all. We cruised slowly up and down the distant waterfront, the outline of Diamond Head enticing in the distance. I felt shortchanged.

In Yokohama, Cliff guided me to the local train station for the ride to Tokyo. He wanted to show me the nooks and crannies of Frank Lloyd Wright's Imperial Hotel that had enchanted him as a child, the majesty of the Imperial Palace grounds, the drama of Japanese kimonos and signs written in ideographic characters. But what struck me were the barriers in bleak railroad stations separating the Allied military personnel from the defeated Japanese, even bleaker families hovering in makeshift living quarters in openings under the railroad trestles, bomb craters where buildings had once stood, and an overall sense of gray landscape and gray people. When we got back to the ship that evening, I turned to Cliff with a pronouncement: "Cliff Forster, I know I married you for better or for worse, and that I signed onto a life in the Foreign Service, but let me tell you one thing—I will never, *never* go to Japan!" Little did I know I would relish fifteen years living in that fascinating country.

In Hong Kong, the oriental magic captivated me. Cliff of course took me for a rickshaw ride and up the Peak Tramway. We crossed the crowded harbor on the Star Ferry. And we wandered through a wonderland of Chinese shops with intriguing food displays and narrow streets exploding with color and designs new to my eyes. I certainly wanted to return here!

A few days later we sailed into Manila Bay. As the pilot boat pulled alongside the *President Wilson* on Friday, September 16th, we noticed another small craft that had come out to meet the ship before we docked at the pier. A group of Cliff's old pals, some of whom had returned before he did and some who never left after liberation, formed an advance welcoming committee. They shouted up to where we hung over the railing. "Mabuhay"—welcome—"Cliff! Tonight we're all going to the tuberculosis benefit ball at the Manila Hotel. You'll sit at our table!"

Waiting on the dock were Filipino members of the old Red Cross staff, those who had survived the massacre of wounded civilians and the nurses and doctors who were caring for them in the Hall of Mercy during the final days of the war. As soon as the gangplank was lowered, one of the senior State Department officials from the U.S. Embassy strode up to welcome us. He waited while we greeted all our well-wishers, then escorted us to our temporary accommodations at the Bayview Hotel across the boulevard from the embassy, where the prisoners of war had gathered before their internment at Santo Tomas. The stories Cliff had been telling me since we first met were now coming vividly to life.

That night at the ball, I was escorted from table to table and introduced to my husband's (it seemed like) five hundred best friends. Cliff was home—the home of his memories, the home-to-be of his new life, the home-to-be of his bewildered wife.

The remembered home was a sorely wounded city. Manila had suffered hand-to-hand fighting and scorched-earth tactics by the cornered Japanese forces, which left the heart of the beautiful colonial city in ruins. The destruction here was second only to that of Warsaw in World War II. Now, four years later, reconstructed buildings were rising from the ashes and the Filipinos were eagerly rebuilding their lives, nurturing their exuberant culture, and experimenting with the levers of independence—and their own brand of democracy.

One of the families Cliff had told me stories about was the Hoffmans, his next-door neighbors before the war. He'd been good friends with Marge Hoffman and her younger brother Bill both before and during internment. Decades later, I would read the letter Cliff sent after his repatriation to Marge and Bill's grandparents, assuring them that the internees had "very few unpleasant circumstances to contend with."

In the remaining months of the war, when food had become ever more scarce, all internees lost a great deal of weight, especially Mrs. Hoffman, who was very weak at the time of liberation. Restored to health back in the U.S. and anxious to pick up their lives and the family printing business, the Hoffmans returned with their daughter to Manila after the war. When Cliff and I sailed into Manila Bay in September of 1949, Marge was among his friends who greeted us as we docked. I was quickly being drawn into the recurring cast of characters of Cliff's life.

Years later, Marge told us that her mother confessed to deliberately denying herself food in Santo Tomas in order to keep her husband healthy "since he would be needed to support the family after the war." Ever generous, Mrs. Hoffman helped us get a small apartment in their building for the few weeks we would be in Manila before heading south to Cliff's first Foreign Service assignment on the island of Mindanao.

Those first few weeks were a whirlwind of activity. Every day, Cliff was introduced to embassy colleagues and briefed on current politics in the Philippines and what to expect in his new territory—an island five hundred miles south of Manila, half the size of France, plus the Sulu Archipelago stretching southwest to within thirty miles of Borneo. Evenings we were at dinners with some of those "five hundred best friends." Cliff's homecoming was a steep learning curve for his new bride.

We spent weekends with Red Cross staff, who told us their war stories and took us for exploratory trips out into the country. They showed us the Red Cross building, rebuilt on the site of the destroyed original, and posed us for a group photo in front of a portrait of the widow of the late President of the Philippines. The portrait was draped in black cloth. Mrs. Quezon had been the honorary chairman of the Red Cross in the Philippines. A few months before our arrival she had been traveling north of Manila when her car was ambushed and she was shot.

The Hukbalahap movement, a successor to the prewar Sakdalistas, had fought the Japanese very effectively as the "People's Army to Fight the Japanese." Now, flush with victory and maintaining their cache of weapons, they picked up the cause of agrarian discontent—long simmering resentment against harsh working and living conditions on plantations owned by wealthy landlords, many of Spanish descent. Many "Huk" leaders were pro-communist and sought to overturn the democratic government in favor of a new Marxist regime. Their command posts were in central Luzon and the widow of the first leader of the democracy was, for them, a target of opportunity. For the Red Cross staff it was a profound loss on top of all they had suffered previously.

In addition to battle-scarred buildings, wounded and killed family members, and the Hukbalahap insurgency, the Filipinos were faced with economic challenges and political corruption—all the growing pains of being a new, developing nation while recovering from the ravages of war. And, as the Filipinos often said of their colonial history, "We spent four hundred years living in a convent and forty years in Hollywood." What would be their lifestyle now?

Our own lifestyle was due for another change, the journey to our final destination on the southern island of Mindanao and settling in for a new routine of work and domesticity. Cliff made the four-hour flying trip to Davao in mid-October, to survey what had been established at the USIS Center there and to make preliminary arrangements for his arrival as its first American Director, and the only U.S. government representative south of Cebu, in the central Philippines.

For our journey together, Cliff wanted to approach Davao by sea, slowly cruising out of Manila Bay past Corregidor and Bataan, weaving among the islands south of Luzon, stopping at the city of Cebu, then following the coastline of Mindanao until we reached the southern port city at 4 degrees north latitude.

The *Mindanao* was scheduled to sail from Manila at 7:30 p.m. on the 20th of October, and we were aboard the interisland freighter well ahead of time, with plenty of time to observe the loading of cargo, including our own luggage. She finally was underway at half past midnight. We would make the trip in two stages, laying over in Cebu for a few days to meet with Cliff's counterpart, the American Director of the USIS Center there. We would then pick up a sister ship of the *Mindanao* for the rest of the trip south.

While we were in Cebu, Cliff wanted to visit the island of Mactan, about half an hour by small boat across from the port. Our goal was to find a monument he had read about, dedicated to the memory of Ferdinand Magellan.

Over the next few years, Cliff wrote several articles for the *Foreign Service Journal* about our time in the Philippines. The first, about Mactan, was published in the November 1951 issue. He used a professional writing style in these articles—quite different from the humorous storytelling style he used among friends—but his words take me back to that early adventure, discovering a new place as we embarked on our new lives.

It was on this island that Ferdinand Magellan met his death at the hands of Lapu-Lapu, a tribal chieftain, in the year 1521. It was also here that other men came to interpret the event in stone. The interpretations are revealing from the standpoint of national psychology as well as history.

Magellan had made the very serious mistake in April of 1521 of getting mixed up in tribal politics more than half way around the world from home. It cost him his life.

After "Christianizing" Rajah Humabon, the ruler of the fortified town now known as Cebu, Magellan was approached by a Mactan tribal chief. Zula. Zula presented Magellan with two goats and in return asked for Magellan's support in crushing a rival on Mactan—Lapu-Lapu. Magellan agreed, and on April 27th he led his small Spanish force ashore. Lapu-Lapu and his followers were there to meet him and in the ensuing conflict Magellan was speared to death. The expedition returned to the Old World without its leader.

Mactan is not much to look at when you approach the Cebu landing strip by air. The island is nothing more than a raised coral reef lying eight to ten feet above sea level. As the plane loses altitude coming over the central mountain range of Cebu you can see Mactan's flat terrain lying across from Cebu City, now the second largest in the Philippines. You also can see the submerged parts of the coral reef sloping away from Mactan's shore line. In some places the water is so clear that the submerged part looks as if it were above water.

The day we visited, we crossed by boat from Cebu to Opon, the main settlement of the island. Shiny Caltex and Standard Oil storage tanks dominated the landscape. We walked up a steep road to the small, rustic "town," where the only vehicle we could find to take us across the island to the historic site was a huge truck with seats in the open back and a radio blaring "Stormy Weather" in Visayan. Some twenty minutes later we passed through a tiny settlement of thatched houses and stopped at the beach, fronted by a monument inside a tall iron-grill fence.

The monument was of yellow stone, standing about twenty feet above the ground. We could almost visualize Magellan and his company wading in over the coral reef and passing through the inshore swamp to meet head-on with Lapu-Lapu's forces. We found a record in stone of two empires of the past, one glorifying its hero, the other glorifying its conquest. And we also found the spirit of nationalism, likewise in stone, which offered a third interesting interpretation of the event for which Mactan is famous.

First there was the monument built by Spain in honor of Ferdinand Magellan. This was the largest monument, now in a state of disrepair. It was erected in 1866 during the reign of Spanish Queen Isabel II. The name of the Spanish governor of the Philippines at the time of its construction, Don Miguel Creus, was also inscribed in the stone. At the top of the monument was the date, 1521, the year of Magellan's death on Mactan. Under this, in very large letters, was the inscription:

GLORIA ESPAÑOLA
A HERNANDO DE MAGALLANES

This was the monument built during the Spanish colonial regime in the Philippines and dedicated to the memory of the famous explorer, who symbolized for the Spaniards the glory that was Spain's in the 16th century as she took to the seas to settle new lands for an expanding empire.

Close to the Spanish monument was an historical marker on a large stucco and tile-surfaced platform. This marker had been placed on the platform by the Philippine Commonwealth Government, just before the war broke out in 1941. It declared:

This spot marks the scene of the battle fought on April 27, 1521, between the Filipinos led by Lapu-Lapu and the Spaniards led by Magellan. Magellan was killed. Since then Lapu-Lapu has been considered the first Filipino to have repelled European aggression.

The story had changed! What fascinated us was the spirit of nationalism that had inspired the Filipinos, then on their way to full independence, to place their own marker opposite the Spanish monument. They saw Lapu-Lapu, not Magellan, as the hero of that April day in 1521.

An objective historian, however, legitimately could question whether Lapu-Lapu had any idea of "repelling European aggression" when Magellan went ashore that morning. Whether or not Lapu-Lapu was merely a tribal chief warring against another tribal chief on a small coral reef does not alter the fact that here Lapu-Lapu is viewed as a hero. Significantly enough, no mention whatsoever is made of the aggressive part played by the rival chieftain, Zula, whom Magellan offered to aid in defeating Lapu-Lapu. But our history, too, often is colored in deference to the pride generated by nationalism.

In 1942 Japan came to Mactan. That island empire also left its mark on the site of Magellan's death—rough letters painted in black on the south side of the Spanish monument to Magellan. Some of the letters are no longer legible. Small arms fire has torn into the stone and removed parts of the surface writing. The inscription below is all that remains today:

The Japanese have occupied completely whole Mactan Island by this April 10, 1942, 400 years after Magerran's coming. By E Commander Watana... Murat... And 66... of sub... yer... KYO

With this crude letter work (notice where the Japanese substituted Rs for Ls) the Japanese wanted all visitors to know that their forces had "completely" occupied the island in 1942. The Japanese forces were not out to glorify Magellan or Lapu-Lapu; both historical figures had nothing to do with their history. So they glorified their own conquest of this island, possibly because of the feeling of elation at the thought that they, the Japanese, had occupied an area of ancient historical significance.

As we left the island we talked about the clash of civilizations depicted in this simple place. What a tragedy that Magellan, the intrepid explorer who had endured so many hardships getting this far on his attempted circumnavigation, was killed in a tribal skirmish on a remote

island. It was interesting to ponder how men with very different backgrounds and aspirations interpreted the same event. Cliff asked:

Who was the aggressor? Who was the hero? Magellan? Lapu-
Lapu? Zula? I guess it all depends on whose glasses you are looking through and what monument you happen to be building,
marker you are placing, or letters you are painting.

Magellan had been sent on his voyage by the Spanish rulers because,
after years of battling the Muslim conquerors of Spain (known as "Moros"
to the Spaniards), the Muslims had been conquered and pushed back into
North Africa. The nation had been unified and there was now money in
the treasury to fund other ventures. After journeying halfway around
the globe, Magellan found himself faced with people professing the same
faith as the erstwhile North African conquerors and he gave the Filipino
Muslims their name—Moros.

In the years since our 1949 visit to Mactan, the nationalism of the
fully independent nation of the Philippines has had the last word in
this spot. The monument complex has been enclosed inside an open-air
pavilion dedicated to the heroism of Lapu-Lapu and decorated in panels
just below the roofline with colorful murals showing the progression of
battle on that day in 1521.

17

DAVAO—A FRONTIER CITY

W^E CONTINUED OUR OWN VOYAGE a day after our Mactan excursion, on the *Masthead Knot*. It made the *Mindanao* seem like pure luxury. This small cargo ship had one passenger cabin, located below decks. Without any air conditioning, two tiny portholes at deck level provided the only access to ocean breezes and longed-for relief from tropical heat. We then discovered that the deck was jam packed with carabao—the huge domesticated water buffalo used as beasts of burden in the Philippines—being shipped for sale to farmers opening new lands to cultivation in the south. After one whiff of their strong animal odors, opening the portholes no longer seemed such a good idea. We rejoiced when we reached the port of Davao City at 11 pm on the fourth day of this leg of our journey.

I would make it a habit to write to Cliff's mother and my family every week or two, long letters with carbon copies, keeping one for myself as a pseudo diary. In the one I wrote shortly after we reached Davao I described our welcome.

We were met by the Center staff and the Mayor's wife, all of whom had been waiting since three in the afternoon. We were smothered with leis and corsages. They had planned to have a brass band and fifteen-car parade until Cliff wrote them asking to prevent all fanfare at our arrival, since any type of noise made by or for an American these last few weeks has been interpreted as interference in the November 8th national elections. The mayor sent his wife because he had been making so many campaign speeches that he had lost his voice.

We were delivered to Suite A (a semi-partition between twin beds and a chair made it a "suite") in the Apo View Hotel, Davao's finest. A "private" bath was merely an extension, partition open at the top, of the public men's room. Early the next morning we were blasted awake by the combination of an off-key brass band practicing and loud hammer blows building a new grandstand for the national athletic meet to be held here in December.

The hotel was named for Mount Apo, the Philippines' highest mountain, which loomed over the countryside in symmetrical splendor and attracted daily rain clouds that burst into cooling afternoon storms.

Cliff's work life was to take place in one wing of a different kind of hotel, the other wing still catering to guests of an operation, according to rumors around town, of less than high moral repute. Before our arrival, space had been rented for the American Center and Filipino staff hired to service a library collection and run a media program. Books had been received and placed on shelves and plans were being made to show documentary films to audiences around the city and upcountry.

Milagros Aquino, a woman of stature around town, was the head librarian and acting director. She took pride in her role, ran the organization with a tight rein, and was not happy to relinquish her power to a young American official. Her welcome was between clenched teeth. Her final power play was to assign office space to Cliff. "Mr. Forster, you see that we have no more space in the building. The library is overcrowded, the one office is needed for myself and the other librarians as workspace" (indeed, uncatalogued books were piled in high stacks on the floor), "and the downstairs rooms are all occupied by the media staff." She escorted

Cliff's first office in Davao was on an open-air porch of the hotel that housed the American Center. The pretty ladies in the other wing enjoyed waving at him.

him to the office she had selected—an open-air porch at the top of the entry stairs, overlooking the street.

Cliff accepted his lot, arranged his furniture and office supplies on the porch—pushed against the wall to avoid the heavy tropical rains that came every afternoon. He was grateful for the cool breezes that swept across this open office, and charmed by the pretty ladies who would lean out the windows of the hotel wing and wave at him.

Davao in 1949 was a boom town. New settlers were coming off ships in the port, up to eight thousand in one week. They sought refuge from the insurgents on Luzon. They sought land. They wanted to try their luck on the abaca (Manila hemp, the raw material for rope) plantations, now neglected and without their prewar Japanese managers. They wanted to challenge the forests where every imaginable kind of lumber waited for the enterprising lumberman.

The city couldn't keep up with the demands made of it. Houses, schools, hospitals, roads—all were desperately needed. There wasn't time to pave sidewalks; planks of wood were thrown over mud and across open sewers. Everyone was full of life, enthusiastic, optimistic. El Dorado! San Francisco in gold-rush days! They came originally from Luzon, Bohol, Cebu, Leyte, from different provinces and speaking different languages, getting to know each other through a new hybrid Filipino English.

Once Cliff was settled in his breezy office, we were anxious to find a home other than the Apo View Hotel. There seemed to be only two possibilities. One was outside of town, near a new Coca-Cola bottling plant. It had no plumbing, no partitions between second-floor rooms, and needed paint inside and out. The rent would be due for a year in advance and any renovations, including the plumbing, would be at our expense. The second was being built by a local man-about-town, Mr. Neri.

Neri had achieved modest prosperity with dealings in the lumber business, a trucking firm, and the sale of crushed coral to the government for road building. His "dream house" was a compact two-story frame structure boasting fourteen different tropical woods in the interior, and was ready for occupancy except for exterior paint. When he learned that an American government official was to live in Davao, conferring prestige on this remote city, Neri offered to rent his dream house to the Forsters. To drive home the point of prestige, he would paint the exterior all white and the house would henceforth be known as "The White House of Davao."

A van containing our household goods had reached Davao while we were still in Manila and furniture purchased by the embassy on our behalf was waiting in storage. We were ready to create our first home in Neri's white house. It wasn't until after we moved in, only four days after the *Masthead Knot* deposited us, that we discovered the home's spacious yard was a commercial enterprise. On three sides it was a carabao sales lot. The forty beasts of burden that had been our shipmates traveling south from Cebu had been brought here to await purchase by their new owners. Each had a scooped-out "wallow" where it could slither in the muddy water and keep cool.

We had barely unpacked when our first houseguest arrived, Frank Gibney, then the bureau chief in Tokyo for *Time* magazine. He had been briefly assigned to the Philippines to cover what was turning out to be a very contentious presidential election and opted to travel to the remote south to see democracy in action in the provinces. It was dark when he arrived. Before we ushered him to the guest bedroom he proudly showed off the new cameras he carried, a Leica and a Canon—marvels of postwar technology. By dawn he had discovered our garden zoo and we found him flat on his stomach next to a carabao wallow, using his high-tech cameras to get a full-face shot of a particularly muddy beast. "Fantastic!" Frank told Cliff. "Have you ever seen such contentment?"

Frank's visit was an excellent opportunity for Cliff, as well, to learn firsthand about the election dynamics in the region. He escorted Frank to interviews with the mayor, the governor, local reporters, and civic leaders, hearing accounts of violence (a man in an outlying village was shot in the head when he leaned out his thatched hut to brush his teeth) and corruption (a constabulary officer's wife had been writing out ballots to fortify the position of her candidate).

As would be the case for decades, I enjoyed hearing Cliff's account of his experiences at the end of the day. Governor Miranda spoke about Davao's feelings toward the Japanese. "Before the war," said Miranda, "the Japanese were the most law-abiding citizens here. But now it is too soon after the war for the Filipinos to forget their bitterness and trade with Japan. As for elections, in the Philippines it is always a battle of personality rather than issues."

"And what is your biggest problem here in Davao, Mr. Governor?" asked Frank. "Roads! Most of them are impassable and the Province is cut off without them." How right he was. We were to feel the magnitude of his number one problem to the marrow of our bones in attempts to cover the island by jeep.

From the Governor's office, Cliff and Frank drove south nineteen bumpy kilometers to Mintal, an old Japanese village. Frank wanted material for his story on the former Japanese residents of the Davao area. The village was deserted. Walking through overgrown orchards and farms they stumbled upon the jungle-choked ruins of a shrine built in the memory of a Japanese plantation owner who had died there in 1917. They wondered what had become of his coworkers and his family in the following years.

Frank was just the first of an unending flow of guests. Our four nights in Davao's finest hotel had convinced us that American visitors would find its sole private room a severe challenge, so anyone with a remote connection to USIS was invited to stay with us. During our entire two years there, visitors occupied the guest room on all but a few nights. I had to reinvent myself as a hostess.

Devoid of any significant cooking experience, my first challenge was putting food on the table, and in particular dealing with food available in the local market. We had been told to avoid uncooked vegetables and unpeeled fruit due to risk of intestinal disease. There were two basic choices for meat, both daunting—live chickens and huge slabs of carabao meat. I retreated to the safety of the groceries that had come in our household goods shipped from the U.S. My father, reconciled to our marriage but still concerned about my coping with housekeeping in the remote tropics, had insisted we bring along a substantial supply of canned goods. I protested at the time (my war bond savings would pay for the groceries), but was happy to have this cache once on the scene.

One night, we had finished dinner and Cliff felt impelled to comment. "Uh, Nancy," he said, "this was a delicious dinner. But couldn't we have something else tomorrow?" I burst into tears. It was the fourteenth night I had served the only food I could cope with—canned corned beef hash, canned spinach, and canned peaches.

The next day, help arrived. Miraculously, a thirty-year-old Filipino man appeared in Cliff's office, looking for a job. Dan had cooked for sailors on freighters crossing the Pacific and for a while served chow to cowhands in the American southwest. "Mr, Forster, I also play the guitar and can serenade you and your wife after dinner." Cliff was sold, brought Dan home that evening, and this man with tattoos covering both arms and the ability to read and recreate the recipes that I had been copying from magazines in the USIS collection became my right hand in the business of diplomatic hospitality.

Information service, we discovered, was a two-way conversation, listening and learning as well as providing resources and giving advice.

People-to-people diplomacy called for learning about the community, discovering what were the most pressing needs, and using what tools were available through the American library, the media collection, specialists and materials coming from the embassy in Manila or—with a much longer delivery time—from the U.S. to alleviate local problems. Mindanao is the second largest island in the Philippines, divided into twenty-five provinces, including the Sulu Archipelago. Davao City, four degrees north of the equator and today the nation's third largest city, was at that time frontier territory. Though sparsely settled, its burgeoning population was eager for what the Americans had to offer.

The USIS Center was making its mark as a leading institution in the city. After several months, and a few visits by high-ranking officials from Manila, Cliff was instructed to negotiate with local authorities (with whom he had become good friends by then) for the U.S. government to take over the entire building and upgrade the facilities to accommodate USIS in a more dignified and efficient manner. By then he and Milagros were also congenial colleagues and she facilitated his move into an indoor office.

Meanwhile, I found myself thrust into an unanticipated career, that of teacher of English at a newly established college, the brainchild of Guillermo Torres, a Davao "booster." He took pride in this raw new city, and embraced the opportunities it offered to men of vision. His particular vision was that of a university for Mindanao, a center of learning in the south to rival the respected institutions of Manila. His dream had started with a few prefabricated buildings with sheet metal roofs on a vacant city lot. This dream was "Mindanao Colleges." Instruction started with practical subjects: engineering and accounting, typing and English. Later he would add law and history and literature. Classes were mostly in the late afternoon and evening to accommodate faculty and students who had daytime jobs.

When we came to Davao they needed, "right now," a native speaker of English to handle a course in grammar and composition. I was hired to teach twenty-three students, several twice my age, for a one-semester course. It was challenging, but I forged ahead and we reached the end of the semester. I turned in my grades and heaved a sigh of relief. But it wasn't over. Mr. Torres called me into his office for a conference. "Mrs. Forster, I see that you have given grades of 60 percent to three students. And 65 percent is passing."

"Yes, Mr. Torres," I agreed. "Their grades really should have been lower but they try so hard and I want to encourage them."

"But you don't understand, Mrs. Forster," he said. "They have *paid!*"
I said that I could not change the grades, but since it was his college he
was in control...

Though young and fresh out of college, Cliff Forster—and by extension his wife—was an instant and sought-after celebrity in Davao. The
diplomatic community consisted of the Chinese Nationalist (i.e., Taiwan)
consul Mr. Mih, consular agents for Great Britain and Spain who were
expatriate businessmen, and Cliff as the one and only American official.
When there was a ceremony, Cliff was often asked to speak, or at the
very least sit in an honored spot. If visiting dignitaries came to town, we
were to join our official vehicle to the caravan that went to the airport to
greet and escort the visitors into the city. This presented a problem: Cliff
was usually placed third or fourth in the motorcade; however, his official
vehicle was an open jeep, hardly up to the standards of the chauffeured
sedans that bore mayor, governor, judge. The mayor offered to loan Cliff a
city vehicle to add more dignity to the parade, but Cliff felt that if the U.S.
government wished to transport him in a jeep, in a jeep he would parade.

One Sunday, the vice president of the Philippines was scheduled to
visit Davao, accompanied by several senators, three secretaries, an American general and his wife, and our boss—the head of USIS Philippines and
his wife. We were at the airport with all of official Davao in time for their
four o'clock arrival. We waited. And waited. And waited. It was the radio
operator's day off, so there was no radio information to explain the delay.

A little after five the radio operator, roused from his holiday, came
bouncing across the runway. The vice president's personal plane had been
trying all afternoon, with no luck, to contact Davao. Finally they made
contact with another Mindanao city, which contacted the Davao office
of the Philippine Constabulary, which located the radio operator and
told him to hurry to the airport. Meanwhile, low clouds prevented the
military pilot from locating Davao City or Mount Apo. He was nervously
circling over the seas south of the island. By the time the plane found
Davao it was getting dark, and there were no lights on the runway. The
nearest airfield with lights was at Cebu and there wasn't enough gas to
make the trip there.

The motorcade came to the rescue. All the officials waiting to greet
their vice president lined their cars up facing the runway and turned on

their headlights. We sat waiting anxiously in our jeep, our headlights playing a part in guiding the plane to a perfect landing.

If it was arbor day and a tree was to be planted, Cliff was handed a shovel. An English oration contest to be judged—call on Mr. Forster. A baseball game between the American business community and the sons of Mindanao—Forster at the bat. The oration contest Cliff judged at the College of the Immaculate Conception lasted three hours, one hour each of elocution in English, Spanish, and Tagalog. The grand finale of the afternoon was the crowning of the college queen. Cliff raised the crown and uttered his assigned proclamation: "I proclaim you the Queen of the Immaculate Conception!"

One of the most renowned orators on the island of Mindanao was Mayor Jaldon of Zamboanga. His Spanish grandee blood came to the fore whenever he was near the podium. He praised beauty, womanhood, music, poetry, flowers, and life in all its glory. Cliff was present when he was asked to give the opening address at a fashion show presented by the graduates of the Largos Fashion Academy. The novice seamstresses were presenting to the public their original creations.

"It is a shame," began the Mayor, "that this ceremony today is not being held in a graveyard. Yes, in a graveyard, for the beauty of these ladies we have here today is so great, it is so great, ladies and gentlemen, that it would be causing the dead to rise!"

That was a hard act to follow and Cliff felt humble when the podium was his. He found his topics in the current issues of the season: the cold war, the "fall" of China, rural development, civic responsibility.

I, in turn, was asked to speak to the Rotary Anns at their monthly meeting "on something cultural and intellectual—like knitting, crocheting, or birth control."

These activities filled our days. Evenings too. And I continued to teach at Mindanao Colleges. Second semester, I was assigned a class in English conversation, in the largest room on this raw campus. There were seventy-two students in the class. I went to Mr. Torres and told him there was no way I could have a conversation with seventy-two people at once. He clucked sympathetically, and promised he would decrease the numbers. When I came for the next class the student population had been reduced—to sixty-five. Conversation became an oral drill. The room had

Cliff hired my student Bernardo Saludares for his media team; Bernardo (on the left) later became a lawyer and a judge.

a corrugated tin roof. Our class met in the afternoon and almost without fail the daily downpour came in the middle of the session. The noise of rain pounding on that tin roof drowned out conversation/drill and we all just smiled at each other, students from their seats and I from the teacher's desk, until the torrent subsided into a less noisy rainfall.

Bernardo Saludares was one of the outstanding students in that conversation class. When he told me that he was looking for a job before going on to law school, I suggested he go and talk to Cliff. Bernardo was hired and became one of the most valuable members of the USIS media team. After leaving Davao, we exchanged Christmas greetings with Bernardo for many years, and were thrilled as he completed law school and prospered in his career.

By spring of 1950 both the library and media sections of the center were flourishing. The library collection grew, with reference books, current (as current as a four-to-six-week land and sea voyage allowed) American magazines, biography, history, economics, politics, fiction, and books for young children. Students and workers and professional men and women crowded the now expanded reading room. The librarians took books from the children's collection out into the barrios and hosted story hours in poorer neighborhoods of town.

The media section received more and more educational films— content which would not satisfy today's sophisticated audiences, but a star attraction in areas where movies were rare, if seen at all. A Belgian-built mobile unit was shipped to Davao, to take USIS on the road. This vehicle was a movie projection booth on wheels with four wheel drive and a generator that produced electricity to run the film equipment in those areas which lacked power. The film crew reached Surigao in June, a grueling many day trip over seemingly impassible roads (a winched rope on the front of the unit could be attached to a nearby tree to haul the vehicle out of jungle mud holes) at the northern tip of the island. When they set up their screen and speakers and projector for the first showing, over ten thousand people, by their estimate, crowed the public park to see the show.

Forty years later, Cliff would describe his Mindanao work in an oral history interview with Lewis Schmidt, a former Tokyo colleague. Lew was one of several retired officers recording the stories of USIS "old hands" for diplomatic archives to be kept in the Library of Congress. The transcript of the full day of conversation, which took place at our home in Hawaii in 1990, was among Cliff's files. I reread it after his death with great interest, and many memories of my own.

There was a lot of unrest in different parts of Mindanao while we there, with Huk infiltration and the Moro uprisings in the area. It was an exciting time for both Nancy and myself, because at that time both husband and wife were very much involved in the work. You both had to be. She would go with me on our mobile unit trips with our films and publications to reach the distant areas. She also helped on office chores, taught English, and entertained constantly.

I should also mention that it was pretty rough politically under the Quirino regime. Voters were beaten up at the polls if they didn't vote for the party in power. What little democracy existed was going under fast along with the economy, and the communist-led Huks were making the most of it.

The USIS team faced numerous challenges on Mindanao's unpaved roads.

The Quirino administration, with the help of some of the constabulary and Philippine Army elements, were violating the constitutional rights of the people. As time went on, however, many of the Philippine Army leaders and the Constabulary were opposed to this kind of autocratic rule, but in the early years you had Quirino in charge with his political hooligans.

The answer to so much of the problem was Ramon Magsaysay, the Defense Minister in the Quirino government. He launched a movement to curb these excesses. He was remarkable, going right out to the provinces to work with the disaffected and promising the Luzon Huks that if they surrendered they would be given a piece of land in Mindanao to start fresh. He set up two very successful resettlement projects for surrenderees, one in northern Mindanao and another in Cotabato, southern Mindanao.

The USIS operation was unusual, because we were tasked with the job of providing information materials on the conduct of good government and how to educate voters on democratic processes, including polling. We were sent around to give talks on these democratic procedures and to provide information on organizing groups modeled after the League of Women Voters. We even went into the camps where the Huk surrenderees were located to assist on the reeducation program.

Looking back on that period, I would say that we were quite successful. We were working with so many good people, so many Filipinos who felt strongly about what was going on in the Philippines not only with a corrupt regime but also with an insurgency capitalizing on this corruption and the deterioration of the economy. We were involved in nation-building in a very real sense, in a country we had administered for many years and where Americans and Filipinos had fought and died together against the invaders in World War II… We had a common experience and we did not want to see a newly independent nation succumb to a totalitarian rule of the right or left…

In an article published in the *Foreign Service Journal* of June 1953, Cliff described an example where local energy, American know-how, and a USIS outpost joined to address a serious economic problem and win friends among Filipino farmers.

We called it "Operation Abaca Mosaic" and it all started when a few people got together and decided to pool their resources. Bartolome Espino, the energetic Filipino agricultural supervisor for Davao Province, had been working for several months with Julian Agati, another Filipino agriculturist, to rid the area of the crippling effects of abaca mosaic disease. The Davao-Cotabato area is one of the world's major suppliers for hemp, the important plant from which rope is made, and the United States is just one of several countries heavily dependent on this area for its fiber supply needs. The economy here rests on abaca. You are strongly aware of this when you ride for miles past row upon row of abaca plantings, when you see men, women, and children out in the fields cutting down and stripping the plants, when trucks loaded high with abaca bales pass you on the narrow roads en route to the warehouses for export from Davao City.

Dr. Otto Reinking, American Agricultural Adviser to the Philippine Government was the first to discover the cause of the disease. It was carried by plant lice or aphids working on healthy fiber after feeding on diseased plants. With Bartolome Espino and Julian Agati, Dr. Reinking had established the headquarters for abaca mosaic control in Davao City. The task of combating the disease was extremely difficult. Infection to the extent of 50 to 100 percent had become common over wide areas by the summer of 1951 and it was apparent that growing discontent among the farmers presented a very grave problem. Espino and Agati wanted desperately to reach more farmers, to inform them how this disease could be controlled and eradicated. They had a problem of their own—how could they get their message across to the farmers and with a minimum of delay?

One afternoon Bart Espino and I were talking about the problem, when I suggested that we might come to his assistance by diverting our mobile unit from a run to northern Mindanao in order to go into the critically diseased regions. We could use Dr. Reinking's excellent color slides on disease recognition for a film strip which the mobile unit could carry to distant farms. Also, since the facilities were available, why not turn out simple local dialect leaflets on control for distribution to the farmers?

Working together as a team, a forty-five day itinerary was drawn up for the mobile unit in order to reach the hardest hit areas in the provinces of Davao and Cotabato. As Espino rechecked the itinerary one afternoon, he suddenly looked up and leaned forward in his chair: "We must have a name for this project," he said. "Let's call it Operation Abaca Mosaic."

One of our first stops was Toril, a small town lying south of Davao city close to the foothills of Mount Apo. The area around Toril had once been a rich abaca area. Now it was disease-ridden. We set up our equipment in an open field near a schoolhouse. It was one of those hot, damp nights following a tropical thunderstorm and the unit, weighted down, began to sink into the mud. Farmers, notified earlier, began to arrive in a steady stream. We could see them coming along the provincial road with their kerosene lanterns—their yellow lights casting strange shadows among the abaca plants. Many were curious and gathered around the unit and the projector. One old farmer approached the projectionist and wanted to know what he was doing. The projectionist explained that the farmers were going to learn how to fight and destroy abaca mosaic disease.

"You are going to help us then?" the farmer asked. He rubbed his chin as he read over the words "United States Information Service" on the side of the mobile unit. "You are working with the Americanos?" he asked. The Filipino projectionist nodded.

"Then the Americanos are helping us also?" he asked. The projectionist nodded again as he worked with the filmstrip. The farmer shook his head slowly as if thinking to himself. "This is a very good thing," he said. "The people will not forget." It was this curious interest mixed with a new feeling of assurance and gratitude which was to greet us as we visited more communities in the days and nights ahead.

Following the forty-five day operation that had reached over 47,000 farmers, a second month covered Cotabato, the largest province in the Philippines, and reached an additional 35,000 in remote rural areas. Although understanding of this destructive plant disease has increased over the years, full eradication is still elusive. This early program, however, did a great deal to control abaca mosaic and give farmers more confidence in their crops and their lives. Statistics and evidences of satisfaction were collected for official reporting to Manila and Washington. Cliff had a favorite:

> The source of my greatest gratification, however, was the Filipino farmer who appeared in the office one morning with his own abaca plant. It was rather startling to see this large plant come through the door, half hiding the small bearer. He had traveled considerable distance to tell us about his successful efforts to control the disease on his farm. He had been on hand at one of our showings. Pulling his bolo (machete) from its sheath, he cut into the stalk. It was a quick stroke which sprayed items on my desk with plant juice. "You see" he said with a wonderful smile, "my plant is like a strong man. Its sickness is gone."

This, Cliff felt, was U.S. public diplomacy at its finest, building bridges across cultures by forming a partnership between experts with solutions to practical problems, the agency with the mission and tools to communicate, and those local citizens who needed help. He relished the challenges and encounters of his daily work. And, all the while, his family's past in this country was never far from his thoughts.

That past came to life in an encounter while he was traveling between Zamboanga and Davao on an interisland ship. Cliff learned that the captain was Julian Tamayo, the man entrusted with the dangerous mission of the *Mactan*, the Red Cross' hastily assembled mercy ship that had left besieged Manila on New Years Eve in 1941, heading for Australia with its cargo of wounded soldiers. With great excitement, Cliff sought out the captain, and learned the details of the perilous voyage to Australia.

In 1951, Cliff recrossed paths with the intrepid Julian Tamayo, captain of the World War II rescue ship the Mactan.

The Mactan had been the first mercy ship of World War II, overseen by Irving Williams, Cliff's father's Red Cross field director. Cliff had already learned that when MacArthur met Williams in Sydney, the general stated it was a miracle the little ship had been able to get through— first the American minefields and then the Japanese submarine and air threats—safely.

Captain Tamayo, competent and steady as ever, was pleased to cross paths again with Charles Forster's now-grown son, and confirmed the hazards of the month-long voyage. He then described how, when they reached their destination, the Sydney harbor had been lined with well wishers gathered to greet the *Mactan* with cheers, flags waving, and a rousing chorus of "Waltzing Matilda."

18

MINDANAO AND SULU

PERSONIFYING THE U.S. GOVERNMENT AND the people of America to the sizeable area of Mindanao and the Sulu Archipelago was a many-splendored vocation for Cliff, infinite in its variety. Occasions for USIS-linked activities in "culture" and "information" and "people-to people diplomacy" ranged from inspirational to off-the-wall, both at home in Davao and on the road throughout the territory.

Cliff was frequently on the road and I was able to join him on many of those trips. In an article published in the February, 1952, *Foreign Service Journal,* "Assignment to Mindanao," he described the routine he'd established when moving around this large area with the terrible roads and visiting the capital cities of the various provincial regions.

Official calls came first: the governor of the province, the mayor, the constabulary commander. All were very interested in the function of USIS and before I knew it, I was delivering speeches all over on our functions and purposes—and answering questions. A small businessman wanted information on how to run a retail shop. A teacher wanted to know about the best methods for counseling students. A farmer came to find out what he could about contour irrigation. A delegation of students requested materials contrasting communism to democracy.

Our librarian, Milagros Aquino, came to my office one afternoon. "The Bagobos hope that you will visit them soon," she said.

"Is it difficult to reach them?" I asked.

"It is not easy," she replied.

On our first visit to a Bagobo settlement we had to leave the jeep at the end of a provincial road and continue on foot along a mountain trail southwest of Davao. Our guide told us that retreating Japanese had used the same trail in 1943. We made our first contact with the tribesmen literally in the clouds. The jungle trail widened at about 2,500 feet and we caught sight of the most ingenious water system we had ever seen. Long green bamboo poles zigzagged down the mountainside, one above the other. Cool spring water gushed from the end of one pole into the one below it, and so on downhill, with branch poles providing spring water on tap for each house.

The small settlement was a compact clearing with several houses surrounding the community center and a bamboo picnic table and benches out in the open. "Welcome! The gongs are ready for you," said the village elder, dressed in a colorful woven abaca sarong with a large cowry shell inserted in each ear. Nine brass *agongs* were tied together in three rows on a scaffolding and could be heard for many miles. A short concert was followed by a feast of roast pig and traditional tribal dances.

On another trip we were able to take the newly arrived mobile unit, although at times we were in mud up to the hubcaps. Datu Monkay, a Bagobo chieftain in the Gumalang district, had invited USIS to come and entertain his followers. I accepted and we were off early in the morning loaded down with films, records, and a projector.

Datu Monkay was waiting for us with his five hereditary subchiefs. All were in full costume. One of the wives of the datu, who spoke some English, came forward to greet us. Suddenly *agong* music was underway and two young girls danced very slowly in a circle. They plucked on taut abaca strings inserted in a bamboo pipe. These bamboo guitars were held away from the body at a forty five degree angle and the players had to devote full attention to them while dancing. The girls were doing the "Harvest Dance in Honor of the American Air Force." The dance depicts two girls harvesting in the fields during the Japanese occupation. Suddenly American planes appear. There is much shouting and the girls are overjoyed and run to the village for a celebration. Another dance, the "Village Warner," shows with elaborate pantomime how Bagobo villages notified each other of the approach of Japanese soldiers.

To reciprocate, we rigged up our electric lights, played some American Indian music and folksongs of the West, and then showed movies. The datu's followers were very enthusiastic. One of our pictures which showed New Englanders eating lobsters— all in Technicolor—caused no end of excitement. Another scene in the same picture which showed skiing in Vermont aroused the curiosity of the datu's wife. She wanted to know why it was that Americans "liked to slide on cement."

Bogobo tribesmen welcomed us to their
village on the slopes of Mount Apo.

Although motion pictures are often not comprehended in areas such as this, the mere fact that USIS comes such a distance to entertain and meet together with a tribal group makes a very great impression. And sometimes a movie will have an impact where a group has never seen a movie before in their lives. The best example of this was a showing made several weeks later by the mobile unit to the Mandayas, a tribe in northern Davao Province. We showed a Walt Disney health cartoon on hookworm. The very graphic presentation of an ugly-looking worm entering through bare feet to feed on the intestinal tract made such an impression on the Mandayas that they besieged the local shoe dealer the next morning with so many requests for tennis shoes that he had to come to Davao City to replenish his supply and meet the demand.

The shoe merchant made a personal call on Cliff in his office to thank him for the boost to his business.

A trip of several days took Cliff and me to the provincial capital of Cotabato Province to the west of Davao. We stopped at Kidapawan, a fast-growing frontier town in central Mindanao. Cliff was to be the commencement speaker at the Central Mindanao Colleges graduation. We stayed in the home of the Filipino woman who ran the growing institution, Mrs. Sabulo. We had been driving for four hours in the jeep, over bumpy and dusty roads, and arrived dirty and tired. We stopped in front of a tiny house made of split bamboo and nipa leaves, raised five feet above the ground on wooden poles. Our hostess ran down the steps to greet us and quickly made us feel at home. Her hospitality was limitless; we were given the one bedroom, with the only bed in the house, while the rest of the family slept on mats which were laid out on the bamboo floor.

In the morning we were awakened at dawn by the sounds of pigs and chickens under the room where we slept. We washed our faces in a pail of water and found the family already awake and active in the preparation of a very special American style breakfast for us. Our hostess was frying eggs over her wood stove. She told us how she, the housewife in a modest Filipino home, had been to the United States and graduated from Columbia University. Mrs. Sabulo had been offered prestigious jobs

in Manila for much more money than she could ever make in Kidapawan, but felt that Mindanao's heartland offered the more important
challenges. Her husband also felt the call to be a pioneer and now was the
District Judge. Here, in the wilderness, she was giving to the students
all she could of the things she had seen and learned in the United States.
She was proud of her students' ability to run a school honor system and
participate in self-government. "You see," she said, "how the lessons of
one of your great universities are being learned as far away as our school
in Kidapawan."

Kidapawan had only a few nipa houses, the school, the courthouse, a
movie theater, and a market. The commencement ceremony was held in
the movie house. Before Cliff's turn came there were the class prophecy,
valedictorian's speech, school song, vocal solos, and a long introduction
of the speaker—him. Afterwards came the diplomas, then the dance.
Farmers and their children, a Moro chieftain and family, the students and
their teachers. Most of these people were pioneers in a new land trying
to build a community on the southern and hitherto unsettled frontiers of
their newly independent nation.

Our next stop on this trip was the provincial capitol, Cotabato City.
As we walked into his office, the American editor and publisher of the
Mindanao Cross (a weekly paper, six pages, 4,000 circulation, largest
in eastern Mindanao) sat in a dirty white cassock, his feet on his desk,
hands behind his head, raptly listening to a scratchy record of "Bye Bye
Blackbird."

Father Cuthbert Billman jumped to his feet and greeted us warmly,
shouting to be heard over the noises of the phonograph record and the
presses in the next room. "Well! The Forsters! Welcome to Cotabato and
the offices of the *Mindanao Cross*. How do you like my new phonograph?
And look at this pile of records! Parishioners back in Boston sent them.
All of them are getting long playing records so I get the old fashioned
ones."

There was no doubt that the phonograph was old fashioned; Father
Billman reached over and wound it before starting a new record. "I like
to play music—it keeps my pressmen happy as they work on the paper."
We wondered if the men at the presses cold really hear the records over
the clatter of their machines.

Next door was the school, Notre Dame de Cotabato, run by Oblate Fathers, young and energetic men who were popular throughout Cotabato Province, one of the homes of the feared (by Catholic Filipinos) Moros. Billman, a keen and courageous newsman, ran his paper while Father Sullivan ran the school. The interests of the two didn't always harmonize. Cliff told Father Billman that we wanted to meet Father Sullivan and discuss the problems of his school library with him.

Billman snorted. "What do you want to meet Father Sullivan for? He's nothing but a goddamn New England educator!" Evidently, there was an ongoing disagreement between the newsman who wanted to run his presses during school hours and play his music over the loud speaker to keep his men happy, and the educator who complained that the racket seriously hindered the progress of education and argued that the presses could be run at night.

Father Billman showed us around his plant, unsuccessfully trying to cover up the tremendous pride he felt in his operation, which with scanty equipment but a strong esprit de corps was putting out one of the best papers in the country. Billman was a fearless reporter and any scandal he could unearth, whether it concerned an unimportant citizen or a high government official, would be exposed in his paper. As a result, he was forever involved in a series of libel cases. "You know," he said, "It's getting so I spend as much time in court as I do on the job. Maybe I should go into the law." But somehow the father managed to work his way out of every lawsuit, unscathed, and having enjoyed himself thoroughly.

When time came for dinner we drove through the dusty unpaved streets to the city square with a faintly Arabian style city hall, a large park filled with waterless fountains and statueless pedestals, and Lee's Hotel. This, the most prominent hostelry and eating spot in Cotabato, was located on the second story of an office building, furnished in the bedrooms with the hardest beds this side of marble slabs, and bare and rickety tables and chairs in the restaurant, which was thick with flies.

Mr. Lee, the Chinese proprietor, greeted us and gave a poetic description of the delights of his Chinese cooking. But Billman wasn't convinced. He brought out a bottle of whiskey from his cassock and grinned. "Very special guests, Lee! For Mr. and Mrs. Forster we will have whiskey and scrambled eggs." As we ate our eggs and drank our whiskey, the father thanked Cliff profusely for the USIS assistance he had been getting from Manila in the form of news releases and cuts for pictures and cartoons. "Without your materials we would have shut our doors and sold our presses long ago. You keep us in business. And I think it's worth your investment. After all, this is the only publication in an area larger than the country of Belgium that is waging the battle for honesty, decency, and democracy. And with the strong appeal of extralegal activity in these parts and the threat of the Huks moving in down in the valley, the people need to be reminded about what they should fight for."

Billman continued, "I'll tell you one thing though. Your news releases aren't colorful enough. They're just facts. People here don't want to read plain facts, so I color it up a bit. Stick fairly close to the facts, jazz it up a bit, then you've got a good story." The padre had given us his formula for the success of the *Mindanao Cross.*

We met more of the fighting priests of Mindanao when we traveled a few months later into southern Cotabato where, indeed, the Huks were trying to gain a foothold and poor farmers were struggling to make a living on isolated plots of land. We had flown a Philippine Airlines plane into the port of Dadiangas while the mobile unit was being shipped by sea. No roads connected southern Cotabato with the rest of the island. The vehicle would come with a load of printed materials to be distributed to schools and community centers in small towns and villages.

I was intrigued by these two American priests in the small settlement of Lagao at the entrance to the southern Cotabato Valley. They had already succeeded fabulously with the first white potatoes ever grown in the area, and would have been right at home in a Stanford fraternity house.

"I was in the Battle of the Bulge and that was plenty rough," Brother Paul was saying as he puffed on a Philippine cigar in the twilight. "But I've never been as scared as I was the other night when three guys jumped me. They came in the window just as I was locking up for the night. Of course they knew I had the money there. Everyone in town had been to the bazaar in the afternoon when we made 3,500 pesos for building the new church."

"Oh, you know you were having the time of your life. Thought you were fighting a war. A hero!" Brother John grinned at the lean young man who had been talking to us. "Besides, I kinda helped you out, re-member?"

Brother Paul continued: "Sure, you helped. You answered my shouts in time to scare them away. By then I'd already had a battle royal on the floor with the leader and managed to grab his gun! Anyway, they didn't get the money and I got to the bank the next morning. The real trouble though is we'll probably be seeing them and their likes again. They need money and guns and they'll do anything to get them. And the mountain is full of them." Brother Paul looked up at Mount Matutum, an almost perfect cone rising straight out of the valley floor, as it was outlined in the last rays of the setting sun. Up there malcontents were being orga-nized by trained Huks from the north, with the aim of creating in the relative peace and quiet of Mindanao a replica of the civil strife that had torn Luzon since the war. It was from the thick mountain forests that the Huks had sent their three men to get the church money in order to buy themselves supplies.

"But they won't bother us any more if the people can be persuaded not to join them or even assist them. Then the government can wipe them out," Brother John burst in. "And the people will just laugh at them if their stomachs are full today and the fields are high with produce so their kids can eat next month. That's why we hope your library can send us down the latest stuff on peanut growing and pig raising. We fellows know nothing about peanuts and less about pigs. But we plan to show these people how to get the best peanuts out of their land and to have the fattest pigs in the country. That's the best way we know of to make those fellows quit the mountain."

And Cliff was convinced the Catholic Oblate brothers would prosper in their self-taught agricultural experiment. Already their potatoes were adding to the economic stability of southern Cotabato.

A different trip, this time to the north, interested me in particular, as it gave me the opportunity to meet Moros for the first time, the subjects of the research paper I had written for Claude Buss at Stanford.

Cliff had visited the province of Lanao as a boy, accompanying his fa-ther on a Red Cross mission to the northern region of the island and meet-ing the ruling datu—Philippine chieftain. He would now make a return visit wearing a different hat, paying his respects to the Moro governor,

Mandanagan Dimakuta, and making arrangements for the USIS mobile unit to operate in the province, with the governor's sanction.

We flew into Cagayan de Oro on the northern coast of Mindanao and Cliff made his usual calls on officials there. When the governor of the province heard that our next destination would be the city of Dansalan in Lanao, he indicated that this could be dangerous territory and offered us the use of a provincial government car. Accepting his gracious offer, we started south for Dansalan. We were excited—and nervous—to be venturing into the land of the Moros. After all, they were famous for their ferocity in battle and hostility to Christians, and the Moro population here was second only to that in the islands of Sulu.

In his 1952 *Foreign Service Journal* article Cliff wrote:

> The Misamis Oriental Governor's parting words were that he would send a telegram to the Lanao Governor informing him that we were coming. I explained that this would not be necessary since I had sent a letter the week before. I thanked him just the same.
>
> In late afternoon the car was climbing rapidly into the hills. It was an entirely different world. There were red fezzes on the men and they wore red and black shirts. Kris swords hung at their sides. The women wore small vests and chewed betel nut. Mosques with tin roofs were much in evidence as we traveled southeast toward Lake Lanao.
>
> We were ascending a steep hill when the engine sputtered and died on us. Two Moros by the side of the road stood up and moved in closer when they saw we had come to a complete standstill. Our driver tinkered for a few minutes, then told us that it would be quite a while before he could get the engine started again. Nancy and I decided to hitchhike to Dansalan. We started walking up the road. A few minutes later a San Miguel Brewery truck came along and we thumbed a ride. The truck was picking up empty Coca-Cola cases and turning over new bottles. In the cab of the truck we had a first-rate opportunity to see how Coca-Cola has caught on with the Moros. Whenever the truck did not stop angry boys would throw rocks at us.

We alighted from the truck in front of the Governor's residence outside of town. About thirty Moros were sitting on the porch, and one spoke English. "The Governor? Oh, he is gone." "Where?" He didn't seem to know. "Is the Mayor in town?" He didn't know. "Is there any way to find out?" "Yes, a man could walk there." The Moro called a guard over to where we were standing and spoke to him for several minutes. He pointed to the guard. "You follow him."

We followed the guard down the street across the Bailey bridge which led into town. It was just past noon and the sun beat down on the dusty street. We finally stopped in front of a two-story house. "Datu Ali!" the guard shouted. An old lady appeared at the window and shook her head. The guard motioned and we followed him back up the street. Suddenly, I saw what had once been a country club on the military reservation. We decided to stop here and said goodbye to the guard. We were hot and dusty and all we wanted to do was to sit down and cool off. Nancy grabbed my arm. "What do you make of that?" she asked. In large blue letters, hanging above the entrance to the club, was a greeting: "WELCOME MEMBERS OF THE AMERICAN EMBASSY."

I shrugged it off as an old sign, possibly welcoming General James Henderson when he had visited the area from Cebu months earlier. It's common for signs to remain hanging long after the event.

We found two chairs at one end of a very large room. No governor, no mayor, and no one so far—except the Moro back at the governor's residence—who spoke English. Nancy called my attention to two Moros who were preparing a long table and had set several places. I walked over and asked if they served lunch. "No." "Is there going to be a party?" "Yes." "For whom?" "Colonel Forster," was the reply. "He is coming from the American Embassy." "Where is the governor?" I asked. "He has gone down to the border to meet the colonel."

It dawned on us: The parting words of the Governor of Misamis Oriental! He was sending a telegram that we were on the way. And I was now a colonel!

When the governor and his party returned from the border, where they had been sitting on benches looking north in antici- pation of our arrival, their laughter was uncontrollable. The cir- cumstances surrounding our arrival at Dansalan—particularly the fact that we hitchhiked into Dansalan in a beer delivery truck—were, and still are we hear, the cause of much hilarity in the Lanao Province capitol.

"You Americans always have a different way of doing things," said the Judge of the Court of First Instance. It was late when we left Dansalan. "Goodbye Colonel Forster," someone said.

An interesting post script: when the mobile unit arrived in Dansalan two months later, shooting broke out in the audi- ence during the movie. The USIS film operator later explained it this way: "The Moros were not interested in a film on Ameri- can school life. I think they became bored. When the shooting started I changed the film and showed the Marines at Iwo Jima. The Moros liked this film and the shooting stopped."

As we started back along the road I realized that our job was only beginning on this island of great distance and contrasts. We were bringing America, its people, and its principles to out- of-the-way places at a very critical time in the world's history. The extent of our success will determine to a very large degree how we are to be looked upon here in the years to come. One thing is certain: nothing is more important now than keeping the facts before people abroad. Tyranny over the minds of men can be challenged through personal contact in the field and an understanding of the facts. USIS has come to Mindanao to accept this challenge.

Cliff's assessment of the USIS mission encapsulated what the post- World War II generation of young officers, many of them veterans of that war, had committed to when they opted for a career as "public" diplo- mats. Young, somewhat innocent, they were highly motivated.

On a later northern journey, Cliff was invited to meet with the vet- erans of an earlier war—the Spanish-American. Every Sunday afternoon in Cagayan de Oro, the men would drift into the living room of Joe

Barker. While Joe's young Spanish wife served them tea and cookies they swapped war stories.

Six veterans were present the day Cliff joined them. On his return to our home in Davao, Cliff told me how delighted the men had been to have a new audience for their tales of glory, most of which had inevitably grown bigger and more heroic during the passage of years.

"Now, look here young feller, we can tell you a thing or two about these islands that you don't get in no fancy books," said the old man across the room, cupping his hand to his deaf ear so he could better hear Cliff's reply. "Yessir, we were out in these parts in the days when men were men! Why, when I was a boy walking twenty miles in the morning and another twenty in the afternoon was all in the day's work. And the jungles didn't stop us. Now you weak-kneed youngsters just flit along the national highways in your fancy cars and think you're getting out in the back country."

Cliff recalled the nightmare of ruts and ridges, mud, dust, and washed-out bridges along which he had labored in a jeep at the reckless speed of five miles an hour to reach Cagayan. Walking probably would have been easier and not much slower. But he had to admit, as he looked around the room at these men, that whatever they did in their youth certainly must have agreed with them. A more robust, bright-eyed group of men at their age would be hard to find.

"Now you just wait a minute, Tom Harris, I want to talk to this young man. He didn't drive all the way from Davao City just to spend an afternoon talking to you." A stocky gentleman walked across the room, banged his cane on the rattan couch for emphasis, and squeezed in next to Cliff on the couch. He leaned over to Cliff and spoke to him confidentially. "Did you know, young man, that I got the congregational middle?" He leaned back to watch the impact of this revelation.

"Oh, you did?" said Cliff, wondering what the congregational middle might be. He was about to go into his family's affiliation with the Congregational Church when his neighbor continued.

"Yep! Back in 1925. Mr. Coolidge himself—a fine man, Mr. Coolidge—he came all the way down to Cagayan from Manila and gave me the congregational middle. He said to me, 'You showed yourself a brave man, Charlie Johnson, and I am only sorry you didn't get this here

middle many years ago. You were a big help to us in that war of 1898.'"
Charlie Johnson beamed triumphantly at his audience.

"Oh," said Cliff, "the Congressional Medal of Honor! Congratulations
to you, Mr. Johnson."

"Now Charlie," said the man on Cliff's left, who had been intently
blowing smoke rings with his black native cigarette, "you know perfectly
well that the horse and not you should have gotten that medal. If the
horse hadn't been frightened by the gunshot and bolted through the enemy lines 'cause it was so darn scared, you'd still be standing up on that
hill wondering how to get your message through to the general."

Charlie turned red, too excited to protest, and Tom Harris jumped
in with one of his own stories. Cliff surmised that on any given Sunday,
at Joe Barker's, the eager student of history could learn about exploits of
the war of 1898 unsung in the textbooks.

Harry Hudson was Cliff's immediate boss in Manila. He was a "can
do" man, and once he latched onto an idea he expected it to be carried
forward. For example, he decided USIS reading centers should be established in some of the towns of the Sulu Archipelago. In vain, Cliff argued
that the English reading materials that would be sent to these islands
wouldn't be relevant to the Moros (most of whom knew no English) and
that this segment of the Filipino population was otherwise engaged at
the moment, either coping with or participating in a rebellion against
Manila's Christian governance. That rebellion dated back to the days
when Spanish priests first tried to convert these Muslims. Sulu had always been a place apart, more attuned to the Islamic culture of Indonesia,
and in constant revolt for over four centuries, against the Spanish, against
the Americans, and now against the independent Philippine authority.
"You won't know until you check it out," was Harry's reply, and so Cliff
headed for a fact-finding trip to the islands of Sulu, taking me along.

We flew into the capitol city on the largest island, Jolo. The superintendent of schools met us at the airport. He had a meeting planned for
Cliff that afternoon at his office. He looked at me and then pointedly told
Cliff, "Your wife must be very tired. We will leave her at the house so
she may rest." Thus dismissed, I was ensconced at the Jolo residence of a
Davao friend, a longtime Spanish resident of the Philippines who managed Mindanao and Sulu light and power companies.

When I wrote my paper at Stanford on "The Moros of Mindanao and Sulu," I learned about long years of Moros fighting Catholic Spain and the uneasy truce established under the Americans after General Pershing challenged the Moro weapon of *juramentado* with the guns of his battleship anchored offshore. Juramentado was a local custom, a precursor to today's suicide bomber, not approved by Islamic authorities in Mecca but enduring here in Sulu. Seeking martyrdom, a man would gird his loins with coils of heavy rope, go to his imam for a blessing, and burst forth brandishing his wavy-bladed kris. His goal was to cut down as many Christians as possible in a killing frenzy, clearing his pathway to paradise. His rampage would be stopped only when he himself was killed.

Not long after Cliff and the superintendent had left for their meeting, I was comfortably reading in the living room when I heard what I thought was firecrackers. Two excited maids ran into the room. *"Juramentado!"* they shouted, as they frantically pulled and latched wooden shutters across windows and bolted all the doors.

When Cliff returned some time later, he described the scene where he had been. He and the superintendent were strolling through Jolo's central plaza. His host was planning to arrange a meeting the next day on the far side of the island with the leader of the current Moro insurgency, Datu Kamlon Kamlon. "You know, Mr. Forster," he said, "you Americans are welcome anywhere in Jolo. The Moros as well as Christian Filipinos have tremendous respect for Americans. You will be very safe with us." As they stepped around women selling sweets from baskets in the middle of the sidewalk, Cliff noted that the feature at the local cinema was an old Buck Rogers film. To entice customers inside, the film's soundtrack was broadcast across the plaza from the theater's loudspeakers.

"Juramentado!" When the cry went up, the superintendent grabbed Cliff's arm and pulled him into the nearest house, where people were already shuttering windows and picking up small children, whom they wrapped in straw mats and stashed on top of a portable closet. "You're American!" he gasped. "You're the best target in town!"

While they waited for the man with the kris to be brought to a standstill, Cliff could hear the Buck Rogers sound track, still broadcasting from the cinema across the plaza, and gunfire. There were two fatalities that day: A man who stuck his head out a window to see what was

going on and was beheaded, plus the *juramentado*. Also several injuries.
When the cry was raised, every person with a gun began running towards the source, firing as they ran, and several innocent bystanders were
shot before the martyr was brought down.

Cliff never did get to meet Kamlon Kamlon, but the next morning
we made a visit to Princess Tarhata, a woman I had written about, in her
home on stilts over water near the port. As a young girl she had traveled
to the States. The American colonial authorities believed that a Western-
educated daughter of the sultan might come back to Sulu as a voice for
moderation and modernization. As her forefathers had led their people
into Islam, maybe the Princess would lead her generation into literacy
and constructive citizenship.

We walked through a maze of floating huts, past skittering children
and chatting housewives, and stopped at a house that looked like all the
others. A piece of embroidery on the wall, a photo of her late father on
the table—these were the royal regalia. She was a simple middle-aged
matron, apologizing for having forgotten much of her English. She had at
one time taught some English classes for young children. Nowadays she
was a member of a woman's group. Life was very simple, very routine.

She said that there had always been great respect for Americans
among the Moros because Americans gave them education and were tol-
erant of their religion. Tarhata appreciated her own education, but said
that the old customs of the Moros were now threatened by education.
The younger generation becomes "civilized and forgets the good things
in its heritage. This is particularly true of high-school students." The day
before the superintendent of schools had told Cliff that illiteracy in Jolo
was the highest in the Philippines, 82 percent. The unrest on the island
of Jolo, he said, had caused a drop in enrollment at the high school during the past year; so fewer of the young Moros were being exposed to the
"civilization" that Tarhata felt was a threat.

The princess's family, Kiram, had produced generations of Sulu sul-
tans and they claimed North Borneo because formerly they ruled there
as well as in Sulu. They had signed an agreement (the Bates Treaty)
with the British who agreed to lease the territory from them. In fact, the
previous month Tarhata had gone to Borneo to collect her annual rent.
Unfortunately, the Kiram copy of the lease was stolen some years before

when her father, Sultan at that time, was visiting Singapore. Her family, she added, was related to the Muslim rulers of Singapore and Malaya. The last Sultan of Sulu had died the past November and at this point (1951) three men, two of them Kiram, were claiming the title.

This journey was to continue by boat, island-hopping along the Sulu Archipelago to the last inhabited island of the Philippines, Sitangkai, which lay thirty miles off the Borneo coast. The *Jovito* was disturbingly small, and all out of proportion. The superstructure, consisting of the captain's quarters and the one passenger cabin grafted on top of a narrow hull, made the vessel taller than it was wide. We edged our way through the turbaned, sarong-clad Moro crowd on the Jolo wharf, walked up the single plank that served as gangway, and settled into our cabin. This one, at least, was above decks and the porthole opened to fresh sea breezes.

Motorized Moro *vintas* sped past us, headed to Borneo where they collected contraband cargoes of liquor and cigarettes. We were establishing personal contacts with inhabitants of fishing villages, many of whom had never seen Americans. At the tiny port of Bongao, a proud Moro educator showed us his shabby school, "the bastion of democracy in Sulu," he declared. Bongao's town leaders assembled on the *Jovito* and, through interpreters, Cliff conducted the town's first "town hall meeting," discussing personal, local, and international affairs.

As the boat approached Sitangkai we could see the dim outline of North Borneo in the distance. At six a.m. we docked at a pier that jutted a couple of miles out into the shallow water. This was the closest the *Jovito* could get to Sitangkai, which was surrounded by a coral reef and waters from two to two and a half feet deep, at high tide. The island itself included about ten acres of land and from any shore we could see the entire island, but houses built out from the land on stilts doubled the real estate. Only the school and one house were actually on the island. The houses, twelve feet above the high tide, were connected to each other and the land by bamboo walkways.

At nine the mayor came aboard, accompanied by six rifle-toting Moros. This was an honor guard (all of the policemen in the town) to escort us through Sitangkai. We wove through channels in the reef in a flat-bottom boat that had been imported from Borneo to navigate the shallow coral-lined waters. It was poled along by a man in front and one behind, a journey of an hour and a half. In the center of town we scrambled up and across bamboo walkways to meet the district supervisor, customs officers, and merchants, then stopped for a coke at the Chinese community headquarters. We went on, past the cemetery (on land), peeking into classes at the elementary school (they were discussing the role of United Nations troops in Korea). We returned to the Chinese hall for lunch. There we were joined by the village nurse, the only nurse within seventy miles. She told us that she herself did operations, for which she had no training. Her greatest handicap was the lack of medical supplies to fight rampant malaria, tuberculosis, and leg and arm ulcers.

After lunch we waited for the tide to rise so that our boat could again glide among the coral reefs back to the *Jovito*.

Coming south we had stopped mid-archipelago at Siasi, the largest island south of Jolo. The resident foreigners (a Swiss coconut planter, an American Oblate priest, and a lone American woman missionary) had urged us to come ashore and have breakfast with them on our return voyage. They relished the prospect of new faces and new conversations.

A short walk from the harbor, the planter's home was reached by narrow wooden walkways across the tidal shallows. Though yet another thatched house, inside it had the look of a cozy Swiss cottage. The breakfast table was set on the veranda overlooking the town's plaza. As we walked through the town we had sensed tension. There was none of the organized chaos that is part of a tropical morning; no shouting, no jostling market activity, no dogs and chickens and children underfoot. As we ate our Rice Krispies—a treasure that had been saved for a special occasion—the men mulled over the local news.

The previous night, in the hills behind town, a Moro bandit had raided the Philippine Constabulary outpost, wounding several soldiers. But he had been caught and now was a prisoner of the Christian Constabulary. The town rumor was that there would be a *juramentado* to avenge the indignity of capture.

My back was to the plaza and I was intent on the conversation. "Oh, no! Get your wife's attention! Don't let her look out at the plaza!" I of course immediately looked to see what had troubled the Oblate priest. The constabulary had come to town, bringing evidence that crime does not pay—the bandit's head. One of them found an old oil drum, rolled it out into the center of the plaza, and set up the severed head for all to behold. A crowd was slowly, sullenly, gathering. The tension mounted.

Behind us the whistle of our ship shattered the silence with three long blasts, a signal that it was ready to sail. Guilty at eating and running, more chagrined at leaving our hosts behind to see the drama played out, we selfishly welcomed our refuge as we sailed away from Siasi.

When Cliff submitted his travel report to Manila and asked Harry Hudson what he thought now about setting up reading rooms in the Sulu Archipelago, the boss admitted that maybe USIS effort could be better invested elsewhere.

19

JAPANESE IMMERSION

A S WE WERE WINDING DOWN our first overseas tour of duty in Davao, our feelings about the experience could be summed up by a verse written by Rabindranath Tagore:

> I slept and dreamt that life was Joy.
> I awoke and saw that life was Duty.
> I acted, and behold—Duty was Joy.

We left Mindanao October 30, 1951. While entertaining three final houseguests, we packed our rattan chairs, our Chinese teacups, my seashell collection, the Mayor's farewell testimonial engraved in teak, and our other household bits and pieces.

In our two years of Foreign Service apprenticeship we had logged a good deal of mileage, seen and done things we never could have anticipated, and grown enormously in self-confidence and the conviction that in the Foreign Service we were following the right career path for both of us. We were being educated by our friends and our clients and we left feeling that, indeed, "duty was joy."

Cliff had been promoted in October of 1950. The United States government recognized his worth by increasing his annual salary from $3,570 to $4,830. In the interstices between caring for guests, road trips with Cliff, teaching, and doing my part in community activities, I had completed three courses from the University of California Extension Division to satisfy Stanford's graduation requirements. Milagros Aquino relished the fact that she was the mandated "official proctor" who certified that my final exams were taken under her supervision, without any cheating. I would receive my diploma in early 1952, and was still considered a member of the class of '50.

Armed with all this wealth and recognition, we set off for the next leg of the journey. After two years, Cliff was due for home leave and reassignment, either in the U.S. or to another overseas post. We learned that we could travel home via Europe for $24 more than what it cost the government to send us directly to the East Coast across the Pacific. For that price, we planned an itinerary that would take us on a Pan American flight through Hong Kong, with stops in Beirut, Athens, and Rome. From there we would go overland, catching a flight home from London.

But our plans abruptly changed. The State Department wanted a formal evaluation of the USIS program work in the Philippines. Cliff was temporarily assigned to Manila, to head up a team investigating what kind of success there had been with USIS activities and publications in countering Huk propaganda. To provide ongoing funding for this new form of diplomacy, Congress was demanding "evidence of effectiveness." During a three-month study Cliff would be traveling to all the outlying USIS Centers and asking questions to obtain substantive data, which would later be analyzed in Washington.

We lived for three months in Manila—in a second floor walk-up apartment, cooking on a hot plate plugged into the living room wall— while Cliff completed his temporary assignment. Instead of taking our European route in October, we did so beginning in late January, which still got us back in time to visit with family in New York, Michigan, and California and to touch base with friends like Barbara and Dick Moore before heading in June to New Haven, Connecticut, for Cliff's new—and surprising—assignment.

We had hoped our second post with USIS would be someplace close to the Mediterranean, not a nation's capitol but again in a secondary city. Perhaps Naples in Italy, or Izmir on the coast of Turkey, or Alexandria at the head of the Nile in Egypt. When the assignment came, it was unequivocal. Cliff was to report to Yale University for an intensive summer course in Japanese language training, followed by an academic year of more language study plus coursework in history, political science, and the fine art of evaluation. Japan had signed a peace treaty, and a chain of American libraries had spread from north to south and east to west, centers that had been set up by the U.S. Army during their occupation of Japan and would now be taken over by the Department of State. A team of center directors was being recruited to man the posts and all would be taught enough Japanese to function at a basic level.

Japan? Japanese language study? This would have been inconceivable at the time Cliff was interned, or after his return to Manila when he saw for himself the wake of destruction and bitter feelings left by the Japanese conquest of his homeland. He discussed his misgivings about the assignment with his boss in Washington, and later described this conversation during his interview with Lew Schmidt.

> I wasn't keen on going into Japan but I was virtually told by the East Asia Area Director, "This is it. You're going in." I said to him, "Well, look, I had this experience during the war. I just don't know how I'll do there." He said, "That's all the more reason you should go in, because you'll know both the minus and plus side of these people." As it turned out, it was a great education for me as time went on, and I hope it was as useful for the Japanese in developing a greater understanding of America and the American people.

Underlying Cliff's anxiety was a fascination with the possibility of being in postwar Japan, experiencing the mood of the defeated conquers and participating in the endeavor to build a lasting peace. This could be a real test of his conviction that dialogue between peoples with different world views was of prime importance. And it would certainly be something new. His first post had been for him a homecoming. Not the second one.

Somewhat to my surprise, given my "never will I follow you to Japan, Cliff Forster" reaction to our Yokohama-Tokyo day in 1949, I, too, was game for this new adventure and curious to learn more about Japan, albeit with some trepidation.

We arrived home from the Philippines at the end of March in 1952, with two months of home leave to get reacquainted with family before Cliff would report for duty. Our first stop was Rye, New York, to visit with my mother, stepfather, teenage sister Vail, and half-sister Cindy, who was now age ten.

Cindy's pride and joy was her collection of tropical fish. She was cleaning the aquarium one Saturday morning and complained about the difficulty of removing slime from the decorative items; being older, wiser (I thought), and an experienced traveler, I offered my advice. "I collected seashells from the beaches of Mindanao," I told her, "and cleaned them in a solution with chlorine." She gleefully took my advice, returned the glistening objects to the aquarium, filled it, and returned the fish to their home. Predictably, all died. Consolation came in the form of a family trip into New York City to purchase an entire new assortment of fish. We continued our home leave with visits to my father, stepmother, and brother Roddy in Michigan, then onward to California to see Cliff's mother, sister, and nephew Charles.

Cliff began his classes in early June. Over the next weeks and months I maintained that another woman had come into our lives. Late into the night, on the tape recorder plugged in beside our bed, the voice of Eleanor Jordan repeating Japanese phrases was funneled into Cliff's ears. As an adult he was learning language the way a child learns. Basic phrases and sentences were to be mimicked, memorized, and repeated over and over in practical conversations.

Right after the attack on Pearl Harbor, Yale University had begun training American soldiers in oral Japanese to remedy the nation's lack of speakers in that language. The designers of Yale's curriculum were now training civilians for the State Department, as well as military officers. Four mornings a week the class of three State Department officers and two men in the military met with native language speakers. Class was conducted in Japanese only, for four straight hours. No questions were to be asked or answers given in English. Just listen, repeat, and learn to use new vocabulary in different contexts. Afternoons and evenings were dedicated to independent drill (using that intrusive tape recorder!) and memorization. On Friday the linguist, an American, ran the class and in a concession to the fact that these students were mature adults, he allowed time to explain, in English, the convoluted grammar of spoken Japanese, the three sets of ideographic and phonetic symbols used in writing the language, and the differences in spoken language used according to the social status of speaker and listener.

After spending the summer in a cramped and hot apartment, we found a house rentable for the winter in a summer colony on Long Island Sound north of New Haven. Our household effects had followed us and our rattan furniture, those Chinese teacups, and other Asian memorabilia were temporarily placed in a pine-paneled New England cottage. No longer did the oriental furnishings of the Forsters' home in Oakland that had astonished me as a college sophomore seem so strange and out of place.

I went to work to supplement that forty-eight-hundred-dollar salary in a women's clothing store on New Haven's main shopping street. It didn't take long for me to realize that selling was not one of my skills, or pleasures, and I was delighted when I was hired to work for a professor of European languages at Yale's graduate school. My secretarial skills were minimal, but Professor Anderson was very patient. He liked Cliff's and my story, and even allowed me a double lunch period twice a week so I could meet with a Japanese tutor. The State Department wasn't funding language instruction for spouses at that point and I knew that I might well need conversational Japanese more than Cliff, since he would have Japanese assistants at whatever post was to be his.

In the spring of 1953, the three Foreign Service officers received their travel orders. The two State Department officers would spend another year in full-time study at the American Embassy's language school in Japan, enabling them to achieve moderate fluency and reading ability in this complex language, and Cliff, the only USIS officer, was to proceed to Matsuyama, where he would take charge of the center that had been established by the U.S. Army and currently was being run by a woman librarian.

Matsuyama?

Cliff asked his Japanese teachers where in Japan the town was located. None knew. It required a trip to the library to discover that our new home would be on Shikoku, the fourth and smallest of Japan's major islands, a port city with a feudal castle and famous hot-spring baths. Matsuyama was on the Inland Sea, across from the city of Hiroshima on the island of Honshu, and was accessible only by boat. We would stop first in Tokyo, where Cliff would be briefed by officers in the embassy and at the consulate in Kobe where he would meet his immediate supervisor, Walter Nichols, who was in charge of the central Honshu and Shikoku USIS operation.

After another American President Line voyage from San Francisco to Yokohama,, we traveled by train from Tokyo to Kobe, relying on our elementary Japanese to find our way through the station and to the right seats on the train. Conductors made announcements over a loudspeaker system before each stop along the route. After a while it seemed to us that a lot of the stations had the same name, "Mamonaku" something or other. We later discovered that *mamonaku* meant "in a little while" and the something or other was the upcoming station's name.

The sights from the train windows were far different from those we had seen on my first trip to Japan. Instead of families huddled under overpasses and scenes of destruction, we looked out at newly constructed commercial buildings, tidy patches of farmland, orderly villages of wooden houses with thatched or tile roofs. And there was no segregation of allied and conquered passengers in station or train; our fellows on the second-class coach were confident, purposeful Japanese businessmen and families.

Walter Nichols and his wife Franny very quickly became much more than the boss and boss's wife. They would become lifelong mentors and friends. He was a third-generation resident of Japan, fluent in the Japanese language and wise in its culture. He had served in the U.S. Navy during the war but returned to Japan at the beginning of the military occupation to work with SCAP, the occupation government, on cultural affairs. She, a daughter of the antebellum south with a soft Virginia accent, had met Walter after the war, come to Japan as a bride, and enthusiastically embraced all that this fascinating land had to offer. Franny never learned much Japanese during the many years they lived in Japan, but she was one of those people who could communicate successfully in a universal language of smiles and gestures and had no trouble understanding or being understood.

While Cliff was being briefed at the Kobe American Consulate, Franny taught me how to navigate the efficient Japanese intercity trains and introduced me to her favorite places. In Kyoto, the ancient imperial capital, we walked up the street lined with shops selling Buddhist religious articles, handmade ceramics, and special spices to the massive Kiyomizu Temple that overlooked the city. We sat in the garden composed of raked sand and artfully placed rocks at Ryuonji, walked through the vermillion arches and manicured gardens of Shinto Shrines, and trod the halls of the feudal castle of the medieval military rulers of Japan. She took me to her favorite antique shops, doll shops, and handmade paper shops, and we ate food such as I had never tasted before in small Japanese restaurants. This was the best possible tutorial for me, before heading to a remote castle town where very few people would speak English and I would need to explore the new environment and set up housekeeping on my own, without the embracing community that had eased my acclimatization in the Philippines. Now I sensed that the adventure I had anticipated with trepidation could truly be fun and fulfilling.

20

MATSUYAMA SUMMER

IT WAS AN OVERNIGHT VOYAGE on the interisland passenger ship from Kobe on the island of Honshu to Matsuyama, on Shikoku. Our first-class accommodations were very different from our be-low-deck cabin on the *Masthead Knot,* when we'd traveled to our post in the Philippines. This time we had a comfortable private cabin and bath and good-sized windows with a view. When we woke up in the early morning we were gliding through a thick fog. Tiny islands with wiz-ened pine trees clinging precariously to jagged rocks would appear and disappear. Then a small boat with a lone fisherman. We were floating through an ancient Japanese scroll! Emerging from the fog, we pulled up alongside the dock where the staff of the American Cultural Center waited to greet us.

The center, located within the confines of the moat and at the foot of Matsuyama Castle, had been built by order of the Governor of Ehime Province to provide adequate facilities for the Americans' mission. The grandson of the last *daimyo* (feudal lord) to live in Matsuyama Castle, he had in his younger years been to the United States and returned home with an abiding respect for our nation and its culture. One of the few citizens of Matsuyama who spoke English, he was a welcome visitor when he dropped in to talk and share a cup of tea with Cliff.

The building was in the shape of the letter U, on one wing a small auditorium, on the other a children's library and reading room, and in the center a two-story library flanked by office and storage spaces. Cliff's office had a sink in one corner; at the foot of a wide staircase was a single lavatory. The center was well situated and well equipped. But where would we live?

For several days we traveled around the city, stopping at Japanese residences in search of a place to rent. If not a house, then just a wing, or a room in a house. Any place where we could put the few pieces of government-issued furniture that had been shipped ahead for our use. But nothing was available. The intensive bombing of Japan's cities at the end of the war had taken a huge toll among the communities along the Inland Sea, preceding the devastation of Hiroshima. Specific military installations had been destroyed, but so had many residences and those that remained were far too crowded to make room for a pair of foreigners, with every spare room occupied by homeless relatives and friends in the summer of 1953.

Our only recourse was to carve out a niche in the American Center. We moved bookshelves in the upstairs reading room forward from the wall, making space for our bed, a dresser, a small refrigerator, and a dining table with six chairs. A portable oven and a hotplate, basic cutlery and dinnerware, and a few cooking utensils rounded out our kitchen supplies. We set up one of the library tables as a kitchen workstation. Adjoining our cordoned-off territory was a balcony that overlooked Matsuyama Castle, an elegant view by day and magically lighted up at night. We moved the dining table and chairs outside there, enjoying our evening meals not by candlelight but by castlelight.

For running water we relied on Cliff's office sink and the single lavatory downstairs. We timed our morning ablutions to occur before the library's opening. The janitor's four-year-old daughter would come into the lavatory and sing to Cliff while he shaved. After lunch I would carry dirty dishes in a dishpan through the upstairs reading room, down the wide staircase, through the downstairs reading room, and onward to Cliff's sink, washing up while he was trying to maintain a Foreign Service Officer's dignity in the presence of a visitor.

Given his wartime experiences, Cliff was surprised to be posted as a diplomat to Japan. Our first lodgings were minimalist, with a magnificent view of Matsuyama Castle.

Each morning we would have the center staff make an appointment for our daily bath at Dogo Onsen (the city's famous hot spring where reputedly a Chinese princess came in ancient times to take the waters, and where a crane with a broken wing—the symbol of Dogo—upon bathing in these waters was healed and flew on its way). The reason for the appointment? We were newcomers to Japan and as yet were not ready to immerse into the communal bathing that was so much a part of the culture. There were two private "family baths" that could be reserved, and using one of these was our choice. Whatever time of day one would become available, we would stop what we were doing, grab our soap and towels, and head for Dogo.

Cliff talked about his Matsuyama experiences with Lew Schmidt during the 1990 interview:

The USIS Director in Tokyo had given instructions to the officers heading to the field centers to erase all vestiges of the Army information program. "You're going to be taking over from this Civil Information and Education (CIE) program. And I want you to paint out all the CIE markings on the shelving and the desks and so on. This has got to be *USIS* now!"

So we all went out to our posts gung-ho to eradicate CIE. But I'll tell you, once I got down to Matsuyama (where I was hoping they would lose my personnel file, since it was such a delightful place), I could see right away that CIE had made a darn fine contribution. I mean, those libraries were really *service* libraries, which was a completely different concept in those days. They were actually community centers in every way. We had square dancing, for example, introduced I under-stand by a Colonel Niblo at the American Center in Hokkaido. The Virginia Reel was going on down below in the audito-rium right into the night and I began to wonder, coming from the counterinsurgency program in the Philippines, "What am I getting into?"

Back to CIE, I do want to say that I have a great admira-tion for what they did. As a matter of fact, I think the old-style Army officer would not have done what MacArthur arranged to have done. Of the twenty-four centers which we took over from the Army, two were in Tokyo, one out at Shinjuku, and one downtown. We soon closed the Shinjuku center, but we still had twenty-three for another year and a half or two years.

Schmidt, who had been USIS Executive Officer in Tokyo and served as stern but kindly uncle to the men in the field, commented, "They got the Japanese involved in those centers and displayed a completely new concept of how to operate a library and what the U. S. could do for them." Cliff continued:

That concept is carried on today, you know. Many of those centers are now run by the prefectures and the cities and still have the old name, *bunka*—which means culture—center. It's a

little known story, isn't it? I think it's one of the exciting chapters of cultural relations that the institution has survived.

Most of the directors we replaced were women librarians,
and they were fantastic. I was in shock at first—I guess we were
more chauvinistic then—that I as a Foreign Service Officer was
taking over from a woman librarian. But years later when I was
questioned about the advisability of sending in our first American woman officer to Kyoto and there was a lot of opposition to
this in the Agency, I said, "No, no. Long ago these centers were
run by absolutely outstanding women who were very well received and who have not been forgotten to this day."

I think our major problem going into Japan, particularly
those of us who had the information-officer background, where
our previous assignments were in insurgency areas, was adjust-
ing to this new role in an occupied country. Earlier we had
specific policy objectives and country plans to work with. So
we couldn't quite see the advantages of just the goodwill thing,
working out of a library in a broader cultural scene. But I'll
tell you, in retrospect, that this was terribly important at the
time. I mean, both should go together. There should be some
kind of mix of the political and cultural, because we have a
mission to do. I felt in later years that our program should be
more balanced. It was much more than going in to pound the
table on policy points of view without having that other kind
of goodwill approach, the give and take of these libraries and
the students in there using our books. I think the later loss of
the libraries is one of the tragedies. I feel we've lost a lot in our
centers, not having them more open to the public than they are
today.

One evening we retuned from our trip to the Dogo baths to find
half a dozen people waiting for us. One boy, the most fluent in English,
spoke for the group. He told us how they met several times a week to
speak English together and had just finished a meeting. We asked them
inside. The same boy explained to us that he worked days in a law office, studied law at college at night, and studied English in his free time

as his "hobby." Right after the war he had been an interpreter for the Australians. The two other boys, he said, also worked days and studied nights. The two girls in this group just worked, one in a dressmaking shop, one in the city's lone department store. All these people were in their early twenties.

The sixth member of the group was in his forties. He told us in broken English that he had graduated from the military academy in 1930, that he was sorry for this and did not like to fight now. He asked if we would like to see his photograph album sometime. When we said yes, he reached into his briefcase and pulled out the album and a notebook, sat down between Cliff and me, and began turning pages. All the pictures showed him in Manchuria, a straight military figure, with wife, with young son, on ice skates, etc. His English was shaky and when he saw we weren't getting the fine points, he told us to wait a minute, then opened the notebook and started to read as he turned the pages of his album: "... and in Manchuria very cold. Water on ground at night freeze. Morning we skate." (A pause while he pointed out a picture of himself on skates.) "In spring many flowers..." (And here we paused to view a photo with a flower in the distance.)

This group would return again to practice their English with us. We marveled that the ex-officer with his conservative background joined a group of people half his age to converse in English.

Few people in Matsuyama could speak English well. The exception was Shigeo Imamura. He spoke it faultlessly, as he should, having been born in California in 1921 to first-generation immigrants and lived in San Francisco until he was ten. He'd recently spent two years at the University of Michigan studying linguistics and returned to Matsuyama on the same ship that brought us to Japan. He'd come to the center to call on Cliff shortly after we arrived and offered to be of help as we settled in. It was a relief to find there was someone in town with whom we could shed all formalities. We would become fast friends that summer.

As we got to know him better, Shig began to reveal his unusual background. We learned about it in greater detail when we received a copy of his memoir written a few years before his 1998 death, *Shig: The True Story of an American Kamikaze.*

While he was in fourth grade in California, Shig's parents decided he needed to learn more about his heritage than he was getting in two hours daily at Japanese school, and the family moved back to their village just outside Matsuyama. By the time he graduated from high school, he had imbibed eight years of repetitive instruction in the nation's unique and glorious history, the duty of all citizens to revere and sacrifice for their Emperor, and Japan's mission to unify an Asia independent of American and European domination—a "Greater East Asia Co-Prosperity Sphere."

Shig enlisted in the Naval Air Reserve in the spring of 1943 and was soon promoted and trained as an attack pilot. By 1945 the war was going badly for Japan. On February 11th, 1945, Japan's National Foundation Day, navy pilots were asked to volunteer for Special Attack Forces. Shigeo Imamura stepped forward, knowing what the mission was even though the word "suicide" was avoided. July 29th, with Tokyo in flames after massive bombing raids, an announcement came over the unit's public address system: "All Hands, prepare for Operation Ketsu-Go." This was the code for the entire Japanese military to defend the nation against the invasion of the Japanese mainland. All the pilots at Kasumigaura Air Base, thirty miles north of Tokyo, were told to "Go back to your quarters, clean up your possessions, and return here for final orders by three zero zero."

Shig wrote in his memoirs:

I arrived at my plane. The navigator was already there. Men were working on the plane. A 250-kilogram bomb was about to be attached to the fuselage. The gas tanks were half filled because that was all that was needed to reach our targets, I was told.

The field telephone rang. Takeoff already? No, it was an order for all the pilots and navigators to return to headquarters immediately.

That was his last (and first) scheduled kamikaze mission. Shig's, and his nation's, war ended on his twenty-third birthday, the fourteenth of August, 1945.

As summer was coming to an end, Cliff received orders to move on to a larger post, Fukuoka on the island of Kyushu. Just before we left for Fukuoka the city of Matsuyama was observing its end-of-summer festival. *"Wasshoi! Wasshoi!"* Keeping in time with their chant, some forty young men dressed in cotton kimonos with red bands around their heads were coming down the street at a slow run, zigzagging from one side to the other, carrying the heavy *omikoshi,* a portable Shinto shrine. Every hundred feet or so the procession would come to a brief stop and the bearers would have a drink of sake, which was conveniently carried in the *omikoshi.*

Since traffic was tied up by these festivities on the main street, we turned down a narrow side street. Here we found ourselves blocked by a crowd watching a lion dance. In the center of the road straw mats had been laid down as a stage for the dancers and a drummer sat with his back to a fruit stand, beating out a fast rhythm. One man manipulated the shiny red head of the lion while another writhed and turned its green body behind him. Little girls dressed in bright flowered kimonos shrieked when the lion playfully lunged at them and little boys teased the lion by jabbing sticks at him, while their elders laughed indulgently. A Shinto priest stood at the edge of the circle of observers, waving a stick with white papers attached, assisting the lion dancers in their task of warding off evil spirits.

The rice harvest was in and the citizens put on their finest kimonos to join in the celebration of thanksgiving to the beneficent gods of Japan who had provided such bounty. The celebration continued three days and three nights as the lion dancers performed in front of houses and stores throughout the city and the young men carried the *omikoshi,* brought out of the city's shrines for such festivities twice a year, up and down Matsuyama's narrow streets.

During their oral recording session, Cliff told Lew Schmidt about his disappointment at being pulled out of Shikoku after such a short time there.

Matsuyama was my first post in Japan. You may not recall,
Lew, but you called me up one summer afternoon after I had
been there a few months to say, "Cliff, pack up your bags with

Nancy. You're being assigned to Fukuoka." I was really quite distressed because we loved that little castle town of Matsuyama.

For us—and for Cliff in particular, given his memories of the past—Matsuyama had been a great introduction to the kinder, gentler, traditional face of Japan.

21

HEARTLAND OF THE RISING SUN

OUR SUCCESSION OF UNUSUAL HOUSING arrangements would continue. No carabao wallows or library living this time, our initial Fukuoka residence would be the annex to a country inn with the grand designation of *bekkan,* or villa. This was in Futsukaichi, about twenty bumpy minutes' ride from the American Consulate where Cliff worked. It was a charming bungalow, set in a classical Japanese garden, at the foot of a mountain famed as the retreat of a ninth-century scholar who was revered as the patron saint of students.

Running water ran only when coaxed from a well by a hard-to-manipulate hand pump. The Japanese bath was a wooden tub filled with water heated by a wood-burning stove outside the house. Winter's cold air could be somewhat warmed locally in the living and sleeping rooms, with portable kerosene heaters that we carried from one place to the next.

The senior Japanese employee for the consulate, Nose-san, lived nearby and he and Cliff arranged to ride together to the office in Cliff's official vehicle, leaving me mobility with the Dodge sedan we had brought with us to Japan. As Nose-san sauntered into our yard to catch his ride for the first time, he found me at my early morning chore, forcing that hand pump up and down, up and down, so I would have water to clean up the breakfast dishes and wash some clothes. He turned to Cliff as he got into the vehicle and I overheard him say: "That's good, Forster-san. She is doing woman's work." I was not amused.

Kyushu was the historic heartland of the country. And in many ways it was the most conservative area of Japan. Americans were often viewed with suspicion here, and establishing cordial relationships would take effort and patience on our part.

Cliff's new USIS domain extended from Yamaguchi Prefecture on Honshu to Kagoshima on Kyushu's southern tip, Oita in the east and Nagasaki in the west. He was Regional Public Affairs Officer, overseeing four centers: in Fukuoka where his office was located in the American Consulate building and Kokura, Kumamoto, and Nagasaki. Kokura and Kumamoto would be closed shortly after we arrived.

We were aware of some of the region's history and were learning more as we traveled and built up our personal reference library. We were eager students.

The lineage of Emperor Hirohito, who had remained Japan's ruler after the war, was traced back 125 generations to an ancestor reputedly descended from the Sun Goddess, on the island of Kyushu. The founder of the Yamato clan, his descendents conquered their way north to Nara in central Honshu where the first imperial capitol was established in the seventh century. Objects found in tombs located in central Kyushu indicate the existence of an aristocratic community from those early days, people who prized jewelry similar to that worn by ancient Korean rulers and displayed in that nation's museums.

Written history affirms that cultural innovations from the Asian mainland—the Chinese writing system, Buddhism and its accompanying arts—traveled to Japan via the waters that separate Kyushu from the Korean Peninsula. Kyushu was also where the first Europeans came to Japan, bringing the Catholic religion, firearms, bread, clocks, and books on medicine. During the seventeenth to nineteenth centuries the nation was sealed off—to avoid the incursions by European missionaries, merchants, and gunboats that the Japanese had witnessed in China and Southeast Asia.

On Kyushu a window to the West was kept open with a small Dutch settlement on an island in Nagasaki harbor, Deshima. The Dutch were allowed to stay, virtual prisoners, and to receive an annual shipload of commerce (and ideas). Emissaries arriving on that yearly voyage were escorted north to Tokyo to present to Japan's rulers gifts showcasing the latest technological advances in Europe. And in feudal domains on this island, the remotest from Tokyo's control, nineteenth-century sons of samurai were to become the founders of a new Japan's Western-style navy, army, banking, parliamentary and educational systems, following the opening of Japan by U.S. Commodore Perry's ships in 1854.

Shortly after we arrived in Fukuoka Jim Martin, the consul, and Cliff planned an excursion to circumnavigate the island of Kyushu where they would meet with government and media and academic leaders in each major city as they progressed. Betty Martin and I joined them. We all traveled in the USIS van, with Cliff's assistant Kenji Hirano as our guide and the USIS driver at the wheel. The roads at that time were in terrible repair and regularly we would blow out a tire. Usually it was around lunchtime, so Betty and I used the repair interlude to forage among our picnic supplies and prepare a sandwich lunch. After one such pause, a farm woman came out from her house with a pan of warm water and towels, so the men could wash up after their labors.

It took us fourteen days to complete our Kyushu circumnavigation. About the same time, a high school students' marathon covered the same route. It seemed it was faster to run these roads than to drive—the youngsters made it in ten days. But our fourteen days were filled with cordial meetings, learning about the concerns and aspirations of the leaders in this part of Japan, launching relationships that lasted for years. We were also following a path of history. We made detours to see prehistoric burial mounds, to visit the cave where the imperial lineage was first believed to have rested, to the shrine at the foot of the mountain where history and myth intermingled with the descent of Japan's primogenitors—in one myth, the islands of Japan were created from drops of cosmic matter falling from a "Heavenly Downward Pointing Spear," a replica of which we were invited to inspect—to sites where Europe first came ashore in Japan and from where the young visionaries of the nineteenth century set forth to change the way of life in Tokyo.

In 2008 Susan Martin found among her deceased father's papers three single-spaced pages of rough notes he had made to himself during that Kyushu journey. They were filled with accounts of long drives on the difficult roads, fruitful visits with local leaders, personal delight at historical sites. He concludes his notes with a comment on the status of vehicle and travelers at trip's end: "Only visible strain on car three flat tires and *galumpff* sound in front that might be no more shocks or springs. Visible strain on passengers: deep dark bags under eyes."

The other strain for Cliff and me was shellfish, that allergy which had attracted each other's attention when we were at Stanford. At each stop around the island the city fathers feted us with local culinary treats. Unfortunately, most meals centered around shellfish. Being good soldiers in the service of our country, we ate at least part of everything that was served, and paid the usual price. We would suffer from our own peculiar brand of food poisoning throughout the night. At journey's end we made a decision: henceforth we would simply tell our hosts abut our allergy, joke abut how it had been at the heart of our courtship, and thus could preserve our intestinal comfort.

Our circumnavigation had bypassed the peninsula with the remaining center supervised by Cliff—Nagasaki, one of his favorite destinations, which had developed into a thriving international community after the opening of Japan to the West. He went early and often, getting acquainted with that beautiful city, supporting the work of the USIS Center there, and becoming immersed in Nagasaki's cosmopolitan history. He frequently visited the city library to browse through their old English-language newspapers; the librarian was delighted to have such an enthusiastic customer and urged him to take the bound volumes back to Fukuoka to read at leisure and return on his next visit.

He met longtime foreign residents who recounted tales about the visits of people like Pierre Loti who wrote the original Madame Butterfly story, and was taken to "Madame Butterfly's house." At Baishinji Temple, the Buddhist priest showed him a picture of a group of Russian naval officers, a young Czar Nicholas among them. Nagasaki was used as a winter haven for the Russian Pacific fleet when its home port of Vladivostok froze over. Some locals maintained that a geisha living on the other side of the mountain had been the real Mme. Butterfly, that a man still living in that village and running a small inn was her child, descended from Russia's last Czar. The Russian residency was before the Russo-Japanese War of 1898 when the Japanese navy surprised and destroyed the Russian flotilla sent out from the Black Sea to augment Russia's Pacific navy. This encounter was the Battle of Tsushima Strait between Kyushu and Korea, and signaled the debut of Japan as an imperial military power.

Using resources from Kyushu's mines, coal-burning ocean liners on transpacific voyages made regular stops here prewar to replenish their fuel supply. Cliff had traveled through the port as a youngster, the last time in 1939 when he and his sister were en route to California from Manila ahead of his parents. This was where he snapped a picture of the harbor, not realizing he had aimed at the Mitsubishi Shipyard (in which a super-size warship was under construction behind super-size matting), and his box camera was confiscated and smashed by a Japanese soldier.

Nagasaki had not been the first choice for the second atomic bomb; the prime target was Yawata north of Fukuoka, where Asia's largest steel mill fed Japan's war effort. Because that city was under cloud cover on the day of the raid, Nagasaki with its shipyard was the victim. Directly across from the shipyard was Japan's largest Catholic church, which became ground zero for the bomb. Though there was considerable collateral damage, the rest of Nagasaki was spared the kind of destruction Hiroshima suffered. The former was shielded by its fjord-like geography; the latter, shaped like a shallow bowl, endured much wider damage. Nevertheless, in both cities and throughout Japan the scars and memories were raw and bitter, and this was to haunt Japanese-American relations and challenge the skills of diplomacy.

Japan had regained sovereignty over most of its island nation when the Treaty of Peace was signed in 1951, but the Ryukyu Archipelago—including Okinawa, which had been scene of bitter fighting at the end of the war, and stretching some 700 miles between Kyushu and Taiwan—remained under allied control. In December of 1953, the U.S. Government gave the Japanese a Christmas present: the reversion of Amami Oshima, which lay closest to Kyushu, to Japanese sovereignty. Ambassador Allison didn't want to ruin his Christmas, so he assigned Cliff and Jim the honor of travel to Amami to make the official presentation on Christmas Day. They sailed from Kagoshima at the southern tip of

Kyushu, participated in the ceremonies, and returned by ship to the same port. They were stopped by Japanese immigration authorities.

"Where are your passports and visas?"

"We have none; we weren't out of Japan."

"Oh, yes, you were; Amami Oshima was not Japan when you left so you have come from what was a foreign country."

Diplomacy prevailed, and the two men managed to make it home to Fukuoka the day after Christmas.

A different kind of diplomacy was called for when Joe DiMaggio came to town in the fall of 1954 at the invitation of the local baseball team, the Nishitetsu Lions. He was to serve for a week as visiting coach for the Fukuoka ball players. Seizing the opportunity for a great bit of cultural interaction, Cliff scheduled the opening session of the coaching workshop at the USIS Center auditorium on the second floor of the consulate building. What heightened excitement over the event was the last minute inclusion on the visit of another baseball hero, Lefty O'Doul, plus a superstar who outshone the athletes, Joe's new bride—Marilyn Monroe.

Their arrival at Itazuke airport was pandemonium. Japan's paparazzi were in full force and the force didn't end at the airport. Photographers had staked out positions on the roof of the Nikkatsu Hotel and lowered themselves by rope to the window level of the DiMaggios' fourth-floor suite. Cliff, knowing that Marilyn would be free during the days her husband worked with the team, suggested I arrange a tea party in honor of the distinguished visitor at our home. I was not sure tea with a group of Japanese ladies would be Marilyn Monroe's idea of fun, but gave it a try and called her at the hotel.

"Hello, Mrs. DiMaggio? I am the wife of the American Foreign Service Officer here in Fukuoka who is facilitating your husband's schedule. I'm calling to see if you would like to come to my home in the country— it's a Japanese style house in a lovely garden—for tea one afternoon. I could invite a few Japanese ladies for you to meet." Silence on the other end of the phone...then, "That's very nice. But I have a sore throat and I really don't think I can. But thank you."

The sore throat didn't keep her from accompanying Joe to the meeting that night at the USIS Center. She emerged from the car, surrounded by the relentless photographers and illuminated by flashbulbs, wearing a jaunty beret and swathed in a full-length mink coat. The three visitors were escorted to seats in the back of the small auditorium, Joe on the aisle, then Marilyn, Lefty, and next to him Cliff. When Joe and Lefty were invited up to the podium to be introduced by the owner of the Nishitetsu Lions, that left Marilyn, with a vacant seat between them, seated next to Cliff. How do you make conversation with a film goddess? Cliff tried: "Do you like baseball, Mrs. DiMaggio?" She indicated that she really didn't care all that much for the game, then stretched out a leg in his direction. "Oh dear, I seem to have a run in my stocking!" Commercial photographers had been barred from the building, but a USIS camera was set up behind Cliff and this moment of glory was recorded and is hidden someplace in American government archives.

Her sore throat also didn't prevent Marilyn Monroe from going to Korea the next day. The trooper decided to do her thing while Joe did his, and her picture was on the cover of *Life* magazine the next week. On a November day with a light snowfall, Marilyn was on an outdoor stage, mike in hand and clad in a slinky black dress with spaghetti straps, singing her heart out for the American troops who were stationed near the Demilitarized Zone where North and South Korea were separated by a fragile truce.

Cliff discovered another Marilyn Monroe fan when he escorted a visiting dignitary to the industrial cities of northern Kyushu and stopped to pay a courtesy call on the mayor of Moji. His office was in a building that had survived the war; it was a Victorian monument with high ceilings and large public spaces. Photos of his predecessors as mayor, since the late 1800s, lined the upper part of the office walls. Starting with Meiji period men who sported Victorian styles and impressive beards, the fashions morphed into those of the early twentieth century, into the forties, and at the very end of the line this Mayor had added Marilyn—a poster shot of her coquettishly looking back over her shoulder at the mayoral lineup.

Shortly after the DiMaggios' visit our first child, Tom, was born. My pregnancy was the impetus for our moving out of our Japanese country villa into a more functional home vacated by an American major who had worked at the military hospital nearby. This new house was centrally located near the Martins and within an easy drive of the consulate. Winter warmth was still provided by localized heaters and baths were again in a wooden tub, but now we hired some helping hands, two wonderful women who took over the chores of keeping the warming fires burning, cooking for us and our growing number of dinner guests, and helping with the baby once he made his appearance. That military hospital, a MASH-type operation for casualties from the Korean War and later the medical center for the Air Force and Army personnel stationed in northern Kyushu, was Tom's birthplace. Before the war it had been a Japanese mail-processing center. We have told Tom, "Dear, you came to us via special delivery at a Fukuoka post office!" My prenatal care was like a revolving door; each time I went for a checkup, a new army doctor was temporarily on maternity duty, but Tom arrived and I survived in good health.

The year before our arrival in Japan, South Korean President Syngman Rhee had established the "Rhee Line," banning Japanese fishermen from waters traditionally considered theirs but now proclaimed to be Korean. This was the focus of one of many protests held during our time in Kyushu. The American Consulate, with the USIS library and center offices on the ground floor, was at the dead end of a wide block-long street that had the City Hall on one side and Prefectural Capitol on the other. A perfect combo of all institutions against whom disgruntled citizens might want to demonstrate!

Saturday was a favorite day for "demos." University students had no classes and, unlike in America, at that time there were no frivolities in their lives. Instead of cheering the home team on the sports field, these students would join in a demo snake dance through the streets, shouting a rhythmic *"hantai! hantai!"* ("opposed! opposed!") as they marched. On this particular Saturday, the leading students carried a pole with John Foster Dulles in effigy, assigning blame for the fishermen's predicament to the American Secretary of State. As they passed through the porte-cochere that sheltered the entrance to the consulate, the top of the pole struck the overhead light, breaking a couple of light bulbs. Nothing serious. Shortly afterwards, the demo was over and everyone went home.

Monday morning Cliff was met at the entrance to the building by his Japanese assistant. "Forster-san," he said, "there are three students here who would like to meet with you." Cliff urged Kenji Hirano to bring them into his office. All three, dressed in their black student uniforms, seemed very nervous. One had a shoebox that he shifted from one hand to the other. Kenji translated for their spokesman.

"Forster-san, we have come to apologize. We were part of the demonstration against the Rhee Line on Saturday and our effigy of Mr. Dulles broke two of your light bulbs. We are very sorry for this. We have nothing against the Americans and very much like your American Culture Center. We come here often to use your library and to study. Please excuse us. We have brought you two new light bulbs and hope we may continue to use your library."

Cliff assured them that they would continue to be welcome and thanked them for their thoughtfulness in bringing replacement bulbs.

In these days of heightened security around the world, the mere suggestion of nervous students carrying a box into a U.S. Consulate boggles the mind—as does the thought of an American protester returning to visit the object of his displeasure with replacement for damages inflicted!

In his 1990 interview with Lewis Schmidt, Cliff described some of the more serious challenges faced by USIS on Kyushu.

Fukuoka was a far more complex and difficult area to work in than Matsuyama, which was a rather laid-back agricultural town. Kyushu had the large industrial area of Yawata with its steel mills and chemical plants. There were strong leftist labor unions carrying out massive strikes in the depressed coal mining areas. There was also our large Itazuke Air Base with our jets flying over Kyushu University all the time, resulting in demonstrations. So you had one issue after another and a great deal of anti-American feeling.

We were all working together in the consulate in those days under the same roof. I had the information and cultural-exchange side of it. At first we spent much of our time continually putting out fires. I was working with our Air Force officers at Itazuke trying to explain their position to the Japanese as an important operation to protect Japan during the Korean conflict. So we did a lot of work on base relations, inviting fighter-jet pilots and others at the base to meet with the students, often teaching them English. Our plan was to try to establish personal relationships between base personnel and the university professors and students to get more community support for our largest air force facility in southwestern Japan, just across from Korea.

Overall, our USIS mission then was to try to achieve a better understanding of our policy positions, and Japan's security was one of the major ones. Of course the "Rhee Line"—demarcating the seas between Japan and Korea for fishing access—was a major problem in our area, and elsewhere in Japan, because they felt it affected their fishing rights. We also had the "Bikini ashes" incident, following our nuclear test in the Bikini region when atomic fallout resulted in the death of a Japanese fisherman. His fishing boat had not received, or observed, the warning the U.S. broadcast telling all vessels to stay clear of a specified zone around the testing area. The anti-U.S. feeling was very strong and once again we had to defend our position. Then you had the case of the U.S. soldier firing on a Japanese entering one of our target ranges in northern Japan to pick up shell casings. It was known as the "Gerard Case" and once again there was a lot of hard feeling since the Japanese felt our military court had let Gerard off too lightly. There was one public relations issue after another in those early days, and it was our job to deal with them to keep U.S.-Japan relations on course.

Nagasaki was also in my region of responsibility. The atom bomb hostility was still running quite high at the time, although it was not as strong as it was in Hiroshima. I've often thought about Nagasaki bombing as contrasted to Hiroshima and I think the long association with the West and the strong Christian community there—mostly Catholic—made the big difference.

Beyond the shorter-term policy issues I would say that it was the cultural exchange effort, the Fulbright program, which really paid off as time went on. The International Visitor program was another very positive long-range effort, since we were able to get many younger Japanese journalists, writers, government officials (city and prefectural) to go to the States. When they retuned you could see the changes. Many of them had not been there before. We selected a socialist leader, for example, Masao Takahashi, and there were a lot of questions about why we were sending him. I even had to do a special waiver on him. Well, he was the fellow who took on extreme leftists when he returned from the States and challenged them effectively, resulting eventually in more moderate socialist positions. Though he remained a socialist, he could see that just going along with the Soviet line was not the answer for Japan.

Then you had the whole labor situation with the more leftist Sohyo unions, and the embassy was working to try and alleviate some of that by bringing in our own labor leaders to meet with them, to see if they couldn't become more moderate. In the beginning the Nikkyoso, the Japan Teachers' Union, and the Zengakuren student unions were very extreme and the coal depression was serious in Kyushu. There was plenty of ammunition for the far left in Japan, and they were using it effectively, very effectively.

I think USIS played a fantastic role working with the more moderate elements in the labor movement through the years. The terrific selection of labor grantees by USIS officers in Tokyo and in the field and the creation of the USIS labor officer position in Tokyo were instrumental in bringing this about. Over almost a thirty-year period you selected those leaders who were concerned—they were not necessarily pro-U.S., but they were concerned about the way the extreme left was taking over their unions. They were far more interested in the kind of labor movement which was closer to the Scandinavian or the British model. I remember we worked with Professor Yoshihiko Seki when I was in Tokyo later. He had been to Oxford and had written the most comprehensive Japanese book on Socialism and the labor movement in Britain. We made it possible for specialists like him to have access to their colleagues not only in the United States but also in Europe through Asia Foundation grants.

Charlie Medd was a fine example of a USIS officer who got out around the country and taught himself Japanese. He was a center director at first in Nagasaki. Charlie studied the Japanese union movement and reached out to the labor unions, really got to know them backwards and forwards. He later became labor officer in Tokyo where his knowledge of Japanese, and his ability to relate to these labor leaders at all levels. made him one of our more effective communicators.

As Cliff told Lew, there were efforts by the Fukuoka Consulate to create better understanding, and thus better relations, between the U.S. airbase at Itazuke and the citizens of Fukuoka. One of the Air Force officers proposed a joint outing of schoolchildren, those from the dependents' school on base and those at a Japanese elementary school. The site and project selected was at Ohori Koen, a classical Japanese garden surrounding a small lake. The children were brought here with their art supplies: paper, pencils, and watercolors. The project was for all to participate in a drawing exercise, each child rendering his or her vision of Ohori Koen. Groups of Japanese and American children were intermingled on the shores of the lake and proud teachers stood behind them, keeping watch over their charges. Cliff strolled around to observe the artists-at-work. The Japanese children were faithfully producing renditions of a classical Japanese landscape. The Americans were less restrained. One boy had created a lake with some likeness to the one in front of him, but he had added a feature: On his paper there was an ocean liner, smoke coming out of its two funnels, cruising across the lake. *"Arr-ahh!"* Several Japanese boys had clustered around him and were viewing his work with amazement. One wonders what lessons each child took home from that intercultural event.

During the time we were in Fukuoka I was again asked to teach some English conversation classes, this time to students at Kyushu University. Formerly an imperial university and the most prestigious tertiary institution on this island, it was hub of a combination of ultra-conservative prewar professors and restless postwar students, like those who had demonstrated against the Rhee Line. The university building where I taught was in the direct path of planes landing and taking off from Itazuke Airbase, which as a symbol of American intrusion into their sacred land was a target of protest. A replay of my classes in Davao, halting to wait for the noise to cease—then of tropical downpours and now of jet engines—happened during those roaring takeoffs and landings. I smiled nervously the first few times, but the students grinned good naturedly and I relaxed, then continued the lesson.

When we first invited Japanese media men or professional men or scholars and their wives to dinner, the men accepted but politely declined on behalf of the wives. "She speaks no English" or "She doesn't know how to act with foreigners" or simply "She is too busy caring for our home" were the excuses. But some of those women were anxious to meet the American wives at the consulate and to learn about what made us tick. They took the initiative and an invitation came from a group of several who had grown up and gone to school together. Would we be so kind as to come to their humble home one afternoon? They would like to prepare lunch for us and, if we would like, show us how they make some of their typical meals. We were of course delighted, accepted, and then reciprocated with a cooking demonstration and lunch in the Martins' house. That began an ongoing routine of alternate cuisines, moving from one house to another. And the cooking demonstrations branched out. The Japanese ladies had heard about a game called "canasta." Would we teach it to them?

Cliff and I had home leave, bouncing baby in tow, during the summer of 1955, then returned to Fukuoka in the fall. We were greeted like old friends by our Japanese acquaintances, including the crusty English professor who felt that nothing worthwhile had been written in this language since Shakespeare and that American literature was unquestionably substandard. The fact that we had invested the time and energy to return was a signal for them to accept us wholeheartedly.

During the time we had lived on Kyushu, we Americans in the consulate had discovered age-old pottery villages tucked in the mountains inland from Fukuoka. Here we met the descendents of Korean potters who had been brought to Kyushu as war booty by leaders of Japan's

failed attempt to conquer northern China in 1600. We became avid collectors of the handsome and practical ceramic art, as we discovered more
kilns scattered throughout the island. As a project to raise funds for relief
to impoverished coal miners and their families, several wives created a
map of Kyushu pinpointing the location of all the kilns we had found. It
was sold on the military bases and at local tourist facilities.

In early 1956 we were told to pack our bags again and head north,
to Kobe, where Cliff would take over as Regional Public Affairs Officer
at the American Consulate General. His territory now would be Japan's
cultural heartland and the western prefectures of Honshu. He would
coordinate activities for USIS Centers in Kobe, Osaka, Kyoto, Hiroshima,
and in Takamatsu, which had replaced Matsuyama as the only center on
Shikoku.

The editor of Fukuoka's leading newspaper assembled for us a farewell gift that touched us deeply and continues to grace my kitchen today.
Knowing that we were enchanted by folk-art pottery, he assembled additions to our collection, including a storage jar from traditional kilns in
every prefecture that would comprise Cliff's new domain.

22

THE KANSAI

B Y 1956, WALT NICHOLS HAD been assigned to Tokyo to oversee all the USIS Centers in the country. It was our good fortune to move into the large modern house where he and Franny
had lived in a suburb between Kobe and Osaka. It was perched on a
ridge overlooking a valley with rice fields and in the distance the homes
of another upscale suburb. Again, no central heating and thus cold in
winter—except for when we had one of our large official receptions and
the gathering's body heat would make the large living room pleasantly
toasty—but this house was a source of joy from April through October.
Part of the yard was a forest of small pine trees, among which were interspersed large azalea bushes that burst into a riot of lavender in the spring.
Nearby was a Shinto shrine, Ashiya Jinja, which was a favorite destination for a leisurely stroll. And halfway down our hill was the local train
station, with trains going regularly to all those places Franny had taken
me to when we first came to Japan—and many more.

In our new territory, there were treasures galore to explore for pleasure, unlimited opportunities for cultural interaction, and centers in five
very different cities for Cliff to visit regularly.

The Kansai is where Japan's political and cultural and economic power had consolidated under the original Yamato rulers; from here it spread out from their first capitol in Nara, to the subsequent imperial capitol in Kyoto, and eventually to Tokyo. But Nara has remained the repository of Japan's earliest treasures, Kyoto the guardian of the country's enduring arts, and Osaka an economic powerhouse. Generations of emperors and their retinues supported generations of fine artists in Kyoto, who created elegant paintings, ceramics, lacquer, and scrumptious garments to adorn the nobility. Simple but imposing temples with elegant gardens were built to glorify Buddhism. Stately shrines were dedicated to the pantheon of Shinto deities in Japan's indigenous religion and inspired colorful annual festivals. The military shoguns who unified Japan at the dawn of the seventeenth century were from Osaka, and later ruled from Tokyo. They put their own stamp on Japan's culture. In contrast to the refined arts of Kyoto, a more boisterous art emerged to satisfy the tastes of the rising merchant class. Osaka's Bunraku puppet theater and Kabuki with its historical dramas were featured in woodblock prints. These were arts for the populace. Prints featuring courtesans from the "floating world" and scenic views along the main routes between Tokyo and Osaka were occasionally used to wrap Japanese artifacts taken back to Europe by the Dutch emissaries who had called in Nagasaki and visited Tokyo. European collectors were charmed and European artists were inspired.

And the heritage of all this historic culture was accessible to us by an easy train ride.

We settled in quickly. Our two household helpers accompanied us from Fukuoka, so we were well cared for personally and had an experienced team to produce and serve food for the parties we were expected to give. Since we were located out of town and our guests would travel from any or all of the three cities in the Kobe/Osaka/Kyoto triangle, I didn't want people to leave our receptions hungry. The answer was a buffet table amply stocked with savories from my growing collection of recipes.

Two-year-old Tom's routine barely missed a beat, with those two ladies who were part of his family and the same growing collection of household goods he had known in Fukuoka now part of his new environment. The maids' English was limited, and we urged them from the beginning to speak to Tom only in Japanese, while he would speak

English with us. Actually, because we were out of the house many days and evenings, this bilingual child operated much of his day in Japanese. His cultural context was evident in a conversation in Japanese that we overheard one evening when we were preparing to go out and Tom was having dinner with the maids in the kitchen. "Isn't there any *nori?*" he asked in a petulant voice, referring to dried seaweed. "How can you expect me to eat my rice without *nori?*"

In the 1990 interview with Lew, Cliff talked about his two years in the Kansai and how the USIS program in Japan was successfully creating cultural bridges between America and the Japanese.

You have to understand the situation in the fifties, when many of the younger Japanese literature professors were really not given an opportunity at their universities to get into American studies and were told to avoid the young "upstarts," as their mentors would call them, authors like Hemingway and Faulkner. Theirs was not really English literature! I remember in particular the Dean of Literature at the University of Kyushu, who had studied in England before the war. His whole program was built around Chaucer. It was pretty deadly for many of his younger professors who were far more interested in contemporary American authors.

So we used to have meetings at the American Centers with the younger Japanese professors. We brought in our own specialists on many of our great authors and the young Japanese scholars became the nucleus of a whole new generation of American literature specialists. This happened throughout Japan, a real groundswell and, as was the case with the labor program launched by Charlie Medd, USIS played a very important role in introducing American studies and, thereby, American culture and our values, so the Japanese would know more about us.

The visit of William Faulkner bought it all together. Because those professors who had been coming to our Fukuoka center to escape the Chaucerian dean, all went to the Faulkner seminar in Nagano. Many of their students also went, as did students and professors from other parts of Japan. This exposure reinforced the determination of the younger Japanese scholars to get a strong American studies underway at their tradition-bound universities.

1956-58 was a very interesting time. This is when we started working with younger professors of international relations and studies at Kyoto and Doshisha Universities, professors who were concerned abut the Marxist domination of the curriculum, particularly at Kyoto University. We were able, as with the labor leaders, to arrange for them to go to the States, not only to meet their counterparts, but also to gather materials to bring back. When they returned they were able to attract more students because they were not as ideological as the Marxists. They really wanted to have a more objective presentation of world history for their students and the American experience provided by USIS was a great help to them.

One of the leaders of that movement was Professor Masamichi Inoki. His disciples, or *deshi* as they call them in Japan, were also able to visit our universities to develop the same kind of contact networks and this resulted in a whole new approach to the study of world politics in Japan. That, I think, was very significant, and it not only happened in the Kansai area but also in Tokyo and other USIS Center areas in Japan.

Schmidt made some comments here:

It's too bad that often our program has been judged on what has been an immediate reaction to the political situation. We tear ourselves apart—or did—in getting a lot of material out, motion pictures and pamphlets, that sort of thing, trying to get immediate impact. I don't say these haven't been successful on occasion, because many of them have been, but the long-range impact is so hard to identify as an accomplishment at the time it's going on. You have to wait three, four, six, seven years before you realize its full impact. We have often been unable to sell our case in Congress simply because you can't measure this in terms of one or two years.

Cliff's response underscored his belief that a successful public diplomacy effort must take place over a number of years, building trust as its practitioners and their clients get to know each other and discover areas of mutual interest.

Precisely. There's continuity to it. That has been very important. Like working with Professor Inoki and his graduate students and with other professors who wanted greater objectivity in the treatment of current affairs in the books they wrote and classes they taught. Some became news commentators and they wrote articles for influential magazines. We also concentrated on journalists, sending them to the U.S. over a period of years. Many returned with positive impressions and broader international perspective.

We also had interesting personal interactions during our time in the Kansai. One of them was the Stanford Alumni Club of the Kansai. The members, usually about ten or twelve attending, met monthly in Osaka for Sunday lunch. The meeting place was a private *tatami* room in a Japanese restaurant, where we all gathered on the floor around a low lacquer table. Always hung on the wall was an eight-foot-wide red-and-white banner proclaiming "STANFORD" in large letters above the university seal. The gatherings were unique in Japan's age-stratified society. There were men from the classes of '07, the teens, the twenties; then a big gap through the thirties and early forties when Japanese did not go to the U.S. to study. Cliff and I represented the classes of '49 and '50, and two young men had recently graduated. Distinguished senior business executives, a retired parliamentarian, and cub reporters from the local newspaper met and dined as equals. And all sang lustily two full verses of the Stanford Hymn (except for we Forsters who couldn't remember past verse one and the chorus).

The Stanford Club of the Kansai cut across age and status barriers, providing Cliff—and young Tom—the opportunity for dialogue outside of work.

One Sunday in May the meeting place was outdoors on the patio of our residence in the hills between Osaka and Kobe. The Stanford banner was hung on the side of the house and the menu—reminiscent of weekend trysts at everyone's favorite Palo Alto pub—was hot dogs and hamburgers, beer and coke. Photos of the event show Tom very much the center of attention, playing his version of the role of diplomatic host.

Sending our three-year-old son to a Japanese nursery school in the fall of 1957 was a learning experience for parents as well as child. Shukugawa Yochien was run by Japanese Catholic nuns for three-, four-, and five-year-olds in a neighboring residential suburb. The children, all Japanese except for Tom and two other foreign children in the youngest class, were outfitted in school uniforms: navy blue skirts or short pants and berets, white shirts and cardigans, white tennis shoes and wicker baskets in which to carry lunch from home.

In late fall all the children and their teachers were loaded on buses for a field trip into the mountains, to gather chestnuts. I was among several mothers who had come along. As they got off the bus in the chestnut forest, each class was assembled around a blanket laid out on the ground. When a whistle blew the children were sent off with their wicker baskets to gather as many chestnuts as they could find before the next whistle signaled them to stop and return to their class blankets. Our three foreigners dashed ahead of their classmates, aggressively scooping up as many nuts as they could before the whistle blew. When the children were again circled around their blanket, the teacher instructed them to empty their baskets onto the center of the blanket. Then the teacher proceeded to count out equal piles of chestnuts for each child—one for you, one for you, and one for you. Every child went home with an equal amount of nuts. This was a great lesson for Tom, and for me, in Japanese cultural mores.

One of Cliff's greatest delights was to take to the road, to visit his teammates in the American Cultural Centers, to encourage and applaud what they were doing locally. They individually had become community fixtures, as each center had become a popular and respected community resource. For example, we went to Takamatsu, the remaining center on Shikoku, at the time of Obon, the midsummer festival when throughout Japan people of all ages don their summer *yukata* (lightweight kimonos) to join in outdoor dancing, the Bon Odori. Takamatsu had its own distinctive summer dance, the Awa Odori. As we and the American Consul General sat in the reviewing stand for a festival parade, along came Harry Kendall, our center director. He was leading the city's geisha corps as they danced the Awa Odori.

USIS did not send another American to Takamatsu after Harry left, but as was true for so many officers who were imbedded in outlying cities, many years later people there still spoke fondly of Kendall-san. In the eighties when a bridge was built across the straits from Kobe to Takamatsu, bringing Shikoku a land connection to the rest of Japan, Harry and his wife were invited to come from California to attend the opening ceremony as guests of Kagawa Prefecture.

Men and women from very different backgrounds brought a variety of interests and skills to their assignments as America's representatives abroad. Dan Herget, who was in Kyoto during our time, not only immersed himself in the city's aristocratic culture, but having been manager of a baseball team during his youth Dan also endeared himself to the sports lovers of the area. A successor director, Mark Peattie, was of academic bent and built strong relationships with professors at the leading universities, which endured far beyond his USIS days. Mark went on to another career as a university professor of Japanese history and often conferred with colleagues he had first met in Kyoto. In Hiroshima, Fazl Fotouhi, an Iranian American, and his wife were able to reach beyond the wounds inflicted by the Atom bomb by becoming proficient at playing the classical *koto,* Japan's horizontal harp. All these personal efforts by the American directors to become immersed in their communities were matched by skillful execution of the programs established by the USIS leadership in Tokyo and Washington.

Two very different events during our time in the Kansai illustrate the variety of cultural events in which Cliff was involved. One was a USIS-sponsored visit of American Tom Two Arrows, who came as a representative of New York State's Iroquois Indian Tribe. At a Rotary Club meeting in Osaka he repeated much of the program he had taken to local schools, performing traditional Iroquois music, doing a short dance, and relating some of his tribe's history. The Japanese businessmen were fascinated; they saw similarities to some of Japan's classical age-old music and dance. Two Arrows had been on the northern island of Hokkaido before coming to Osaka. There he met with elders from the Ainu people who had been the original inhabitants of much of Japan, pushed north by Yamato conquests, and were believed to have originally come from Siberia. The Ainu elders had seen even more pronounced similarities between the native cultures of New York and northern Japan. And what they showed Tom Two Arrows gave him a whole new perspective on the possibility of a shared lineage from the distant past.

The other event was a ceremony honoring an American professor by interring his ashes in the grounds of the most sacred temple in Nara. Dr. Langdon Warner was an art historian and professor at Harvard University who had written extensively on Japanese art before the war. He served in the U.S. Army's Antiquities Division during the war and was given credit for advising against the use of firebombs on Nara, Kyoto, and other ancient cities—to protect cultural heritage of Japan. Warner died in 1955 and the priests at Horyuji Temple requested a portion of his ashes. These would be placed in a spot of honor next to the Temple wall, where gratitude for Warner's role would be evermore recognized. Cliff was asked to represent the American ambassador and deliver the urn of ashes in a formal ceremony, accompanied by chanting of prayers and centuries-old dances. As Cliff and I sat through the ceremony, we were transported back to eighth-century Japan. As lovers of antiquity and beauty, we rejoiced that the military decision-makers had paid attention to Warner's plea to save Japan's cultural treasures.

When a couple is married in Japan, according to tradition there is (or at least there was in the past) a *nakodo* (intermediary or "go-between") who helps select appropriate candidates as bride and/or groom and is an important figure at the wedding ceremony. During the fifties and sixties, Japanese and American cities were being joined together as "sister cities," and Cliff was frequently the *nakodo*. On both sides of the Pacific Ocean, the relationship was eagerly embraced by civic groups, schools, government officials, and journalists who wrote long articles about what happened when ordinary Japanese and Americans visited each other's cities. We joined the opening ceremonies in Okayama, to the south of Kobe, when San Jose, California, sent its mayor and a number of leading citizens and their wives to celebrate their union in May of 1957. A group photo taken then shows me, hugely pregnant with our second child.

Decades later, San Jose's Mission Chamber Orchestra commissioned a commemorative work, "Sisters," which was performed by the San Jose Symphonic Choir in February 2003. The president of an organization of California teachers for which I was then executive director sang at that concert and sent me a copy of the libretto whose words celebrated the many years of popular exchange activities.

Kobe married Seattle, and sent as a gift to that city an enormous vase, over six feet tall and covered with the intricate floral designs typical of Satsuma ware. Not to be outdone, Seattle sent a full-sized totem pole to Kobe. We were there at Kobe's City Hall for the dedication of this artifact, quietly wondering to ourselves how this could possibly be incorporated into the Japanese aesthetic. We found out when we returned some years later: the city had been given a flower clock by a German sister city. This was beautifully laid out as a garden in front of the City Hall and looming over the clock was Seattle's totem pole. They were featured in a postcard handed out by the Mayor's Office and sold at newsstands.

Cindy was born in June of 1957. Hers was an exciting arrival. Canadian missionaries had established a small but modern hospital on the edge of a poverty-stricken Korean district in Osaka. The woman obstetrician there was our doctor of choice and under the best of circumstances the drive to this hospital took nearly an hour over crowded and bumpy roads. On the June evening when Cliff and I started off for the hospital the Kansai was being lashed by an out-of-season typhoon, "Virginia." Roads we usually took which passed underneath the railroad were flooded, so we had to take a circuitous detour through unfamiliar back streets. As we neared the hospital, we saw that all the lights were out in the Korean neighborhood. Fortunately, the hospital had its own generator and half an hour after we entered the lobby a healthy baby girl had been delivered. As this little girl filled out and sprouted a head of strawberry-blond hair, friends marveled, "She looks just like Cliff, with curls!"

In April of 1958, Cliff helped organize a triumphant visit of the New York City Ballet to Osaka. A grand new concert complex was being inaugurated by an ambitious Osaka Cultural Festival, featuring international as well as Japanese artists. Our ballet was followed in that hall by the Leningrad Symphony, Salzburg Marionettes, and dancers from India. Since USIS served as facilitator for the ballet, we were rewarded with tickets to each of their four performances. After the show we would meet with the dancers as they wolfed down hearty dinners, and would hear their stories.

Their first few days were challenging, beginning with communication gaps at the hotels. One ballerina requesting stewed prunes for breakfast was presented with a tray of seven spoons. The more serious challenge was on stage. The theater was built to accommodate Kabuki dramas, which require an extra-wide stage, much wider than the Carnegie Hall home base of the troupe. Dancers had to make a running entry before getting to the point where they could begin the dancing so meticulously choreographed and rehearsed. Problems solved, they wowed the audiences. The most respected performing arts critic in the area wrote in his column, "Please, send the New York City Ballet to us again!"

On Sunday the dancers had a free day and Cliff invited the entire troupe to come to our home for a picnic on our garden patio. It was a gorgeous day, with the azaleas in full bloom. The dancers cavorted among the pines and flowers, an incredible customized ballet. Jacques d'Amboise, their premier male dancer, was accompanied by his wife who also was a dancer and their fifteen-month-old son. We put him along with Cindy (now at ten months) in her playpen on the patio, where they happily watched the show.

Monday morning the troupe was off to Australia and New Zealand to continue their international concert tour. And Cindy was covered with red spots—chicken pox. We had exposed that visiting baby at Cindy's most contagious stage and agonized over what impact this might have on the ballet's continuing tour.

In his interview with Lew Schmidt, Cliff reminisced about the value of these visits by American artists.

It was during the time I was in the Kansai, the late fifties, that the Japanese really discovered American drama and modern dance. Up until the time when we started bringing in our big performing artists it was the Europeans and Russians who were receiving top billing in Japan. The only ballet that had any impact was the Bolshoi. So when the New York City Ballet came out in 1958 for the first Osaka Cultural Festival, it really was overwhelming for the Japanese. The USSR-sponsored Bolshoi was there at the same time as the U.S.-sponsored New York City Ballet and it was our ballet that received the rave reviews. The same happened later with the first musicals we were able to bring out, like "Hello Dolly" with Mary Martin. You may recall that we also started programming the first symphonies, the Los Angeles Symphony, the Symphony of the Air, and other musical attractions that were widely acclaimed.

The first one was the Symphony of the Air, which had just lost its contract with NBC, and they didn't know what they were going to do. They were still intact, so they were picked up by the State Department as a cultural presentation. The USIS centers arranged for that complete tour all around Japan. Again, I would like to cite that as an example of our ability to put the American performing arts on the center stage in Japan. Now, of course, we don't need to be involved in programming these groups any longer. The Japanese bring them over continually.

As I review for this book some of the letters I wrote home during this period, I look back from the relaxed perspective of a retiree with renewed wonder at the very rich, often chaotic schedule we followed during those Foreign Service days. While we were in the Kansai I did not do any regular teaching, but my days were filled. American dignitaries frequently visited the region, accompanied by wives who expected to be shown the local sites. This was fun. I met some fascinating people and would use their excursions to indulge in my own sightseeing, selecting my favorite places and varying the menu (there were so many in Kyoto alone!) to avoid going to the same place every time. I had a stint of several weeks at a farmers' cooperative center near Kobe, in response to a request to do a series of demonstrations on American cooking—showing what our people would eat for breakfast, lunch, and dinner. (I knew I had traveled a long road from those early days in Davao when canned dinners were all I could manage! Still, it seemed rather presumptuous to be performing as a culinary authority.)

A fellow consulate wife and I had discovered an ancient Japanese art form at an exhibit in a department store—*bonseki,* the creation of miniature classical scenes on black-lacquer trays, using white sand and pebbles coaxed into place with feathers and tiny spoons. We purchased our instruction books and supplies, engaged a teacher, and after several months were able to create simple landscapes to display on a side table for incredulous guests. The weekly lessons provided a few hours of shelter from the storms of our busy daily lives.

During that same April month when the ballet was in town, I had a bit part in a play put on by the Kobe Women's Club, hosted a home luncheon for fifteen Japanese women to meet with an American official from the U. S. National Council of Women's Organizations, spoke for an hour and answered questions for two more about American students at a congress of high school English Speaking Societies, and with Cliff's genial support scheduled an Easter egg hunt in our garden for twenty-three children and parents from the American Consulate. The day of the hunt it poured rain and we tried to control the mayhem by hiding eggs and confining kids to the upstairs, following the hunt with a rousing game or "pin-the-tail-on-the-bunny." During this time we also had two groups of houseguests. One was our dear friends the Nichols, in town to help with the New York City Ballet and join us at two elaborate parties for 2,500 at the new Osaka Festival Center. The other was the Kendalls, who came to the Kansai from Takamatsu for the birth of their second child, accompanied by their small daughter, whom Tom saw as an invader in his territory and harassed incessantly. Cliff meanwhile was dealing with U.S. representatives who had come to the region to officiate at an international trade fair, a visit by the Secretary of Labor, and a port call by the U.S. Navy, all requiring special attention from him in managing press releases and interviews. All this for him was in addition to maintaining a busy schedule of meetings in several different towns.

April of 1958 was also the month when we learned where we would go after our second tour of duty in Japan ended in June. We had again fantasized about someplace close to the glamour of Europe. But as I wrote in breaking the news to our parents, "Last January I was about to order three new electric blankets from Sears Roebuck when a little voice spoke to me and said: you order those blankets and sure as shootin' you'll be transferred to a tropical post. I'm glad I heeded that little voice, because a collection of electric blankets wouldn't be much good to us in Rangoon!" I continued,

> Cliff has been offered a really wonderful position for one
> of his still tender years, that of Deputy Country Public Affairs
> Officer for Burma. We are of course thrilled that he has been
> offered so much responsibility. Art Hummel, the chief Public
> Affairs Officer there who used to be Deputy in Japan, came
> through here en route for home leave last week and asked Cliff
> if he would take the job.
>
> Rangoon is of course still a long way from those European
> capitols our tourist instincts were leaning towards, but it is cer-
> tainly an interesting and a strategic area and one where Cliff's
> training and interest in the Far East should be put to good use.

The fact that the Hummels are a couple we know well and like tremendously and that Art specifically asked that Cliff come and work with him should make for a very pleasant office relationship.

I did not share with the home families the information we were gleaning from the State Department's "Post Report" on Burma, which we had found in the consulate's files and had been reading with rapt attention—the three kinds of poisonous snakes, the need to be inoculated against cholera and take antimalaria pills along with the more standard preventions, the insurgencies that were festering along all of Burma's borders, and the tenuous position of a struggling, newly independent nation caught as a pawn between the Cold War battles of East and West.

Whatever their feelings about our onward assignment, our family members in three cities were eager to visit with us during our home leave in the summer of 1958. This would be their first introduction to Cindy. And Tom—who had last seen them before his first birthday—would be meeting them as a worldly preschooler with lots of stories to share.

23

GETTING THERE IS HALF THE FUN

WHEN THE *PRESIDENT CLEVELAND* SAILED from Kobe on July 10th bound for San Francisco, the entire Stanford Club membership was at the pier to wave us off, singing the Stanford hymn and unfurling the banner as we pulled away from the dock. Despite our early doubts about the posting, Cliff and I felt wrenched to leave the country that had been our home for five years, the incubator of so many special friendships, and the birthplace of Tom and Cindy. And our two maids were bereft as they said farewell to "their" two children.

At nearly four years old, Tom sensed that something big was happening as the shores of Japan receded, and he began speaking to us in Japanese, something he would not do before. He listened intently to parental conversations about something called "Burma" and one day in midvoyage, with tears in his eyes, he blurted out, "But where is my *home?*" When we reached San Francisco, he turned off his Japanese entirely, even refused to use it when a few months later he was greeted by the Japanese parents of new playmates in Rangoon. Our formerly bilingual boy refused to speak his first language for six years, until we returned to Japan in 1964.

As we sailed into San Francisco Bay and under the Golden Gate Bridge, Tom began to understand why his dad had extolled the magical attractions of the "City by the Bay." We moved into the Forsters' hillside home in Oakland for a few weeks and introduced the children to some of California's beauty spots: Yosemite National Park, the Monterey Peninsula, and San Francisco itself. It too had been married off in the sister-city program. Many years later en route to another tour in Japan we discovered overlooking San Francisco Bay a monumental stone with incised Japanese characters. This commemorated the city's affiliation with its sister city, Osaka.

We traveled in California as a family caravan. Cliff's mother, sister Gerry, and nephew Charles—by now a strapping teenager who had been so impressed by his uncle's descriptions of a geology course at Stanford that he aimed to major in this subject when he went to university—were anxious to share as much of Cliff's time as possible. They were also enchanted with the two newest Forsters.

We had two more stops to make in the U.S., Dayton in Ohio and Rye in New York. Tom had a date in Dayton, arranged on the recommendation of our doctor in Japan, for the removal of tonsils deemed responsible for a series of colds and throat infections the previous winter. Surgery behind him, he bounced back to his usual energetic (and mischievous) self. My father, unaccustomed to all that young energy remarked, with a twinkle in his eye, "You can certainly tell that this child has come from Japan where boys are kings of the roost!"

When we got to my mother's home in Rye, she had a wonderful present waiting for Cliff and me, the repeat of a gift received when we returned from the Philippines—a handful of tickets to Broadway shows, the hits we had missed while overseas. Among the handful was a pair to the New York City Ballet. After that performance, which featured Jacques D'Amboise, we went backstage and found him and his wife. "Come with us to a great nearby sushi restaurant," they insisted. Once our orders had been taken, we asked the question that had been nagging us since they left our Sunday picnic in April: "Did any of you, by any chance, come down with chicken pox?" When the answer was "No," we sighed with relief and told them how Cindy had presented us with a full crop of red spots the day after she had shared her playpen with their son.

Our onward trip to Burma was a mixed blessing. To satisfy some of our hunger for European glamour, we took a ship to Rome, enjoyed a few days in that wonderful city, then went by train to Venice before heading to Frankfurt and a flight to Rangoon. Bundled up in winter clothes (it was now mid-November) en route to a two-year summer, Cliff and I exchanged strong words as we got off the train in Venice and tried to assemble our seventeen pieces of luggage, which included a wardrobe trunk and a huge carton, almost impossible to handle, of disposable diapers. We had been forewarned that shops in Rangoon would offer few of the items deemed necessary for an American home and that deliveries from overseas were sporadic.

"How on earth did you expect to travel with all this stuff?" Cliff grumped.

"It's *your* family, you know, and you're taking us to a place where we can't get the 'stuff' we need!" was my retort. In a foul mood, parents, kids, and stuff managed to get crammed onto a gondola and headed for our hotel. As we were poled along a narrow canal, a commercial photographer—strategically posted to take irresistible pictures of ecstatically happy tourists—snapped his shot of the Forsters and tossed instructions into my lap regarding where to collect the photo. When we went to his

En route to Burma—"Having a wonderful time."

shop a couple days later we found a picture of a glum-looking foursome, with luggage piled high behind them. Having recaptured our sense of humor, we mailed copies to friends and family with the caption, "Having a wonderful time, wish you were here."

The last leg of that trip was the worst. The flight from Frankfurt took many, many, interminable hours and Cindy, who was too young to rate a U.S. government-paid seat and was shifted between Cliff's and my lap, cried most of the way. Finally a resourceful stewardess persuaded a family of three with bulkhead seats to trade with the noisy Forsters (for the sake of surrounding passengers as much as for us) and created a bed on the floor where our babe could settle in for a blessedly quiet nap. Ever since, I've endured crying babies on planes in peace and with sympathy.

This was our road to Mandalay, and the "Land of Golden Pagodas."

24

IN THE LAND OF THE
GOLDEN PAGODAS

WHEN WE ARRIVED IN RANGOON, the British colonial-style home that had been assigned to us had only recently been vacated and was receiving a new coat of interior paint, so we were put up temporarily in the Strand Hotel, located near the embassy in the heart of the city.

Rangoon and Burma have been renamed Yangon and Myanmar by the current military government, but I will use the more traditional names. The Strand has been taken over by the Raffles chain of luxury hotels and reputedly restored to full grandeur, but at the time of our stay it was a faded monument to past glory with lofty ceilings and spacious rooms, Bengalis wearing white uniforms with red turbans serving scrambled eggs for breakfast and curry for lunch and dinner, shabby carpets and drapes, peeling paint throughout, and rust-stained tubs and sputtering water faucets in the bathrooms.

We sorted out our mound of luggage, then went for a walk. Victorian and pseudo-Mughal architecture, more faded elegance, red stains left by the spittle of betel-nut chewers on the cracked pavement, and roving pie dogs—these are my prime memories of that first foray into the city. Glamour? Health and safety for our children? We wondered.

But we soon appreciated that we had come to a very special place. Just beyond the city's faded grandeur was the splendid Shwedagon Pagoda, a shimmering golden spire crowning a hill and approached among stalls of colorful offerings to be purchased by worshippers on their way up the long flights of stairs. The stupa rose majestically from a marble platform and was surrounded by numerous small pagodas. The Shwedagon was the most magnificent, but only one among the innumerable Buddhist structures that we would see dotting the landscape throughout Burma. An older and more venerable one, the Sule Pagoda in the heart of Rangoon, was revered as the repository of a hair of the Buddha reputedly brought to this place by monks from Sri Lanka some 2,000 years ago.

This place would quickly feel like home. We were embraced by a community of instant friends, both within the embassy and among the Burmese who welcomed us with enthusiastic informality. No longer "Forster-san" with an honorific as in the more formal Japanese society, it was immediately "Cliff" and "Nancy." And Cindy and Tom would soon be lovingly tended by a household staff that Art Hummel's wife, Betty Lou, had already engaged pending our approval.

Burma had been part of the British colonial empire, achieving independence in 1948. The new nation was plagued with a host of challenges. On the eve of independence, an assassin broke into the room where the top leadership was holding a cabinet meeting and gunned down many of those most respected by their compatriots—those most prepared to lead the new nation. Dikes breeched during the war had flooded the rice fields with salt water in the Irrawaddy Delta region, which had once produced an export crop of the world's finest rice. Multiple ethnic minorities, some of whom had enjoyed preferential treatment under the British, resisted control by the Burmans of the central valley and fought the government with rebellions along all the frontiers.

A small nation sandwiched between the two giants of Asia, Burma shared frontiers with India and Bangladesh as well as with China and Thailand. The government was uneasy over that border with China— 1,400 miles—and opted to follow India's lead in becoming a declared neutral, a "nonaligned nation" in the conflicts of the Cold War.

On the positive side, the British rulers left a legacy of the institutions of law—a functioning civil service and democratic government. Solid educational foundations (including fluency in English) were based on the British model. The land was rich in natural beauty and contained forests filled with teak and uplands with precious gems. And, unlike the situation in many Asian nations, the population was sparse enough that there need not be competition for scarce resources.

We moved into our house at number nine Washington Park, formerly a residential compound of the British Burma Oil Company and now U.S. Embassy property. It sparkled with its fresh coat of paint and was furnished with our familiar household goods. Our staff, housed in quarters within the compound, was part of a community, sizeable and diversified according to the lingering colonial customs. Hari, a Bengali Indian, was the "bearer"—the head servant who gave orders and filled the role of major domo and butler. Barua, a Muslim Indian, was the cook; he also did all the local shopping and favored heavy menus learned from years cooking for British housewives. Two Karens—members of one of the tribal groups resisting Burmese control—were our nannies, Sheila in charge of the children, and Bepaw in charge of the laundry. Our daughter still recalls with delight the fairy tales Sheila told her at bedtime and the folklore Bepaw shared while Cindy watched her ironing in the guest bathroom. A Madrasi from South India was the "sweeper" assigned the most menial household tasks and Mali, also a Karen, the full-time gardener, who we later discovered was adept at killing snakes with a swift barefoot heel thrust to the reptile's head. Each of these six had a family and most, with their different cultural backgrounds, harbored grievances against their neighbors in the servants' quarters. This was an interesting domestic community!

As had been the case in Davao, our first houseguest arrived a few days after we moved in. Shig Imamura, our "American kamikaze" friend from Matsuyama, was traveling around Southeast Asia on a Ford Foundation grant to share some of his English-language teaching skills with teachers in several countries. Burma was his first stop. We welcomed him, showed him to his room, and invited him to relax and refresh with a shower before joining us in the living room for a drink before dinner.

When Shig joined us he expressed concern: "Cliff, there's a lizard in my bathroom!"

Cliff laughed and said, "That's nothing to worry about, Shig. They're common in Southeast Asia. Geckos." Geckos are small lizards that crawl up the walls and along the ceiling in search of their bug repasts, a creature familiar in the Philippines. "They're good to have because they eat the mosquitoes."

Shig shrugged. "OK, if you say so, Cliff."

A few days later Cliff and I were vying for the shower in our bathroom and I suggested he use the one by the guest room. He dashed back a minute later. "There's a *monster* in that bathroom! It's not a gecko at all, but a lizard a couple feet long with huge gaping jaws! "

The next morning Cliff told Hari that the monster in the guest bathroom must be removed. "Oh, no, Sahib!" Hari protested. "That lizard in our house brings much good luck to you, to your children, to me, and to all the servants and our children. If we remove him it will bring bad luck to you, to your children, to me, and to all the servants and our children."

The lizard stayed. It nested in a hole in the wall below the sink and would come out to air itself on the edge of the bathtub. It would oversee the family's ironing while Cindy sat next to it on the tub and Bepaw told her folk tales. When we had guests we would coax the lizard back into the hole and stuff it closed with newspapers.

Right after we arrived in Burma we were on the road. On later trips, we often traveled separately; communication links were almost nonexistent within the country, and given the volatile political situation in those days Cliff and I did not want to both be away from our children for more than a few days. But the first trip, we took together.

Ambassador McConaughy had been invited by the Burmese government to tour the Irrawaddy Delta region—the same area that suffered catastrophic damage from typhoon and tsunami in the spring of 2008—on one of their military vessels, to view firsthand the war-damaged rice fields and the efforts being made in partnership with the U.S. aid program to revive them. The ambassador asked Cliff to come along, an introduction to Burma from the ground up. Wives were invited to join their husbands.

On our first field trip in Burma, we joined the ambassador
for a tour of the Irrawaddy Delta.

At each small river village where we stopped, we were greeted by performing singers and dancers, local officials, and welcoming citizens. With a military escort, we walked through the villages and along the banks between rice fields then returned to our boat, where the resident armed guards had guns at the ready, and proceeded to the next village. It was a good learning experience—a way to understand the fragility of

Burma's security situation outside of the capitol city and to appreciate the warmth of the Burmese people.

Burma is a land of many ecosystems. The Delta is very different from "upcountry." There one encounters dry lands, dense jungle and teak forests, and mighty rivers (the Irrawaddy's "Road to Mandalay" runs through the middle of the country). Along the eastern and northern frontiers, uplands rise towards the mountains, which on the east comprise "the hump" through which the Burma Road was built and over which American pilots flew precious cargo to sustain the Chinese during World War II. To the north, those mountains rise up to meet the Tibetan plateau.

Cliff's first upcountry trip was to the northern jungle, accompanied by a fellow USIS officer, to get photos and write a story about another kind of U.S.-Burmese partnership. Deep in the jungle where massive teak logs were felled, the heavy work of hauling was done by elephants. The logs were then picked up by tractors provided by ICA (the International Cooperation Administration, which later became the U.S. Agency for International Development or USAID) for the rest of the journey to the Irrawaddy River bank, where they were rolled into the water, lashed together to form massive rafts, and floated downriver to the port in Rangoon. The rafts' river journey would take weeks; resident raftsmen steered the rafts with long poles, living in simple shelters built on board, often with family accompanying and sharing in the tasks of cooking and laundering. Cliff and Mel Brokenshire got their photos and their story, which was published in *Dawn,* an English-language magazine assembled at the USIS printing facility in Manila and distributed throughout Asia. And Cliff, treated to his first ride on a working elephant, was unnerved by the thundering roar that the giant creatures let out with each heave as they hauled the logs.

When one traveled north by road, the only access was through the "Namwan Tract," an area through the mountains, near the Burma Road, that was in territorial dispute: Both China and Burma claimed it, an unresolved legacy of British boundary-drawing. Transit through the Tract was always tense during these Cold War days. And rugged. Roads throughout the country were rough, narrow, dusty or muddy, suitable only for jeeps. Often one would take the train to Mandalay, then hire a war-surplus jeep and driver for the rest of the way. On one trip, Cliff and his driver were stopped in the middle of the Namwan Tract by two armed soldiers. Was this an assault? A kidnapping? After conversation with the driver, the soldiers retreated into the roadside shrubbery and came out carrying a dead orangutan between them. What they wanted was a ride to the next town, along with their hunting trophy. The two soldiers climbed into the front of the jeep with the driver, after seating the orangutan snugly upright next to Cliff in the back seat.

We wives had our separate travel adventures while the men stayed home with the children. Betty Lou Hummel, Lois Rollefson (the wife of the embassy's agricultural attaché), and I would set off in a jeep with our bedrolls, mosquito nets, malaria pills, snakebite kits, and food supplies for a week or two of strenuous but exhilarating exploration. We met with American Fulbright grantees who were working (more in a Peace Corps than a scholarly role) in the northern outposts. We visited the mountain-village markets that moved daily from town to town and drew sellers and buyers from across the border in China as well as the local area. The older Chinese women had tiny bound feet and local tribesmen and women wore traditional costumes.

We witnessed the mining of rubies in Mogok, done by hand-digging deep wells and sifting through the earth that came from below, or by filtering water running downstream though a series of ever finer meshes. In Mogaung we learned that jade is found in huge, unimposing-on-the-outside boulders, sawed into smaller pieces to ship to Chinese craftsmen, each cut showing streaks of progressively more valuable jade. On one return trip to Rangoon, we rode on the top deck of a flat-bottomed paddleboat from Bhamo in the north to Mandalay, experiencing communal life on this river highway—getting stuck on mud banks; stopping at small settlements where food would be off-loaded and unglazed pottery, cotton blankets, colorful toys, and fish would be taken aboard; playing scrabble to while away the long hours between ports while other passengers looked on with fascination (they wondered if this was some variation of the Chinese tile game of mahjong). Frequently we steamed past a teak log raft, with the crew's laundry drying alongside their hut and children running around on their teak playground.

In his 1990 interview, Cliff told Lew Schmidt that he had been excited about this assignment, in a fascinating part of the world at a most
interesting time.

> It was the period from 1958 when General Ne Win took
> over temporarily—an "arranged coup" in agreement with U Nu,
> who was then the Prime Minister. Many in the government felt
> that U Nu had been too tolerant of the communists and other
> insurgents and that there had to be a greater effort to keep
> them out of Rangoon and to turn things around. When we ar-
> rived, U Nu had gone into retreat at a Buddhist monastery and
> General Ne Win was in control. We left two years later, when
> the government had been returned to civilian control and be-
> fore the second coup in 1961. That time there was a real take-
> over by Ne Win, not "arranged." That time the General wanted
> absolute control.
>
> We foreigners were welcome. USIS was in Rangoon along
> with the British Council and all our opposite numbers from the
> People's Republic of China and the Soviet Union. You had the
> Japanese working on construction projects, as we were with our
> AID programs. You had the Israelis helping with agriculture in
> the more arid areas near Mandalay, and Yugoslavia with coastal
> shipping. It was a truly international effort to help Burma de-
> velop and become an open society. It reminded me of the period
> in Japan after its isolation when that country began to open up
> to foreign influence.

At this point in their conversation, Cliff jumped ahead to lament
the changes that took place in Burma after we left in 1960. General Ne
Win, who had been so close to foreigners when we were there (he and
Cliff's predecessor had co-owned a race horse, who they named "Lolita"
and rooted for together at the Rangoon race track), became suspicious
of outsiders. He felt that some, including Burmese citizens of Indian
ethnicity, were aiding the rebellious tribes along the eastern border. In
1961, after returning to power by forceful coup, he expelled foreigners.
The American Embassy staff was drastically reduced, the USIS library

closed, and the Fulbright program ended. The news from Burma in the years following that coup became increasingly depressing as a clique of military rulers held the reins of government tightly, restricted individual freedom, brutally repressed any signs of protest, and steered the once promising economy into deeper and deeper poverty.

Cliff was, however, proud of the successful program USIS maintained in the late fifties:

> We were there during the years when you could travel all over Burma and accomplish a great deal, before the curtain came down. It was, as I say, a very exciting time, because you were getting back into what we had in the Philippines earlier with our "nation-building" type of program. We were assisting the Burmese with their efforts in the fields of education, public health, and government administration. The Asia Foundation was also there with its projects. There were so many of us who were trying to do our very best to help the government which had been so rocky since the war, what with insurrection movements and a fragile economy.

In April of 1959 we were moved into another house. Also in Washington Park, but predating the stolid British-built residences, it was an enchanting Burmese-style house built on stilts and overlooking a small lake. A path led down to the water, with a huge tree on either side. One of the trees was dead; Cliff discovered the skin of a full-size king cobra under the house and learned that the dead tree was home to a nest of baby cobras. He went into the embassy property manager's office, demanding that the tree be removed for the safety of his small children. The official in charge, a hard-bitten old Asia hand and consummate bureaucrat, said absolutely not. "That tree is on U.S. government property, marked on charts which are on file in the Department of State, and it cannot be harmed." Unable to get past the bureaucratic approach, Cliff took matters into his own hands.

The Karens, Cliff knew, liked to feast on snake meat. Cliff made a deal with our gardener: "If you round up your friends and cut down that dead tree, you all can have a barbequed snake feast." The Karens were delighted; the tree was removed; our children were allowed to walk in the garden. And, to this day, Cliff has never received reprimand or request for reimbursement for the damaged government property.

Cliff found an old rowboat and set it at the bottom of our path to the lake, where he spent several weekends varnishing the exterior and oars and painting the inside. On a Sunday morning he was ready to launch and Tom rounded up the other children in Washington Park to watch the event. Into the water went the boat and—glug, glug, glug! It sank. After sitting under the tropical sun those several weeks, the caulking between boards had dried up. Repairs were duly made and a second launching was much more successful. In the meantime Cliff, who really loved to sail, had joined the Rangoon Yacht Club on the other side of the lake, which had several boats for member use. He was out in one on a day when a severe storm came up and he was having difficulty maneuvering the boat back to the dock. Two attendants from the club rowed out to tow him in, but wouldn't attach the rescue line until he gave them an opinion about who was right in the India-Pakistan conflict over Kashmir. He hedged with diplomatic language, but his answer seemed to satisfy these Bengalis and he was rescued.

Entertaining was not only an expected and effective way to cement relations with the local population, in Rangoon it was great fun. The Burmese loved a party, loved to come to our homes, to eat and drink heartily and to stay late. We learned early on that attendance could be fluid, a real challenge if one planned a sit-down dinner. People who had accepted an invitation might not show up. More frequently, they might bring along friends and family who hadn't been expected. Our recourse was to skip the formal dinners with table seating and serve buffet style. Members of the Burmese press corps—and there were many of them with an inordinate number of papers being published in Rangoon—loved to drink, whisky before dinner and brandy after. When we had vacationed in Singapore I came back with a recipe for Singapore gin slings, and decided those would be featured at our next big party. Rather than slow down production with ingredients assembled one by one for each glass, I made an infusion with proportionate amounts of gin and flavorings which was to be used at a ratio of one jigger of infusion to two jiggers of water per serving. Cliff was enthusiastically helping out at the bar but hadn't understood the bit about the two parts of water—his concoctions were dynamite. Everyone loved the drink, and the party was even merrier than usual!

Nearby was the Burma-America Institute, a cooperative venture jointly operated by the U.S. and Burmese governments. With a small auditorium and several conference rooms, and located very close to Rangoon University, it had a lively schedule of lectures by Americans and by Burmese, language lessons (in both English and Burmese—it was an institution for mutual learning), exhibitions, and meetings of all types. Even American cooking lessons, which I was recruited to provide. While assembling a dish from a recipe, I remarked that this cuisine-by-formula had saved me from disaster many a time since my days as a bride in the Philippines. And noted that by comparison, women from other cultures usually were taught by their mothers and when asked by an American like me for the "recipe" for a particular dish we were told there was no such thing, just a dash of this and a handful of that.

At the end of our class at the Burma-American Institute I invited everyone to our house for a potluck luncheon, requesting that they bring their family favorites. This they did, wonderful dishes representing their native Burmese or Indian or Pakistani cuisine, and they did more; as a gift they presented me with their handmade cookbook—carefully calculated and transcribed recipes for each of the dishes brought to this meal.

Another event at the Institute was an international arts and crafts fair. Wives of diplomats from several nations along with Burmese women prepared displays of their work: hand-painted note cards, embroidery and handwoven goods, ceramics, Japanese flower arrangements. Here was an opportunity to show off the *bonseki* I had learned in Japan. On the day before the fair, I meticulously created a landscape with mountain and sea and a full moon with cranes flying by. Unknowingly, I had placed my fragile sand painting under a ceiling fan—which was suddenly turned on. A sandstorm destroyed my creation. I moved the tray to a safer place and recreated my exhibit. When I came the next morning just before the American ambassador's wife would preside over the opening, I discovered there had been small visitors in the night. Ants had left a trail down my sand mountain. "That's OK," I decided. "It looks like there have been skiers on the slopes."

Living in Burma, while fascinating, had its challenges. Public sanitation was substandard. We had to be extra cautious about what we ate and drank—nothing raw and only boiled water. Port calls to Rangoon by the ships bringing frozen meat, cheese, butter, and canned goodies to the embassy commissary came on erratic schedules. We grew tired of goat stews and stringy chicken curries and longed for fresh lettuce and celery and a slab of rare beef. Occasional family trips to Singapore and Bangkok were opportunities to satisfy that hunger. Two longer breaks enabled us to visit Angkor Wat in Cambodia, and take a Dutch ship from Singapore to Jakarta and Surabaya on Java, ending up for a week on the island of Bali. These trips were true adventures for the children. Angkor had lots of neat stones to scramble over and a vine-covered ruin where a monkey frightened Cindy. The Dutch ship had yummy cheese and fresh milk. In Surabaya, Tom twirled around a flagpole and was stung by swarms of red ants crawling from the pole up his arm. On Bali, Mom kept everybody waiting to go to the beach while she bought souvenirs. For all of us, these were precious times to relax together as a family, experience more of the wonders of Asia, renew and refresh body and spirit before returning to Rangoon.

In Burma, one of the most memorable professional experiences for Cliff was when an officer in Moscow's embassy came to the USIS library as a defector. Cliff described this incident to Lew:

My opposite number in the Soviet Embassy was Aleksandr Kaznacheev, their information officer. Just before he defected to us their military attaché, Colonel Mikhail Stryguine had also attempted to defect. But his own wife and Soviet staff caught up with him at the Rangoon General Hospital and dragged Stryguine back to their embassy, then shipped him out on a People's Republic of China plane, which had been flown in for the purpose. That infuriated the Burmese, because they knew Stryguine was seeking asylum and protection from them and they did not like the way he was whisked out of the country.

So Kaznacheev played his cards well. He walked quietly into our USIS library to defect. Zelma Graham, who was the director, called over to our embassy, which was a block away. Following government regulations, Kaznacheev was told to go home and come back in twenty-four hours if, upon reflection, this was what he truly wanted to do. He returned. He was a young fellow, very fluent in English. He said he was not a communist, and had not joined the party. He had come out to Burma to work on a Burmese-Russian dictionary, and said he was conscripted by his embassy. While working there, he became increasingly upset about the KGB and what they were up to in Burma.

The Soviets, of course, learned that he was in our embassy, and they were about to put out a story that we had kidnapped him. When we got wind of this, Art Hummel called upon the press officer, Larry Sharpe, and myself to counter that effort. We were able to get to all the media that night to invite them in to meet with Kaznacheev at USIS the following morning to hear him tell his story. He blew things wide open. His story appeared all over Asia and was also carried by the wire services to the U.S. and Europe. It opened all eyes to what the Soviets were up to in attempting to subvert a neutral country like Burma, and USIS played an important role in getting the story out.

After seeking asylum in the USIS library in Rangoon, Soviet defector Aleksandr Kaznacheev told his story to the world in a press conference arranged by Cliff and his colleagues.

Kaznacheev had fallen in love with the Burmese people. In his press conference, he gave that as one of the primary reasons for his turning against the Soviets' rule; he hated what his government was asking him to do with—and to—these easygoing, independent-minded people. We, too, had become entranced with Burma and hoped to return for a second tour. But our time had run out; according to law, Foreign Service officers were required to return to Washington after extended periods in the field, to become reoriented into their own culture and familiar with the view of the world as seen from Washington. We had been gone eleven years and our home assignment was overdue.

Cliff was assigned to Washington, to serve as USIA's desk officer for Japan and Korea (though still referred to as USIS overseas, the name had been officially changed to the U.S. Information Agency, so as not to be confused with the U.S. Immigration Service). But Cliff and I had never lived as a family in the States. From the first weeks of our first posting we had been blessed with household help. How would we adjust to the harsh new realities of do-it-yourself living? We had a family conference with the children, explaining that in their next home there would be no Hari or Barua or Sheila or Bepaw and we would need their help. I suggested to Tom and Cindy that they should prepare by practicing with Hari, setting and clearing the table. Tom drew himself up with all the dignity a six-year-old could muster: "That would be an insult to Hari. That work is *his* and he's proud of it! Don't you worry, Mom, we'll help you out when we get to Washington."

This was no ploy to get out of chores—Tom was serious. Cliff and I took pride in the fact that our son at his tender age had developed in instinctive understanding of cultural nuances governing East and West.

25

A TASTE OF CAMELOT

WE RETURNED TO AMERICA VIA Europe in January of 1961, picking up a new Mercedes at the factory in Germany. An Indian salesman in Rangoon had ordered it for us in exchange for our two-year-old Chevy—a bargain for him, since imported cars were heavily taxed in Burma. We traveled by ship for the final leg of our journey, with the car onboard, and landed in New York.

That first evening with my mother in Rye, the adults had lots to talk about and we sent Tom and Cindy off for a bath before dinner. Soon we heard uproarious laughter from the bathroom and went to investigate, finding our children gleefully slurping water from the tub. In Burma this wasn't safe, and we'd repeatedly told them, "No slurping here. When you get to America it will be OK." This was their homecoming celebration.

We found our dream house in Washington on the day John F. Kennedy was inaugurated. On January 19th, 1961, Washington had been brought to a standstill by a snowstorm, but the following day brought clear skies as a backdrop to that memorable inauguration. Cliff had been on temporary duty at the Agency and, leaving the kids with Mother,

I joined him for a week of house hunting. Our last Rangoon visitors from Washington, noting that our Asian furnishings might not be suited to a colonial Virginia home, suggested we take a look at a brand new contemporary California subdivision in Bethesda, Maryland. On that snowy day we peeked into the window of the model home—everyone was either at the inauguration or in front of the TV—and agreed that this was exactly what we wanted.

In February, after quick trips to see my father and Cliff's family, we moved into our first American home, an anchor that would serve us for twenty-three years, until Cliff retired. A few days later he was off to New York, on temporary duty with the United Nations. As he described it to Lew:

> John Kennedy had just become president and I was assigned to the United Nations on the U.S. Delegation. Adlai Stevenson had just come in as ambassador to head up our delegation and I had the great privilege and honor of serving on his public-affairs staff. It turned out to be a rewarding but tough assignment.
>
> That was the second session of the U.N. Fifteenth General Assembly, where all hell broke loose with the Bay of Pigs. We in New York simply did not have all the background. As a result, we were being clobbered by the other delegates because we had no detailed information to counter theirs. It was kind of a low period for us, since the whole operation had not been handled well. I could see then that when a policy goes awry, as did that one to deny any U.S. involvement in the invasion of Cuba, it can undermine your credibility overnight. Because up until the Bay of Pigs, we had considerable support at that General Assembly largely as the result of Adlai Stevenson's presence. He was widely admired by the other delegates. While he came through fine in the end, the Cuba fiasco cast a dark shadow over the credibility of the entire U.S. delegation. "You folks must have known," was the usual comment. Just prior to that, I'd had the job of going around talking on disarmament and other

issues, trying to explain our positions, and other delegates had
listened with interest.

While Cliff was in New York he stayed with my mother in Rye and
came to Bethesda on the weekends to be with the family and help us
settle in. Tom had spent a few weeks in the neighborhood school in Rye,
where his first-grade class was using the same books he had in Rangoon
(school there was two months ahead of the U.S. schedule to avoid the intense heat of the pre-monsoon spring). When he entered the local school
near our Maryland home, he was also right in step. That was a relief! As
was the fact that our neighbors in this newly built neighborhood were all
about our age and had children who made ours feel at home.

Cindy wouldn't be ready for kindergarten for another year, and rather
than put her into nursery school we decided she and I would use the
year to explore together, making leisurely visits to Washington's many
museums and the zoo. Walt and Franny Nichols had also returned for a
Washington assignment and their youngest son was Cindy's age, a congenial playmate, so we had our own customized preschool experience.

Cliff had been stimulated by his time at the United Nations, especially the privilege of working with Ambassador Adlai Stevenson and
special envoy Eleanor Roosevelt. Stevenson ran the daily meetings of the
U.S. staff with elegance; even when the situation was grim he opened
with a cheerful anecdote and was always gracious to every participant.
One of Cliff's major assignments while in New York was to facilitate setting up a foreign press center where members of the international media
could gather and USIA press officers would be available to assist them.
That completed, he was glad when the General Assembly ended and he
could return to the family and his assigned job at the Agency in Washington.

It was truly exciting to be in D. C. as the Kennedy administration moved in. The team of bright and personable men and women
were *our* generation. The White House epitomized glamour and this
city felt like the hub of the world, with foreign heads of state constantly visiting and their national flags attached to all the downtown lamp
posts. We read the *Washington Post* from cover to cover. The Kennedys
had young children and Jacqueline's obstetrician was an associate of my

doctor. (Yes, I was pregnant again—our third child was due shortly before Christmas.)

I didn't know my way around Washington at all. Then I heard a radio plea for volunteers to drive one day a week for the Red Cross, picking up blood donors from all over the city. Red Cross service was appropriate, considering the family background. Driving all over the city would familiarize me with my new home. And this would be a good excuse to indulge myself with a weekly cleaning woman who could double as a babysitter for Cindy. Done!

Cliff's Japan-Korea desk in the East Asia division of USIA was in a cubicle next to the China desk, manned by Bill Payeff. Bill was a Chinese language officer who had just returned from his series of Asia posts and had a lively sense of humor, honed by an earlier stint with the *New Yorker* magazine. They shared a zany secretary who was originally from Greece, Kiki Papadopoulos. This threesome worked hard and long hours, but seasoned their days with laughter and the pleasure of each other's good company.

Cliff had long been an admirer of Edward R. Murrow and was delighted when Murrow was appointed as Director of USIA.

> There was an excitement about working at the Agency, a
> real sense of purpose, heightened by President Kennedy and
> Ed Murrow's strong interest in Japan and the assignment of
> the Japan specialist, Edwin Reischauer, as ambassador to Japan.
> There was to be a whole new relationship following the tense
> period of riots there over the U.S. Japan Security Treaty.

Cliff's responsibilities—in addition to serving as liaison between the agency and posts in Asia and making regular inspection visits there—included working with those in Washington who administered the exchange programs and provided the resources needed for USIS libraries and media programs. He also worked closely with counterparts in the Department of State to coordinate policy guidelines—to ensure that the U.S. spoke with one voice overseas—and to make regular visits to Congress to testify before their committees on budget requests, backing up those requests with "evidences of effectiveness" like those he had accumulated in his 1950 assignment to evaluate the program in the Philippines. As he mentioned to Lew, it wasn't easy to provide skeptical legislators with concrete examples of the importance of personal relationships, nurtured over a period of time.

Cliff and I certainly saw the importance of those relationships in our personal life, as friends from earlier assignments stayed in touch. The 1962 Christmas card from Bernardo Saludares, the young man we'd befriended in Davao more than a decade before, brought us particular pleasure.

> I can never forget the Forsters. Whenever I remember them, I am reminded of those days when I was yet a greenhorn student under Mrs. Forster at the Mindanao Colleges; when I received the first "break" in my school life when I was taken by Mr. Forster to work with the USIS; which job contributed immensely to my finishing my college law course and making me what I am now today.
>
> And speaking of "breaks," I wish to inform you that I have had another break last October 2nd, 1962, when without my knowledge beforehand I was sworn in by His Excellency, President Diosdado, as Municipal Judge for the frontier municipality of Kapalong, province of Davao, at Nabunturan, Davao, when the President was on one of his regionalizing trips there. I was just called to the stage after the President's speech and was made to proceed in reading my oath of office—notwithstanding the fact that I was not prepared as I was only in ordinary Banlon shirt, and full of dust all over my body due to the condition of the roads here, and I was not even able to comb my hair.

He proudly signed his name "Judge Bernardo Saludares."

Japan had a huge press corps in Washington, both print and broadcast media. We made a point of getting to know them, inviting couples to dinner and taking newcomers shopping. After I took Hatsue Horikawa to my favorite shoe store and discovered she also wore size 7 AAA, we became fast friends. Cliff introduced her husband, Atsuhiro, to individuals who could provide good stories for his paper or elaborate on the complex ones already in the headlines.

Embedding spokesmen who would inform the public of Japan in the contemporary culture of the U.S. was a win-win situation. One of the most successful programs was conceived by Walt and Cliff. The studios of the Voice of America were opened to Japan's TV correspondents to interview newsmakers and make weekly broadcasts to their home audiences on subjects ranging from politics to popular culture to health and welfare.

Another innovation during the early sixties was the organization of the United States-Japan Cultural Conference, CULCON. This was a convening of leaders from media, the arts, government, and education—counterparts from each nation coming together for an informal, wide-ranging dialogue. One of the Japanese artists we felt most drawn to was Shoji Hamada, one of three folk-art potters who were "living national treasures." He was a marvelous man—modest, thoughtful, embracing new ideas and new friends. Fourteen years later, while living in Tokyo, we would visit the ailing Hamada in his country village of Mashiko.

At the end of the first conference, a Rockefeller grant hosted a weekend at Colonial Williamsburg for all the delegates and their wives. It was fascinating to watch the Japanese members of our group immerse themselves in the daily lifestyles as well as the political philosophy of the American Republic's founding mothers and fathers. CULCON meetings continued annually, alternating between a site in Japan and one in the U.S.

At a subsequent meeting Mr. Maeda, president of Japan's national broadcasting system (NHK), developed a plan with Frank Stanton of CBS to exchange educational television shows. Cliff commented to Lew, "It was a real breakthrough. The direct result was improved quality in American TV programs viewed by Japanese audiences and an introduction to American audiences of Japanese educational films."

Tom and Cindy—once she reached kindergarten age—both settled comfortably into their elementary school. True to Tom's promise in Rangoon, they rallied beautifully as household helpers, performing kitchen duties before and after dinner as well as other household chores. Most importantly, they were delighted to have a baby brother to wheel around in the red wagon that had been under the Christmas tree—"Dougie in the buggy" was the new family member's neighborhood sobriquet—and I was delighted to have had a first-class birthing experience at Georgetown University Hospital, quite a contrast to the Japan deliveries.

But I was getting restless. Wanting to have options in my professional life overseas other than teaching English and demonstrating cooking, neither of which I was trained to do, I decided to go back to college to be certified as a teacher in my own subject, one that fascinated me. I would become a high-school history teacher. This meant taking required courses in education—educational philosophy and curriculum design—and, to fill in a gap in my university transcript, two terms of the history of the United States. I selected the campus closest to home, American University, and managed to complete the two education courses in the summer, with vacationing teenage neighbors babysitting the children. In the fall and winter I attended the history courses one night a week, with Cliff officiating at home.

The final assignment, nine weeks of practice teaching during the fall of 1963, was more complicated. Daytime care for Doug involved a series of sitters and leaving the baby next door when arrangements fell apart. But the teaching assignment was invaluable. I was sent to nearby Walt Whitman High School to work with the instructor of five senior world-history classes. When we met he announced, "Mrs. Forster, I've looked at your record and you're not the usual student teacher. I'll give you one week to observe, visiting classes of every history and social studies teacher in the building, then you'll take over my classes. I've rearranged the course schedule for the year so the chapter on Asia will be yours."

It was a superb learning experience for me—and my "mentor" was able to devote more time to his role as assistant coach of the school's football team. I of course loved having a captive audience, sharing all my tales of living in Asia while trying to put the textbook history events into context. On my final day, November 22nd, one of my classes presented me with a long scroll they had made, an illustrated timeline of Japanese history based on stories I had told them. I was teaching the last class of the day when once again—as happened frequently in the fall, with visitors from various colleges coming to meet with prospective recruits—we were interrupted for a broadcast over the speaker system.

"President Kennedy has been shot in Dallas!" Stunned silence, then a buzz of comments and wails from tearful girls. As do all of us who were alive then, I remember clearly where I was on the day JFK died.

Cliff had a particularly poignant challenge that day and on through the night. A few days previously, President Kennedy had recorded a message to the people of Japan, which would be broadcast on the first transit over Japan by a new communications satellite.

This was a USIA initiative, to be transmitted by COMSAT. It would be the first broadcast by an American president to a specific nation, and an honor for the Japanese. But the broadcast was pulled. When Cliff objected he was told, "We won't be able to use the footage because the president has just been shot."

Cliff persisted. "This was the president's message to the Japanese people when he was still very much alive. He's still alive according to news reports. We can't assume that this is the end until there's confirmation."

Higher authority concurred and the program was reinstituted for the next relay to Japan, launched just prior to the news of Kennedy's death. Cliff told Lew Schmidt about the impact this had on Japan:

> When the relay satellite first came over, the Japanese were getting the president live and listening to him. By the time the relay came around again, they were getting the reports of his death. The NHK correspondent in Washington called us early Saturday morning to see if it would be possible to use the satellite just to send all the weekend coverage. To this day when you talk to our Japanese friends about this sequence of events, they describe the tremendous impact, which has never been forgotten by those who viewed it at the time.

We watched that same coverage on the TV in our Bethesda living room. And when the cortege taking President Kennedy's casket to the Capitol passed through downtown Washington, five Forsters were among the mourners along Pennsylvania Avenue, witnessing the solemn parade.

Early in 1964, Cliff was reassigned to Japan as the Field Supervisor for all the centers throughout the country. We would live in Tokyo. He looked forward to working with Ambassador Reischauer and reaping the benefits of the good will built up in Japan during the Kennedy era. I selected a realtor who could rent and manage our house, started sorting which goods would remain in Washington storage and which would go with us, investigated school options for the children in Tokyo, and made inquiries about a teaching job for myself.

We were on the road again in May.

26

JAPAN, FROM OLYMPICS TO EXPO

W HEN WE RETURNED TO JAPAN in June of 1964, we found a changed ethos from the Japan we had experienced in Kyushu and the Kansai in the fifties. Tremendous strides had been made in recovery from the war, both physical and psychological. The Olympic Games were coming in October, and Japan was preparing to host the world. Superhighways ran through Tokyo and its sprawling suburbs and connected with Osaka. "Bullet trains" were sleek and efficient, cutting travel time between the key cities by two-thirds. New sports facilities designed by world-class architects were rising and multi-star hotels brought Japanese hospitality to new levels of worldly sophistication. Theaters and art galleries had been refurbished to showcase the highlights of Japanese art, old and new.

Tokyo would be our home for most of the sixties and into the new decade, from the summer before the Olympics until the opening of the World Expo in Osaka. Although the capitol was newly modern and thriving when we arrived, fortunately the traditional culture of Japan that had so appealed to us when we lived in the outlying areas was still available as well, as long as you knew how and where to get beyond the neon glitter.

Tokyo was new to us, but we found many old friends. The Nichols Family was back in Japan. Dick Moore had left his broadcasting job in San Francisco, joined the Foreign Service, and his family was also assigned to Tokyo. Barbara and Cliff now enthralled not just their spouses but their children—three each, of similar ages—with their memories of growing up in Manila. And they both marveled at how ironic it was, many years later, to be surrounded by and thoroughly enjoying the company of the Japanese.

We reconnected with Japanese friends, as well. Some from our earlier years here had, like Cliff, been promoted to more prestigious jobs in the capitol. Others who had represented their newspapers—like the Horikawas—or served at their embassy in Washington during the Kennedy era and became good friends were now back home in Tokyo. Here was the payoff for our years of studying the language and culture of this fascinating country and developing personal relationships with its people. Payoff for us personally and for the government that funded us.

We returned to Japan with our new Forster in tow. Doug was now almost three, Cindy seven, and Tom almost ten. Settling in should have been easy—coming back to a country we knew, friends we knew, a job that Cliff looked forward to, excellent schools for the children, and soon a position for me teaching history in an international school. But a smooth move wasn't to be. Embassy housing was in transition and we were moved into four homes in six weeks, shunted from one temporary space to another. In those six weeks we dealt with robbery, personal injury, and natural calamity. Our second home was broken into while we were away with the Nichols family for the weekend. While I was shopping for draperies to adorn home number three, Doug leaned against and collapsed a brass table in a furnishings store and was rushed to the hospital with two nearly severed fingers and a huge bump on his forehead. And a magnitude-7.5 earthquake struck as Cliff was en route for his first visit to the outlying USIS Centers.

The city of Niigata was badly shaken. A major highway bridge collapsed and several new apartment buildings were torn out of their foundations and laid on their sides. Cliff was due to arrive in Niigata that afternoon, but was delayed for a day by torrential rains in the north where he had to change trains. The USIS Center and center director's residence were a shambles of deshelved books and broken glass, and for several days the city had no water or electricity. Despite widespread destruction, only eighty-five lives were lost and the citizens immediately began cleaning and patching up the damage. Disaster was something they had learned to live with. A massive city fire had destroyed blocks of homes and stores a few years before, and paralyzing snows and landslides came every winter and spring.

As soon as the telephone lines were open to Niigata Ted Ashford, the center director, called USIS Tokyo. His first item of business was to report that all USIS staff members and their families were safe. The second item was: "Get Duke Ellington!" The Duke was in Japan on a concert tour and Ted, a jazz fan who had met Ellington, was determined to presume on their friendship to persuade the master musician to give a benefit performance in Tokyo, to raise relief funds for Niigata's earthquake victims.

Cliff and Walt Nichols, who was the cultural officer, scrambled to arrange the concert on very short notice. Ellington was scheduled to leave Tokyo in a few days and had only one free evening. Luck prevailed; the hall of choice was free of engagements, and free of charge, for a "Gala Duke Ellington Niigata Earthquake Concert." Every seat in the house was sold and the aisles were filled with Japanese teenagers stomping out the beat. The Mayor of Niigata came onstage at the end of the concert, teary-eyed, and presented Ellington with the key to his city.

After those first hectic weeks, we finally found refuge in a permanent home in a Japanese neighborhood at the southern entrance to Tokyo. This area, with houses and stores built many years earlier, had escaped the wartime fire bombing. Ours was a compact, European-style house with a hillside garden and one Japanese-style room. Part of an earlier residence, that room had been preserved because it once was a tearoom where the founders of modern Japan met to discuss politics. We were told that in this room the Japanese drafted their terms for the Treaty of Shimonoseki, which ended the 1895 war between Japan and China. The terms of that treaty gave Japan a foothold in Taiwan and parts of the Asian mainland, their first steps towards an overseas empire.

The day we moved in and unpacked our household shipment from the States, Tom took off to explore the neighborhood. Within an hour he had located stores where he could buy candy and Japanese comic books, met the son of the local shoemaker, and brought the boy home to introduce him. With delight, Tom told us that the neighborhood Shinto shrine festival would take place that weekend and he had been invited to join the local children in carrying a small portable shrine from house to house for annual airing of the gods and blessing of the homes. The Japanese language that had been so fluent at age three but not used during the intervening six years had obviously been resurrected, since the shoemaker's son, the local merchants, and the shrine officials did not speak English.

On Friday decorative ropes and lanterns went up all over the neighborhood. A stage was erected on shrine grounds, and citizens were invited to step up and perform. The children went first: playing drums, singing unrehearsed songs, horsing around. Cliff and I heard the noise and went to see what was going on. Tom, Cindy, and Doug, all wearing summer kimonos, were in the center of all the action, on stage with the Japanese children. Offstage, when the adult performers took over, they clustered with their new friends. The next day they all followed the small shrine through the neighborhood, Tom in the lead. With a towel tied around his head, he was weaving down the street, shouldering one pole, in time with the chant: "Wasshoi! Wasshoi!"

While Cliff was picking up the reins of his new job, three members of the family were off to school in September. An international school for boys run with firm Catholic discipline was only a few blocks down the main street below our house. Tom was outfitted with the required grey slacks, blue blazer, and red tie and began a regime under the care of Christian Brothers from New York and Canada. Cindy started second grade at Nishimachi International School, and I began my professional career as a history teacher at the same institution. Doug, in the meantime, joined a play group with several other American preschoolers.

Throughout the summer, and right up to the last few days before the October 10 opening ceremony, Tokyo was torn up in preparation for the Olympics. Streets were widened and trees planted; athletic venues received finishing touches; signs in Japanese and English appeared on the streets and at entrances to the not-quite-finished subway stations. Miraculously all was ready on time, the city sparkled under bright autumn skies, and Japan was able to show the world that she was now a truly modern nation, a cultural and economic power of stature. As fate would have it, I was revisiting those times while writing this book, just as China was hosting the 2008 Olympics. I vividly recalled the mood of the Japanese before and during the Tokyo Olympics, how passionate they were about impressing the rest of the world with their national achievements. As were the Chinese forty-four years, later when they showcased the Olympics in Beijing.

By the winter holidays, we had settled into our new life, and Cliff and I were participating in the rituals of diplomacy. The most formal of these was on New Year's Day, when Japan's Emperor Hirohito and his family accepted respectful greetings from a series of distinguished guests who progressed through the Imperial Palace. The diplomatic corps was presented to their Majesties in order of seniority of the ambassador—the number of years in Japan—and, within each embassy, the rank of the officials and their wives. The protocol for this reception at high noon was very specific. Men wore striped pants and tails, an outfit few of the Americans owned. Cliff joined those who rented the costume from a department store; he didn't feel, or look, at ease, since the trousers were too tight and the coat sleeves too long. Ladies wore dresses—with long skirts, long sleeves, and high necks—and hats, no red (imperial color), white (mourning color in Asia), or black (mourning color in the West).

It was a thrill to be driven across the moat and to enter one of the buildings on the grounds of the imposing stone palace in the heart of Tokyo. This complex had been the center of political power in Japan since the seventeenth century. The reception was in a Victorian-style building and we were guided to a waiting room where clusters of diplomats milled around. There was an easel set up with a diagram of the reception hall. Using a pointer, an imperial chamberlain gave us instructions on how to present ourselves one couple at a time to the imperial family, who would be standing in a line along one side of a large hall. "X" on the diagram marked the spot where we should stop, bow, and curtsy.

Bowing was no problem for the men. This was part of the social culture in Japan; they just had to be sure the bow was deep enough to express sufficient respect. Curtsying was another story—at least for the average American woman. The U.S. wives had been summoned to the ambassador's residence by the embassy protocol officer for a curtsying training session.

When our names were called, Cliff and I slowly walked to the center of the hall. We faced the row of resplendent imperial majesties, the women in ball gowns and bejeweled, the men in their formal suits. We did our bow and curtsy, then—and this was the hard part—we backed up slowly towards the door on the other side of the hall and attempted a dignified exit. In the next room long tables were set with lacquer boxes containing a selection of New Year's delicacies and sake in porcelain cups decorated with the imperial chrysanthemum crest. Standing, we sampled the delicacies and took a sip of sake, then were urged to gather up box and cup as souvenirs and be on our way to make room for the next group of visitors.

Cliff was enjoying his expanded mandate overseeing all the cultural centers. USIS in Japan was a huge and multifaceted operation in those years. Eleven fully-staffed centers ran programs around the country and managed library and media facilities. In Tokyo there were separate information and cultural sections, which supported the field centers and worked with Japanese people and institutions in the capitol and elsewhere. American officers specialized in press, film, labor, women's activities, exhibits, books, publications, press translations (Japanese into English and English into Japanese), and programs for visiting American notables.

Each American worked with incredibly talented Japanese associates, local employees of the embassy. These men and women brought their wisdom about local needs and concerns—what would work in Japan and what wouldn't—to the table, served as institutional memory when the Americans were rotated in and out of Japan assignments, and contributed immeasurably to the success of the program. They became more than mentors and associates; they became cherished friends. They knew and appreciated the USIS mission, saw how it could create an important international dialogue, and devoted their professional careers to this cultural diplomacy.

Cliff worked with his Japanese associates on all facets of the program, as well as visiting the outlying centers regularly. At the same time he and fellow USIS officers—as is the case in all large embassies—worked closely with the ambassador and with colleagues in the political, economic, consular, and other sections of the embassy, assisting with drafts of major speeches and evaluating the impact of current events in Japan, the U.S., and elsewhere in the world.

My day job at Nishimachi School was a wonderful opportunity for intercultural learning, and would remain so for the next six years. The school was the brainchild of Tane Matsukata, the granddaughter of two founding fathers of modern Japan, one a samurai son who was a leader in finance and government, the other a rural mountain villager who moved to New York and established a world market for Japan's silk. Tane had grown up in a cosmopolitan household where the children had tutors in English, French, and the ways of the world. After the war, she established a school in her family home, at first to teach English to young Japanese children so they would have the skill as well as the will to work internationally for peace and understanding. Within a few years, American parents in Tokyo learned about the school and asked Tane to teach their children Japanese. Americans, they said, also needed to acquire the skill and the will. By the time I arrived in Tokyo the school went up to grade eight; it would top off at nine the next year. Those graduates would have the language facility to continue high school either in the Japanese system or one teaching in English. My good fortune was that Tane needed someone to design and teach a social studies/history curriculum for grades seven through nine.

The classes were small and the pupils were citizens of the world. Australia, Bulgaria, Canada, China, Czechoslovakia, Denmark, India, Iran, Israel, Japan, New Zealand, Sweden, the Soviet Union, the United Kingdom, and the United States were represented in my history, geography, and government classes. These students had much to teach each other, and their teacher.

Two of my most memorable students were Zdenek Hrdlicka and Masha Troyanovsky, son of the Czech ambassador and daughter of the ambassador from the USSR. They were elegant students: bright, curious, and highly motivated. I was using an American textbook for the world history class, a book that by its very nature espoused our nation's view of world politics. My challenge was to encourage mutual understanding and oversee lively discussion while maintaining the comfort and dignity of each youngster.

An extra bonus to this job was that Cliff and I got to know the parents as well as the students. When we attended the Prime Minister's annual garden party hosting the diplomatic corps, the Troyanovskys sought us out for a long conversation. U.S. Embassy political officers noticed—Ambassador Troyanovsky was a formidable diplomatic opponent, later to become a symbol of Cold War hostility at the United Nations—and later queried Cliff, "Just what were you and the Soviet ambassador talking about?"

"It was Nancy's conversation," Cliff assured his colleagues. "She was having an informal parent-teacher conference about one of her students."

My other job, as ever, was to help Cliff in his work of diplomacy. Although formal gatherings were always a highlight, informal dinner parties were much more our style. At our cozy home in the Japanese neighborhood we brought together many of the Japanese we had known on our earlier tours with their American counterparts. It was also a good place to become acquainted with new people active in Japan's cultural life: university professors, artists, musicians, journalists, government officials. Visiting American personages sent by USIA to Japan to lecture and confer with their opposite numbers gave us the perfect excuse for a party. In the informal setting of a private home, conversations were lively, meaningful, and relaxed.

Summers in Tokyo were long and hot—muggy hot—and it took a lot of imagination to keep children occupied between weekend trips to the mountains or beach. Plus they relied on their own imaginations. When we were in our first home Tom, Cindy, and Doug started building a tree house in our back yard, joyfully nailing boards onto branches of what was known in Japanese as a "monkey climbing tree." Our landlady, who lived next door, was horrified. "This tree is a national treasure," she told us. "And it is so dangerous for your children to be up in those branches." To lure them to a safer, less destructive site, she unlocked a musty storage area in the hillside underneath our driveway, aired it out, and turned it over to the trio to furnish as their special clubhouse.

The next summer Beanie Erickson, the son of an embassy political officer, organized a theatrical troupe. He had a script featuring an ancient Korean love story and decided to produce it using embassy children as actors and stage hands. This youngster, who would later go on to a theatrical career, had great powers of persuasion. He secured the use of the assembly hall at St. Mary's School (where he was a class ahead of Tom) for a month of rehearsals and a weekend of performances, the services of an embassy wife who had been a choir director back home as pianist and voice coach, the use of our garage for construction and storage of the scenery, and a loan of formal silk attire from the Korean Embassy as costumes. Doug shadowed Tom as part of the construction crew and Cindy had a part in the play. Singing her solo lament, "I remember when" as a nostalgic old man, our little girl brought the house down.

We eventually found refuge away from the muggy city. Tom McVeigh—an American accountant who had lived and would live for many more years in Tokyo—and his wife Maggie had bought a piece of land on a bluff overlooking Sagami Bay south of Tokyo. There they built a cottage for themselves and a guest house that they rented to friends. Tom was invited to spend a weekend with a schoolmate at the guest house; when he returned with glowing descriptions of this wonderful place and mentioned that the current renters were suddenly being transferred to Los Angeles, I got on the phone immediately. For the remainder of our time in Japan, the guest house would be ours for weekends, summer and winter, rain and shine. Over the New Year, when all Japan shut down for four days, we would spend a week. This is where Cliff started sorting out his family photos and created the scrapbooks I would thumb through with such fond memories and use as resource material four decades later.

Meanwhile, Cliff's work of keeping up international dialogue went on under all sorts of disguises. One smashing success, in September of 1965, was the Tokyo run of *Hello Dolly,* starring Mary Martin. The show wowed everyone, bringing down the house with the final Martin number of "Harro Tokyo." The lady was a superstar, with star demands placed on the Cultural attaché's office. Reservations at the posh Okura Hotel wouldn't do; they must be switched to the more famous old Imperial Hotel, Frank Lloyd Wright's masterpiece that had survived the 1923 earthquake and 1945 bombing, only to succumb to the wreckers' ball in 1970. To travel around town, the star would only ride in a silver Rolls Royce. A drive, in Tokyo traffic, was not our idea of relaxation; however it turned out that the owner of the Imperial Hotel had just such a car and would be delighted to turn it over to Miss Martin.

Posted again to Japan, Cliff began to organize family photos and write about his memories during weekends at a rented beach house.

Two months later, Cliff was promoted to Deputy Public Affairs Officer for USIS Japan. Where before he had been in charge of USIS Centers throughout the country, he was now second in charge of all cultural and information activities in the huge USIS operation—press, TV, motion picture, labor, Fulbright, and leader-exchange grants. This bound him more closely to his desk and cut out regular trips to the centers, but it was rewarding to have more command responsibility and there was plenty to keep him busy in Tokyo. The title put him higher on the diplomatic list and generated more ceremonial invitations, like the one, the following year, to the Imperial Duck Netting Party.

It was a gorgeous December day, sunny and mild. The hunting party totaled forty people—eight couples from the American Embassy plus Saudi Arabian, Indonesian, Swiss, Venezuelan, Finnish, Moroccan, and Vietnamese diplomats, the Papal Nuncio, and several imperial chamberlains. Of four teams, ours included the only member of the Imperial family present, Princess Chichibu, the emperor's sister-in-law, a gracious, relaxed woman whose faultless English reflected childhood days in the U.S. and U.K.

We were taken two teams at a time to special canals where decoy ducks would lead some of the 16,000 live ducks wintering in the nearby game preserve into the diplomatic snare. Each of us was given a net, three feet in diameter, at the end of a nine-foot polished-bamboo pole. We waited behind an artificial hill that hid us from the target canal (one of four on our morning agenda). The game keeper, in ancient regalia, gave a signal and our team tiptoed at a trot through the grass, nets lowered to keep us hidden from the ducks. Two teams converged from opposite directions and confronted each other—and the startled ducks—across the narrow water. The ducks flew up, a few were caught in poised nets, and the first round was over.

By the end of the morning, a few of us—Cliff and I not included—had been awarded feathers for having netted ducks, a disgruntled diplomatic wife had insisted the Vietnamese ambassador had cheated, and the Finnish ambassador, who had been coming to these affairs for four years and never caught a duck, had thrown down his net and refused to continue. Returning to our starting point, we enjoyed a magnificent lunch of soy-marinated duck barbeque, and were then encouraged to participate in post-lunch badminton, ping pong, or conversation. I was talking with Princess Chichibu when I felt something bounce off my shoe. She swooped down before I had a chance to react, scooping up the button that had fallen off her suit.

"Mustn't lose this," she said, "because I would have to buy a whole new set of buttons!"

Our children grew up quickly during their time in Tokyo. When we traveled to America for home leave in the summer of 1967, Tom was nearly as tall as his mother, Cindy had honed her natural talent as a storyteller, and Doug had a year of kindergarten at Nishimachi under his belt. We traveled cross-country by car, found more of our roots as Americans, enjoyed time with family and friends, and visited the World's Fair in Montreal.

After returning from America, we moved into a larger house in Tokyo, embassy property designed for entertaining on a grander scale. Grander than we had anticipated. When the ambassador said he was unable to entertain the Los Angeles Philharmonic, Cliff was asked to please give the party. The full orchestra, conducted by Zubin Mehta, played at the symphony hall on the other side of Tokyo, a half-hour drive from our home under the best of circumstances. The concert was at seven-thirty. Musicians prefer not to eat (or drink) before they perform, so the party would begin around ten-thirty. We set the buffet table with sushi, turkeys and ham, and sandwich makings. We planned for two hundred, including the members of the orchestra, Japanese performers, and fans of classical music. Fortunately, it was a warm May night and we could open glass doors to the lawn and let guests spill outside. The musicians swarmed the buffet table and I saw a couple of men happily gnawing on turkey legs.

We had an extra bit of Americana drawn into the party. Also in town that week was Bozo the Clown and, to welcome another facet of American culture, Cliff invited him to come, too. He and Zubin Mehta tied as the most popular stars of the evening!

On the personal front, an auspicious turn of events took place at the end of the school year in 1968, when a husband-and-wife team who had been teaching at Nishimachi School—he doing junior-high science and she the sixth-grade class—decided to move to the States. Tane was traveling to the U.S. East Coast to seek their replacements. I had a suggestion. "I suppose it's nepotism, but my sister's an experienced grade-school teacher and her husband is trained to teach science. He's just finishing his military service outside Washington and they're looking for jobs." When

Entertaining was part of the job description for a husband-and-wife team. At a 1968 reception, we hosted Zubin Mehta (center), the Los Angeles Philharmonic, Japanese music lovers, and Bozo the Clown—a total of 200 guests.

Tane returned to Tokyo she said, "Nancy, I like your kind of nepotism." She had hired my sister Cindy (for whom our Cindy had been named) and her husband Jim, and they would live in the apartment on the third floor of the schoolhouse.

It was wonderful having the Hawkins in Tokyo, filling one of the gaps in our lives as international gypsies. I had a beloved sister and the children had an aunt and uncle with whom to celebrate birthdays and Christmas and share weekend adventures. With the birth of a Hawkins baby—Karen—my mother even came to visit, so we had a resident grandmother for a couple of weeks!

Daughter Cindy wasn't always so sure. The first year her aunt and uncle were in Tokyo, her aunt was her sixth-grade teacher. The next year, her mother was her history teacher and her uncle was her science teacher. The Hawkins had brought their Labrador retriever with them to Japan; "Even the school *dog* is related to me!" our daughter lamented.

As with all our assignments overseas, our lives were a lively blend of personal and professional, local and international, easy and challenging. In the late sixties, numerous challenges worked against USIS's job of keeping the dialogue open between Japan and the United States and fostering respect and understanding. Angry demonstrators took to the streets to protest the docking of American nuclear submarines in Japanese ports, to protest the terms of the U.S.-Japan Security Treaty (up for renewal), to protest against the war in Vietnam. On the university campuses, radical students harassed professors, burned papers, and occupied administrative offices. One Sunday a nationwide TV audience (including us) watched the battle between helmeted students and shield-bearing riot policemen for control over the main tower building at Tokyo University.

Before we arrived in Tokyo, a student had leapt over the wall surrounding the American Embassy and stabbed Ambassador Reischauer in the leg. Another time, Japanese students got inside an American Embassy apartment and unfurled from the roof a red banner with their protest message. When demonstrators threatened the embassy annex building, a small army of riot policemen made a barricade of streetcars and stopped the crowd. Tokyo's sidewalks had been originally paved with concrete blocks. The student rioters discovered that they could pry the blocks loose with crowbars and use them as ammunition against the police. So the metropolitan government took on the task of removing paving blocks throughout the city and replacing them with asphalt. The "demos" (Japanese word for demonstration) were often festive. Red banners flew from trucks in procession, people wore red armbands and neckerchiefs; sometimes they carried balloons, and rousing music was broadcast from loudspeakers.

A big boost to the binational dialogue came with the U.S. moon landing in July of 1969. The Japanese were caught up in the excitement and followed the adventure as avidly as we did. One of the local employees of the embassy, Sen Nishiyama, was exceptionally skilled as a simultaneous interpreter and became a Japanese media star at the time of the landing. He became the narrator on Japanese television throughout the coverage of the journey, the landing, and the aftermath. People recognizing him on the street gave him credit for being part of that epic event. He was "Mr. Moon."

In March of 1970, shortly before we were to leave Japan, the world's fair opened in Osaka—"Expo '70." USIS had had been responsible for the U.S. pavilion's theme and content, and served as in-country facilitators for the design, assembly, and management of the American exhibition. The hall was dug deep into the ground and was roofed over by a fiberglass "skin." One piece of material large enough to cover one and a half football fields, it was floated on a cushion of air over the display area. The construction supervisor explained, "This skin is basically the world's largest sail. A continuous stream of air will keep the skin aloft, like a giant balloon."

We visited Osaka during spring vacation. In three days, according to Cindy and Doug's countdown, we saw thirty-five pavilions. People! Crushes! Lines! One friend had three buttons ripped off her coat in the crunch of the lines at the Soviet pavilion. Police were announcing outside the U.S. Pavilion that the wait to get in was seven hours. The day we arrived, a woman tripped just as she was getting off a moving sidewalk, fell down, and those behind piled on top of her and each other. The nineteen-year-old attendant panicked, forgot the emergency stop button, and ran off for help. Forty-two people were injured, two critically, before the pileup ceased.

But what marvelous crowds! Old folks from the country were in tour groups, wearing kimonos, identified by paper hats or armbands, shuffling behind flag-bearing guides. This was a party for them, a window to the world from which they had been alienated during the thirties and forties Daily, about half a million people congregated in the space of a few city blocks. The wonder was that people actually could move about and there weren't more pileups and crushes.

The design of the U.S. pavilion was hailed as the most innovative of the fair. The sail-topped city was light and airy, exhibits following a maze-like course. We weren't aware of the presence of 7,000 bodies in that below-ground-level space. We entered to face a collection of photos by ten of the country's leading photographers, progressed through American paintings, Babe Ruth's locker (in the sports section), outlandish cars (including a bathtub on wheels), rocks picked up by our astronauts on their moon walk (the hit of the exhibition), sky divers, an exhibition of American folk art, and examples of modern American art.

One of my favorite moments was witnessing the encounter of an elderly Japanese lady and her grandson with a piece of work by Clause Oldenburg—a giant (15 feet in diameter) shiny orange ice bag, which pulsated and undulated. The pair was quizzically eyeing the ice bag, reading the sign on the wall, eyeing the "art" again, trying to comprehend. They couldn't, and stopped me. My Japanese vocabulary didn't include a word for ice bag, but I gestured and explained how you fill this thing with ice when you have a toothache and that helps the pain. *"Ahh...soo desu ka?"* Grandmother now understood the object, but couldn't fathom why it was displayed as art.

As our six-year, double tour in Tokyo was coming to an end, Cliff received his next assignment. He was to attend the Department of State's Senior Seminar in Washington for one year. This would be a sabbatical opportunity for immersion into contemporary Americana, in all its facets and in the company of twenty midcareer officers from a mixture of U.S. agencies.

This tour in Japan was neatly framed for us, with our entry as the country was preparing for the Olympics and exit during Expo. We had observed and been involved in the nation as it showed the world that it was an elegant and efficient modern nation during their 1964 coming-out party, as it consolidated that momentum in years following, and as in 1970 it hosted another world-class celebration. The difference in 1970 was that they no longer needed to sell Japan to the world; this party was a celebration for their own people to go out into the world as it was showcased in Osaka and to enjoy it for themselves.

We felt honored to have lived these pivotal years in a country toward which we both once felt such resistance, and fortunate that our children had spent so much of their childhoods in its rich embrace.

27

AMERICANIZATION

IT WAS GREAT TO RETURN to Washington, with our very own house to move into, our own furniture to be brought out of storage and arranged to reinstate this house as home, and with our former neighbors still there to become a part of our daily lives again. But first we stopped for family visits in California, Ohio, and New York.

In California we made a pilgrimage, as always when in the area, to check out the old campus at Stanford. What we saw shocked us. While we were watching the student protests on TV and in the streets in Tokyo, student protestors at our own university had smashed windows and painted graffiti on the walls of the historic sandstone buildings. This was a wake-up call for us, that we would face more challenges as parents in the U.S. than we had in Tokyo. There we had been relatively relaxed, knowing that our teenagers couldn't drive, that public transportation was ubiquitous and safe, and that all the trains stopped at midnight—not too much opportunity for them to get into trouble, we believed. Here, it would be a different situation.

In Ohio, where my father had moved into a new career as a civilian with the Air Force at Wright-Patterson Field, leaving the family law office behind in Grand Rapids, a new bond formed between him and Cliff. Both now had U.S. Government top-security clearance and the two would retreat for man-to-man talks about "matters of national significance." It was a far cry from the day in 1948 when Roger Keeney expressed disdain at Cliff's potential job with the U.S. government. Cliff had tremendous respect for my father's intellectual prowess and Dad was immensely proud of Cliff's career accomplishments. They also had developed a genuine friendship.

Before Cliff reported for duty in Washington, we spent a week with my mother in a cottage she had purchased on a hillside overlooking her family's ancestral hometown of Woodstock, Vermont. At gatherings of the extended family clan, Cliff had another wake-up call. He was cornered by a posse of cousins who vehemently opposed U.S. involvement in the Vietnam War and accused him, as a government representative, of being one of the perpetrators. He tried to explain that while overseas it was his duty to follow government policy in public, he personally was very troubled by our involvement and like many of his colleagues was voicing his opinions in internal discussions. To these skeptical New Englanders, Cliff's arguments sounded like diplomatic doublespeak.

Another event during our Vermont visit was not on my agenda. Cliff and the children heard an announcement over the Dartmouth College radio station that a student couple was moving and seeking a loving home for their two dogs. Without revealing their mission, my family set off to spend the day in New Hampshire—and came back with "Cao" (an abbreviation of "Cacao" because of his milk-chocolate coat). I was less than thrilled, because I would be the lone adult driving the family from Woodstock to Bethesda while Cliff blithely flew ahead to assume his Washington duties. "You should be glad," Cindy said, "that we only took one of the dogs, not both."

We all were happy with Cao, who was a biological wonder and quickly became a beloved Forster, accompanying us and provoking many an adventure. His ancestry included collie, black Labrador, and Irish setter. He looked more setter than anything, with a lovely white collie bib and the shorter hair of a lab. Cao and Doug were special pals, sleeping together at night.

Cao joined the family in Washington, and would strain international relations in Israel.

As we settled into Washington, Doug was in elementary school, Cindy in junior high, and Tom about to enter eleventh grade. The Senior Seminar lasted only a year, after which we would possibly move on to a post where Tom would spend only his senior year in a school of unknown quality. For that reason—plus the fact that a little space between opinionated parents and son might be healthy, given the intergenerational tensions of this time—we enrolled Tom in boarding school in Andover, Massachusetts.

It was too late for me to land a full-time teaching job, but I was glad to have time to organize the house and be a presence for Cindy and Doug as they made the switch from the family atmosphere at Nishimachi to the very different lifestyle of large public schools. I would do several stints during the year as a substitute teacher, one for a full marking period. And Cliff would become immersed in his Senior Seminar.

The Army has one; the Air Force and Navy each have one; the Department of State has one too—an institutionalized year of professional education. A year pondering the words of distinguished lecturers, considering contemporary political and strategic problems away from the pressures of daily deadlines, a year of refueling. The "students" are senior officers and at each of the military service colleges as well as at the Senior Seminar of the State Department a few slots are reserved for career officers outside the sponsoring service. Much of the education goes on in informal discussions when soldier, sailor, diplomat, and employees of USAID, USIA, and CIA express their opinions and share experiences. The thing that sets the State Department Senior Seminar apart from the others has been its relatively small class size, in the twenties instead of a hundred or more. That means participants, and their wives, all get to know each other well during the course of the year. It also means that the group can be taken on "field trips" with relative ease. A core part of the State Department year is introducing Foreign Service officers to the many faces of their own country, which many people like Cliff Forster may not have experienced in recent years.

Cliff was assigned to the class of 1970-71. Ambassador Matthews, director of the seminar, pulled in an eclectic array of speakers from university presidents to political commentators to urban planners. He scheduled excursions to industrial centers in North Carolina and Texas, to military command posts, to New York City, to Chicago, to the Pacific Coast, and to the North Slope of Alaska. The "seminarians" were briefed by mayors, harangued by university students (during this time of vehement student protests against the Vietnam War), taken along on night patrol by Chicago cops, shown parachute drills and a nuclear submarine.

In the spring each was given time and travel money to do the research project of his dreams, any subject and any place as long as it was not a post where he had served recently and could be justified as informing him for future service.

These were the years when "trilateral" dialogue between the United States, European nations, and Japan was just coming into fashion. Cliff was interested in the strategic studies institutes, the "think tanks" of Europe and the men who did the studies and the thinking. He knew the think-tank men in Japan; his goal was to meet their counterparts in Europe. Here was his project. He visited institutes in England, Sweden, Norway, Germany, France, Switzerland, and Yugoslavia. He met the scholars and commentators who were discussing and writing about international problems and would welcome an opportunity to express their concerns and get to know their colleagues in Japan. Cliff came home exhausted from trying to cover too much territory in too short a time, but he had opened up a new channel of communication. This he made use of again and again in the coming years. Cliff took great pride in introducing the Europeans he had met to the Japanese they sought and in seeing Americans, Europeans, and Japanese working jointly to pinpoint and seek solutions for the problems they shared as industrialized, urbanized societies.

I was able to attend many of the Senior Seminar lectures and joined Cliff for evening gatherings with his classmates. I would have loved to accompany him on his excursions, but Cindy and Doug needed me at home. Doug was pretty well acclimatized, but it was a difficult year for Cindy. Accustomed to a close-knit group of international friends who were eager and competitive students, constant student-teacher interaction, and thought-provoking assignments, Cindy found her textbook-driven, slow-paced classes frustrating. And missed her friends.

The Washington assignment was only for the duration of the Seminar, so we were transients in our own neighborhood. We knew we would not return to Japan right away and assumed Cliff would not be trained in a new language, but that left open a lot of possibilities. We were sitting in the living room before dinner one evening when Cliff told us we might go to Israel. I looked over at Cindy, who was doing something strange with her feet. "What *are* you doing, Cindy?" I asked.

"Curling my toes!"

"What?"

"I always curl my toes when I want something very, very much!"

Her efforts coalesced with the Agency's decision, and when school was out we were en route to Tel Aviv.

28

PAST AND PRESENT IN ISRAEL

W E LIVED AT A "FAST FORWARD" PACE during our two years in
Israel. Conversations with Israelis were intense, meaningful,
rarely casual. Everyone had a story to tell. Cliff's job as the
public affairs officer for the embassy, managing the entire USIS operation and serving as embassy spokesman, was challenging and all of us
lived with the daily tensions of a volatile political situation. Demanding
and intense, but exhilarating. And when we were "off duty," there was
so much to explore. Cliff, Cindy, and I loved the drama of history and
Doug, always good-natured, would grab Cao and join in whatever was
the adventure of the day. Tom, when he was on vacation from Andover,
roamed the streets of Jerusalem and participated in archaeological exca-
vation at Tel Gezer.

There were approximately one-fourth as many people in all of
Israel—a country about the size of New Jersey—as there were in the
city of Tokyo. Yet, as we traveled around Israel, we felt more population pressure than we ever knew in Asia. We decided it was because we
were constantly engulfed by generations of history. Everywhere, we were
in the company of men and women of antiquity, the Middle Ages, and

more recent centuries—all at the same time. We walked with the heroes
and anonymous masses whose exploits were recorded in the *Bible*; in the
histories of Roman, Crusader, Turkish, and British overlords; and in the
accounts of contemporary Jewish writers. Our two years in Israel were for
all five of us a heady meeting with story and history. There was so much
to learn. We had never specifically studied the Middle East. People and
events we had known vaguely came to life as we scuffed our shoes in the
earth and picnicked in the ruins of castles and ancient cities. And, while
we were finding roots, we were meeting the vital, passionate, demanding
men and women of modern Israel.

We arrived a few days before the Fourth of July, 1971, and Cliff and
I attended the customary embassy celebration of our national birthday.
The reception for some five hundred people spread across the lawn of
Ambassador Walworth Barbour's seaside residence and we were to meet
many of his guests that day. The ambassador presented us to the prime
minister, mentioning that we had just arrived. Wearing a long green
gown, chain smoking, and drinking Scotch whiskey, Golda Meir greeted
us in her husky voice: "Welcome to Israel! You see that Israelis come to
your party!"

Indeed, they did: Defense Minister Moshe Dayan, statesman-author
Abba Eban, the director of Israel's National Theater, the London stage
star of *Fiddler on the Roof*. The French press correspondent remarked as he
looked across Ambassador Barbour's lawn: "Right here you could hold
a cabinet meeting, a parliament meeting, and a meeting of the national
defense headquarters."

Our new home was a U.S. government-designed structure in the
town of Kfar Shmaryahu north of Tel Aviv. Several years earlier the ambassador had been asked to select land on which embassy housing could
be built, and he did it in a very interesting way. He had his driver take
him on a ride through new suburbs, looking for vacant lots. Wanting to
avoid the strictures of compound living for his staff, Walworth Barbour
chose a lot here, one there, each part of a neighborhood. We were very
grateful for this; our neighbors were to become fast friends and it was the
proximity that brought us together.

Across the street were the Simons. Yohanan was one of Israel's top artists, producing paintings and prints that exploded into vivid colors and

lively forms. Finny, his wife, was a leading fashion designer. They had a large family between them—children of former marriages and cousins, nieces, and nephews near and far—and they reached out lovingly to our children. Finny decided that Cindy had a sense of fashion tucked away in her heart and started to teach her tricks of design and color. When Cindy volunteered to create seventy-eight medieval costumes for the musical *Once upon a Mattress,* which was being produced by the American International School, Finny took her shopping for fabric and showed her how to convert her rough sketches into patterns then cut out the pieces.

Cao became part of the neighborhood. And he led Cliff, the professional communicator, into several unplanned encounters. Soon after we arrived in Israel, Cliff set off on the Sabbath to try his bicycle on the roads leading to the beach. Cao ran loose alongside, a welcome stretching of those big dog limbs and muscles. They were a happy pair, a man and his dog—until Cao spotted a cat. The cat fled, straight through a back yard where a large family picnic was underway. The cat skirted around chairs and under tables. The dog followed, paw print for paw print, and where the smaller animal had skirted under the furniture the big one sent a food-laden table flying. Cliff cycled on past the scene of mayhem, pretending that he had no acquaintance with the animal that kept circling back to him for a word of greeting and approval. This was just the first Cao adventure in Israel.

We tried to keep Cao contained in our yard, which was fenced in. But, with all of us at school or work on weekdays (I began teaching at an Israeli high school near the Gaza Strip), he jumped over the fence. Cliff built it higher and Cao jumped higher, running the two blocks down the street to join the children at the International School. When we confined him on the upstairs porch, he jumped to the first floor roof, then down and over the fence to freedom. He would find Doug in his classroom, and curl up in a corner. Finally Doug's teacher said, "Let's make Cao a member of our class," and put the dog's name on the fifth-grade attendance list. We gave up trying to confine the dog to an empty home.

The American Embassy in Tel Aviv was a twenty- to thirty-minute drive from our house. From his second-floor office Cliff looked straight out to sea. Downstairs was the center library and auditorium, so the entire USIS Tel Aviv operation was close at hand. Another American Center was in Jerusalem on the second floor of a new building in the middle of town. Cliff would work with Israelis in both cities. He started out with a round of calls on newspaper men in Tel Aviv and visited the university; then he continued to Jerusalem, making calls at the Foreign Ministry and Hebrew University, and met more press and television people. It took ninety minutes to drive between the two cities and we would make that trip often. The trip was a harrowing mix of heavy traffic and aggressive drivers, but we loved "going up" to Jerusalem, and the beauty of that city crowning the Judean Hills never failed to excite us and make us glad we had fought the traffic.

Working with his Israeli staff was a new adventure for Cliff. They had come from Austria, Germany, Hungary, Shanghai, Syria, Yemen, as well as the land of Israel, and each had strong opinions. Cliff soon understood why Golda Meir had once said, "Israel is an impossible country to govern because every Israeli thinks he can do it better than the Prime Minister;" and Zubin Mehta, who was a visiting conductor for the Israel Philharmonic, echoed her saying, "Every musician in this orchestra thinks he's the conductor." At USIS staff meetings each member expressed his or her opinion, each at the same time. But their messages got through, educating Cliff in the ways of Israel, and his messages as public affairs officer were received with respect and affection.

While Cliff was learning to manage his outspoken staff, I was dealing with hair-raising traffic on the road to my teaching job at the Mollie Goodman Academic High School. This was a residential enclave, on the campus of an Israeli high school, for English-speaking children who were sent by their Jewish parents to experience Israel for a year. About twenty each were in grades ten, eleven, and twelve and were following the New York State curriculum. A few weeks before the academic year, the school still sought a history teacher and, even though I made it clear to the principal that I was brand new to the country and as a gentile might not be the kind of instructor the sending parents had in mind, I was hired to fill their academic gap. After experiencing an hour and a half on the two-lane highway that shuttled cargo between Red Sea and Mediterranean ports as I drove there for the interview—with truck drivers passing without concern for oncoming traffic—I made a deal. I would take the job, but only if I could come just two days a week and teach double periods. That year of teaching was a different kind of exposure to life in Israel, working with children from the Diaspora, complying with the New York State standards for history, geography, and government courses but also learning along with my students about the country where we were all temporary visitors together.

In the 1990 interview, Lew Schmidt asked Cliff, "What was the thrust of your program for Israel in those days?"

When we were there, Golda Meir was running the show and doing a very effective job of it with leaders like Moshe Dayan and Shimon Peres. Cairo was under blackout then, fearing attack from Israel, and Sadat was coming out with a strong anti-Israeli line. You certainly had the feeling that Israel was surrounded by hostile regimes, and that they needed some kind of support. I'd say at that time we were generally sympathetic to their problems. We—when I say we, I'm referring to those of us in USIS who were on the cutting edge, because we would continually be up against a very active and vocal Israeli media, people who felt that the U.S. did not fully understand the position they were in. This was when we were pressing them very hard on the U.S. "Rogers Plan" to try and work out some kind of adjustment in the Sinai and to avoid retaliatory raids in depth into Egypt and Lebanon. We felt raids would be counterproductive. Lebanon was not the major problem then; it was Egypt.

At times working in Israel became very intense. As the months went by, we could feel the Arab-Israeli tension building up fast. We were very close to some of this, both in Jerusalem and in northern Israel. There were strikes across the border from Lebanon. A family killed driving home after a Bar Mitzvah not too far from where we were traveling on the road caused great resentment in Israel. You could see and feel the Israelis steeling up. They were mad and they started striking back. They would justify their actions in our sessions. "You see? You see this? How do you deal with this? You have to strike, strike, strike." It was clearly a policy of "an eye for an eye and a tooth for a tooth."

This was when Bill Thompson, who served in USIS Tel Aviv as the cultural attaché, deployed a new kind of resource in the exercise of public diplomacy—Marx Brothers films. We could secure these through U.S. Embassy channels and Bill and his wife Barbara hosted many an evening in their living room screening the old movies, which the Israelis adored. Then we discovered that the flat roof to our house could be turned into an open-air theater and seat even larger audiences. Groucho Marx and his siblings did a great job for us, inserting humor into the binational conversations, lowering the decibel level so we could all enjoy time together as friends.

But by early 1972, after constant exposure to the Israeli points of view, Cliff felt a need to hear the other side of the story. He asked his bosses back in Washington to let him visit his USIS colleagues in Egypt, Lebanon, and Jordan and meet with some of their contacts. In exchange he wanted his counterparts there to visit Israel, also to experience opposing views up close. I accompanied Cliff on his trip and we both started out with clean passports—in those days an Israeli stamp in one's pages prohibited a visit to Arab countries. We played innocent as we crossed the borders, but once in the country our mission was known. The local public affairs officers hosted parties for us, explaining that this was a unique opportunity to meet with someone living in Israel.

In Egypt there were two parties for Cliff, one with editors and commentators from the media and the other with university scholars. At each the guests poured out their hearts, listed their grievances, and stated their dreams. These dreams were the same we were hearing from the Israelis: "All we want is to live secure in our homes and at peace with our neighbors." In Jordan, Cliff met with Palestinians, both Muslim and Christian, who attacked him verbally as if he were the Israeli enemy, demanding the return of their land. Soon after we returned to Israel, reciprocal visits and meetings were made by the colleagues serving in Arab countries. They were introduced to Israeli journalists and scholars to get firsthand impressions of their perceptions. Cliff believed this had been an important learning experience for all.

This was a gamble. I certainly felt it was worth trying and
it got off to a good start. Whether you're in Israel or one of

the Arab countries as an American Foreign Service officer, you sometimes find yourself taking on the coloration of the country where you serve if you're not careful. It's the old problem, rather like China when it went under, all the strong feeling among the Americans over what happened there in '49.

I just wanted to know how the others all viewed the Israelis and our policies there and in the Middle East in general. You can read about their reactions, but I wanted to know in person. I felt this would be an opportunity also for me to try and give them some idea of our positions on Israel and the Arab world as viewed from Tel Aviv. The whole idea was ultimately to arrange very selectively for Israelis, Palestinians, Jordanians, and Egyptians to meet informally at USIS-arranged programs.

However, by the time such informal programs seemed to be a real possibility, it was 1973 and the planned project was a casualty of the Yom Kippur War.

Not long after our trip to the neighboring countries, we scheduled a weekend ski trip. We hadn't counted on being in the midst of an Israeli retaliatory raid into Lebanon.

The highest point in Israel is the mountain slopes of Mount Hermon. Here, at the northeastern tip of the country, the borders of Israel, Lebanon, and Syria converge. Some of the Syrian land was occupied after the Six-Day War, giving Israel a high point overlooking the southern valleys of Lebanon and the valleys of the Upper Galilee. Occupation put Israeli soldiers on the hills from which Syrian guns had pounded the kibbutzim of the north, forcing a generation of Israel's kibbutz children to grow up sleeping in underground shelters.

Israeli policy has always been to make use of every inch of their small land and be a presence right up to their borders. This has the political purpose of, as Moshe Dayan once put it, "creating facts." In 1971 the government of Israel decided to build a ski lift in the Golan Heights. This would bring sportsmen right up to that northeastern frontier. We Forsters had never anticipated skiing in Israel, but by mistake our skis had been put into our shipment of household goods. So we were equipped and eager to try the slopes one February weekend.

Public diplomacy included tabulating 1972 election returns at the Tel Aviv
USIS Center, as illustrated by Israeli cartoonist Ze'Ev.

In August we had met a charming couple at Kfar Giladi, a kibbutz
near the slopes, and now we asked them to reserve for us two rooms in
their kibbutz guest house. We planned to leave early Friday morning. On
Wednesday and Thursday there had been border incidents; two civilians

were killed by rocket attack in one and three soldiers in another by Palestinian commandos who had crossed the border from Lebanon. Friday morning as we were loading the car, we heard on the radio that the ski slopes on Mount Hermon were closed indefinitely, due to "bad weather." We looked up at clear blue skies to see airplanes in formation flying north and guessed that the weather problem was politico-military.

Since we were all set for a holiday, and since we didn't have the nerve to telephone our friends at the kibbutz to say we didn't think it safe to spend the weekend in the area where they had lived and pursued "business as usual" within range of Syrian and Lebanese guns for years, we decided to proceed. We packed a picnic lunch and spent a leisurely day sightseeing en route. The wildflowers were blooming in the Lower Galilee: fields of red, purple, and yellow poppies, almond orchards in white bloom, lush green fields of wheat, all bathed in soft spring air. Our skis seemed terribly out of place.

As we drove north into the highlands, we met empty tank carriers coming back from the direction of the border, many of them, one after another. By now it was late afternoon and military traffic was heavy. But so was the civilian activity. Farmers were busily tending their fields; school children were walking home along the edge of the highway. When we got to Kfar Giladi, our friend Mr. Shalgi was surprised to hear of all the military traffic. He hadn't heard of anything in the way of military operations. However, he did say he was very sad about this week's incidents and felt they might be "terrorist gifts" for Mr. Jarring, who had arrived today as a United Nations mediator to discuss peace with the officials in Jerusalem.

"Please make yourselves comfortable and after dinner come have some coffee in our home," he told us. Doug mentioned that he'd probably stay in the guest house and read his stack of comic books.

"Why don't you come with me now so you'll know how to find us if you decide to come over later?" Mr. Shalgi suggested. It was a thoughtful gesture and, while showing Doug the way, he pointed out the entrance to the air-raid shelter.

When artillery started pounding at ten o'clock, Doug decided to join the coffee party. He dressed in record time and we heard his knock on the door just as the first round of shooting ended. "Don't be worried," said the Shalgis' son as the second round began. "When the shots keep repeating like now, they're ours. They"—the Arabs—"only set up one or two blasts then run back to their houses for cover."

So we continued our conversation about Nixon in Peking, discussed the current state of archaeology in the neighborhood, talked about the coming twenty-fifth birthday celebration for Israel and the two hundredth for the U.S. And the explosions continued. As Mr. Shalgi walked us home in bright moonlight, he pointed up the hill to Misgav Am. The lights on the hill just behind the kibbutz were brighter than usual because the cement factory was doing night work. "As long as their lights are on, we feel perfectly secure," he said. "That settlement is exactly on the border and many small children live there." We wondered where the Misgav Am residents looked for security and comfort.

The explosions were still continuing at dawn the next morning. The BBC and VOA broadcasts reported that there had been raids from Israel into Lebanon the previous day, and that now the action was over and the border was quiet. We couldn't quite agree with that! Just as we were discussing what we should do for the day, since skiing was surely out of the question, Mr. Shalgi appeared with news. "They've just announced it. The mountain is open for skiing. You can eat your breakfast and go."

We drove across the narrow valley, past a Syrian tank left as a 1948 war memorial, past the Banias Falls which Greek conquerors of Palestine in the days of Alexander the Great had dedicated to their god Pan. We drove up above the kibbutz of Kfar Szold, which used to send its children to bed in underground shelters, up the slopes of Mount Hermon. Here was the Crusader castle that was still off limits to civilians; here were the deserted former Syrian villages and their gun emplacements; here were signs pointing out "Air Raid Shelter," arrows directed to drainage ditches and under bridges that spanned gullies. It was a bleak landscape, barren of vegetation and habitation. As we reached the heights, we could look across Israel from the eastern frontier to the western and northern ones, and across the border to towns and a high-perched Crusader castle in Lebanon.

The made-in-Austria ski lift was running and the view from the moving chairs was superb. A few other skiers were on the hill, which was too icy for my skill level because snow had melted and frozen again—but here we were, skiing in Israel! And doing so while a battle was being fought in the valleys. As we skied down, we could see puffs of smoke and hear continuing explosions across the frontier. We watched planes come out of the south near the Sea of Galilee and fly across the border. When we stopped for lunch at the bottom of the lift, we stood in line for hot soup with Israeli soldiers in combat dress. The conjunction of sports and bombardments struck us as theater of the absurd.

The next day we visited some of the nature preserves in the area before heading home. As we strolled through the tropical vegetation around the headwaters of the Dan (one of three sources of the Jordan River) and climbed down to enjoy the full splendor of Banias Falls, the explosions continued. As we drove from one recreation site to another, we met groups of tired-looking soldiers and their heavy vehicles. They stopped by the road in clusters, munching sandwiches, and they ran into tourist canteens to pick up ice-cream bars. Road-building trucks from the cement plants at Kfar Giladi and Misgav Am were going up the road that crossed into Lebanon. They didn't even pause at the border, but went straight on across. Later in the week, newspapers reported that Israelis were carving out a road in Lebanon to cross the valley where the terrorists had been operating.

"Israelis don't like to do this," Mr. Shalgi had said with sadness during the artillery fire on Friday night. "We like the Lebanese; they are our neighbors. But if they can't take care of the terrorists like King Hussein did in Jordan, we simply must go in and do the job for them."

Four months later, violence struck Israel from a very different source. We awoke to the news that Japanese gunmen had shot passengers at Lod International Airport. As Cliff told Lew Schmidt,

It was a surprise attack by three Japanese "Sekigun"—Red Army—members who had been trained in Lebanon by the Popular Front for the Liberation of Palestine, the PFLP. They opened fire indiscriminately on passengers after landing, while they were waiting for baggage in the terminal. The airport was like a battlefield with dead and dying, including women and children, everywhere. Those of us in Israel at the time will never forget the carnage. Many of the victims were Puerto Ricans coming on a pilgrimage to visit the Holy Land, many of them American citizens. In all twenty-six—including sixteen Puerto Ricans—were killed and 166 wounded; prominent among the Israeli fatalities was Professor Aharon Katzir, a biophysicist of international repute whose brother became Israel's president the following year. Many of us in the embassy served as pallbearers the following day.

"Why Japanese?" was the first question the Israelis asked. Many came to Cliff with questions about radical politics in Japan, and he offered what insight he could. Two of the Japanese terrorists were killed in the airport battle. The third, Okamoto, was captured and tried and imprisoned in Israel. In years following, his name has been on the list of prisoners wanted by the Palestinians in return for the release of Israeli hostages. The Israelis refused to discuss such an exchange. At our embassy's Fourth of July reception the month following the Lod slaughter, Cliff and I were talking to the director of prisons. Okamoto, he told us, had asked for some books to read, including books about agriculture and the *Bible*.

We were in Israel at the time the gates had opened in the Soviet Union and Russian Jews were being allowed to leave for Israel. We met one of these at a concert at a small experimental theater in Tel Aviv. The manager was from a kibbutz we had visited and had invited us to an evening of songs based on Hebrew folk music. It was a superb show and we asked the Russian immigrant—a young jazz singer and one of the soloists—if he would like to come to a dinner party we were having the following week.

"Sure, if I can bring along my guitar and sing some songs." We were delighted. His idiomatic English, plus the jazz, blues, and folk music he knew were all self-taught, he told us. He learned words and music through broadcasts of the Voice of America into the USSR. He had been booked for a concert and lecture on American jazz in one of Moscow's largest halls to take place just after President Nixon visited. Posters advertising the event were up all over the city. Two days after the President and accompanying journalists left, down came the posters and he was told the lecture-concert would have to be postponed due to "technical difficulties." It never was rescheduled. He decided it was time to emigrate and now he was studying Hebrew and trying out his music on Israeli audiences.

The adjustments newcomers made to Israel and the roles they found for themselves in their new home were fascinating to investigate. When we had been in Beirut we were told of an Israeli professor, formerly American, living on a kibbutz in the Negev. "Look up the Baileys when you go south," the NBC correspondent in Lebanon had urged us. "This is a family really worth meeting."

Dr. Clinton Bailey had his Ph.D. from Columbia University in both Arabic and Hebrew literature. He had settled with his family in the closest place to the Sinai Peninsula where his children could still get first-class schooling, Sde Boker. He used that kibbutz as a jumping-off place for meetings with various Bedouin tribes. (At the time we were in Israel the Sinai, a trophy of the Six-Day War, was still in Israeli hands.) Bailey's project of the moment was to travel the Negev and Sinai wilderness areas, seeking out Bedouin in order to collect their poetry. What he wanted was the pre-Islamic poems that had been recited around campfires since time immemorial. The recitations had been going out of fashion in recent years. The Bedouin now carried transistor radios and preferred to tune in on Radio Cairo for their evening entertainment. Bailey wanted to record their poems before they were forgotten.

His technique was to present teenage boys with small tape recorders and ask for their help. "As you travel around, ask some of the old men if they have any favorite poems. Ask them to recite while you record them. I'll meet you again in a few weeks and if you can give me poems on these tapes, I'll supply you with fresh tapes and you get to keep the recorder."

We were with Dr. Bailey at one such meeting with part of his teenage network, at a crude shelter that served as an Arab coffee stand on the main road going south through the Sinai Peninsula. A few minutes after we arrived, three young Bedouin appeared fiddling with a tape recorder. They happily handed over their tapes and explained where they'd made each recording. Bailey had a special gift for them that day, some poetry he had recorded outside their territory, at El Arish over on the Egyptian side, and they rerecorded it with delight on their own machine. Not only was the professor gathering poems for his book, he was rekindling enthusiasm for a dying art in the young men of the desert.

The natives of Israel whom we met had a special bond with their land, a special pride in being of the land. Raffi Badhav, Cliff's driver, had been born and brought up in Jerusalem and had family roots that stretched west along North Africa to Spain and south along the Red Sea to Yemen. He had driven for Nelson Glueck when that American archaeologist was seeking lost cities in the Negev. He had gone to Cairo during the war as a soldier in the British army. He had lived in the first public housing built outside the old walls of Jerusalem, thanks to the gift of a British philanthropist. His father was buried on the Mount of Olives across from the site of Solomon's temple. Raffi made it his personal duty to introduce us to his hometown. His was a personalized tour like no guide ever concocted. Not only did Raffi know every place, he knew every body, and the tour took extra time as we stopped for greetings and introductions and a cup of coffee. He was a fantastic driver. The USIS librarian, Eva Weintraub, said he was for her the epitome of Marshall Mc-Cluhan's phrase, "The arm is the extension of the wheel." All four wheels were part of Raffi's arm and he took on the aggressive Israeli drivers with a sportsman's competitive zest.

Eva, who had survived the Nazi occupation of her native Hungary by using false Christian documents and hiding with her family in many different locations, was another very special guide for us into the heart of Israel's culture. Liberated by the Russian army on Christmas Eve in 1944, she was married in 1947 and soon after emigrated with her husband to Canada. In 1950 their journey ended in Israel where other family members had preceded them. "I was raised as a Zionist and it was natural for me to want to live in the land that we knew was our spiritual home," she said.

It was Eva who arranged for us to visit the kibbutzim where USIS would deliver books for their libraries. This was how we met the Shalgis at Kfar Giladi. As we toured the countryside with her books, she detoured us to visit Biblical sites, both Jewish and Christian, and Roman ruins,—introducing us to some of those layers of history which crowded the intellectual landscape of Israel. She took her role as a librarian as much more than custodianship—her mission was to get materials out of the institution and into the hands of appropriate people. Her regular "customers" were journalists, parliamentarians, university professors. One statement she made early after we arrived has stayed with us. Her dream, she said, was one day to be free to cross Israel's borders and meet her fellow USIS librarians in the Arab countries. "We have so much in common. They've been reading the same American books I have and they share the same USIS cultural mission." We were in Tokyo years later when we learned that Prime Minister Sadat of Egypt had gone to Israel. "Maybe," we said to each other, "Eva Weintraub's dream will be realized and one day soon she will meet the USIS librarian from Cairo!"

But in the present blood was being shed and dreams of peaceful co-existence seemed very remote. Perhaps the most pivotal event during our time in Israel took place on September 5, 1972, when eleven members of the Israeli Olympic team were killed by Palestine Liberation Organization (PLO) terrorists in what came to be known as the Munich Massacre. As Cliff told Lew,

That had a devastating effect on the Israelis and we saw them striking back. Over a number of years the perpetrators were relentlessly hunted down and killed. After Munich there was the capture of the Sabena plane, with Israelis aboard, by the Palestinians, right outside of Tel Aviv on the Lod Airport tarmac. Dayan personally led the commandos who rescued the passengers. Israelis were beginning to retaliate in force each time, and the policy made sense to them since these strikes were increasing.

Because of the tensions building up, we were cautioning them to avoid overkill, pointing out that our retaliation raids in Vietnam were often counterproductive. We urged them to work out some kind of solution with the Palestinians, the "Land for Peace" idea. But the Israelis were not prepared to buy this.

I even arranged for a number of leading Israeli journalists to go as a team around the U.S. to get some idea of the feeling that was building up in the U.S. even then about some of the Israeli intransigence. I don't know whether it resulted in much, because they felt they were beleaguered and that we had no conception of the real problem—survival. But at least they had a chance to have face-to-face talks with editors outside of Washington. So many of those Israeli journalists were tied in with the Washington scene. They had not gone around the country previously to get a better idea of American public opinion, and it was both educational and disturbing for them.

For our second year in Israel, I took a position teaching history at the American School in the Kfar Shmaryahu neighborhood of Tel Aviv. Once again, Cindy was a student at the school where her mother taught. Unique to the school was its bomb shelter; part of it had been turned into a lounge for the high-school students—the only place on campus where smoking was allowed—and part was used for overflow classes. Cindy did her year of American history in the bomb shelter. I learned quickly not to ask my grade-twelve students, many of whom were Israelis, what their post-graduation plans were. All the Israelis—girls as well as boys— would be going into the military. And when these alumni came back to visit their school, they often were dressed in military uniform with Uzi rifles slung over their shoulders.

One afternoon early in 1973, *Time* magazine's bureau chief dropped in to see Cliff at the embassy in Tel Aviv. His home was in Jerusalem on the via Dolorosa in the walled city—at the First Station of the Cross in the traditional Good Friday procession. Marsh Clark had been temporarily assigned to Ireland to cover events there and, knowing Cliff often went to Jerusalem to do his USIS business, he wondered if we would like to take over his apartment while he was gone.

Of course we would!

The upstairs apartment was part of a large complex of rooms that were owned by the "Bukhara Sheikh"—an Arab lawyer whose parents had come from Bukhara in Central Asia. At the spot where Pontius Pilate reportedly washed his hands, said "Ecce Homo" (I give you the man), and turned Jesus over to the mob, we found a tiny alley and entered the first door on the left. Arched windows and domed ceilings made each room in that second-floor apartment a magical place. Doors opened onto porches and rooftop patios with views extending across the bubble-shaped domes of the bazaar and the spires and minarets of various religious enclaves. In one direction we looked towards the Christian Quarter with its Church of the Holy Sepulchre, and beyond that to the walled-in city-within-the-city that was the Armenian Quarter. We were in the Arab Quarter. The

Jewish Quarter in the fourth quadrant of the old city was hidden from view by the Arab mosques which crown the Temple Mount, as Israelis called it—Haram al Sharif to the Arabs.

This was the focal point of historic and religious traditions which were central to all three of the faiths that had sprung from the Middle East. Tradition pinpointed the Mount as the spot where Abraham, in the ultimate act of obedience to his God, prepared to sacrifice his first-born son, Isaac. Almost a thousand years later, when King David established his capitol at Jerusalem, he bought the rocky summit from a farmer who had used it to thresh his grain. David's son Solomon, seeking a place to house the scriptures and ceremonial objects that the Jews had carried during their wanderings through the desert, chose the Mount. On that hilltop he built his magnificent Temple, the showplace and spiritual home of the Jews. His temple was destroyed during subsequent centuries of imperial strife and conquest. Another great builder, King Herod, ruling as a Roman satrap had built a new temple on the foundations of the original one. This was the site of Jewish pilgrimage at festival time.

When later Roman rulers became impatient with the religious fervor of the Jews (Rome saw it as political rebellion), they destroyed the Temple and dispersed the people. The treasures were looted, the buildings were torn down, and nothing remained but the ruble and fragments of the western wall of the compound. The Western Wall through the centuries of Diaspora remained the emotional homeland of the Jews who intoned the phrase "Next Year, in Jerusalem!" at the close of their Passover celebrations. During the Diaspora it had been labeled the "Wailing Wall"—a focal point for lament and the longing of exiled Jews to return to their homeland.

According to the *New Testament,* it was during the season of Passover that Jesus and his disciples came triumphantly into Jerusalem, initiating a week of events that was to culminate in the death and resurrection of the man called Christ. At the northern end of the Temple compound was the Antonia Fortress (named so by Herod in honor of his friend, Mark Antony). It was here that the trial, condemnation, and imprisonment of Jesus are believed to have taken place, making this a deeply significant place to Christians.

During Holy Week of 1973, we were able to sublet an apartment in Jerusalem's walled city that incorporated the Ecce Homo Arch on the Via Dolorosa.

Jerusalem had also become a holy city to the Muslims, ranking in sanctity only after Mecca and Medina. The lore of the life of Mohammed told of a Night Journey which the Prophet had made to Jerusalem. He rode through the sky on his white horse, Buraq, came to the rock revered as the sacrificial altar of Abraham, and from that rock ascended into heaven. The Muslims built a magnificent golden-domed shrine above the rock. Their Mosque of Omar ("Dome of the Rock") dominates the Jerusalem skyline and, within the building, visitors are shown the footprint made by Buraq's hoof when he leapt skyward and a cave that was created when the Mount started to follow Mohammed to heaven (the Mount was restrained by the hand of the Angel Gabriel holding it back). At the other end of the Mount, the Al Aqsa Mosque was built for prayers and Friday services. During the Crusader era this became a palace for the Latin Kings of Jerusalem and the cross replaced the crescent on the gold dome of Omar and the silver one of Al Aqsa. When Saladin defeated the Crusaders in 1187, the crescent returned and the compound was reinstated as a principal Islamic shrine.

Thus the faiths converge and compete for the right to pray and to police. The Clarks' apartment was across from a French Catholic convent that had been built over the paved courtyard of the Antonia Fortress. Walled into the church and extending over the street into our apartment as a room was the Ecce Homo Arch. This had been used by the Sheikh as his library until many of his books were damaged by bullets during the battle for Jerusalem in the Six-Day War. The Clarks used it for storage and as a place to view Christian parades when they passed underneath the arch on the Via Dolorosa.

Next door was a mosque and an Arab boys' school. A minaret in the schoolyard broadcast the muezzin's call to prayer before dawn and at four other times daily. It would be followed by the tolling of church bells at the Little Sisters of Sion convent; other belfry and minaret calls echoed each other throughout the walled city.

We stayed in the apartment during Holy Week of 1973. It was spring vacation so we school people were free and Cliff reversed his usual travel, using Jerusalem as headquarters and going back to Tel Aviv a couple of times. On Good Friday we played host to Jerusalem friends, both Jewish and Arab, and embassy colleagues. We watched from our roof as groups of pilgrims gathered by the Arab school. At about 8:00 a.m. the first group—of Germans—carried a large cross and stopped at each of the stations on the Via Dolorosa to say prayers and sing hymns. Later, several French groups led by parish priests carrying transistor microphones came out of the convent. The largest group of pilgrims assembled and began marching at 11:00. This was made up of Jerusalem residents. Arab Boy Scouts led the way and separated the various components of the group. The Latin Patriarch of Jerusalem, with an honor guard in a Turkish dragoon's costume, was in the forefront. Other groups from many nations made the solemn pilgrimage. One bore a sign saying they had come from Poland.

On our Easter Sunday we visited the Church of the Holy Sepulchre. Here we were swept into passionate crowds circumnavigating the Chapel of the Tomb in the wake of the gloriously robed and bejeweled hierarchy of the Orthodox clergy. Children in bright dresses and smart suits carried woven palm baskets of spring flowers, and multitudes of elderly Greek women in black were in the crowd. On the Greek calendar, the holidays came a week later than the Roman one and this, our Easter Day, was Palm Sunday for the Orthodox Church. Many of the multitude had made the trip in chartered ships from Cyprus and Greece for the holy days.

The night before, on Easter Eve, we were summoned to another style of celebration. We were eating dinner in the apartment when the owner of the nearby Arab camera shop came running upstairs and urged us away from the table. "Hurry! Hurry! Come and see the festival fire in the street!" A group carrying candles had gathered around a small fire under our Ecce Homo Arch and before we knew what was happening we were pulled along with the group into the convent church for a candlelit service in French. It was a beautiful event that took us back to the Middle Ages. Ancient chants, nuns and monks in their robes, the flicker of candlelight and shadow, the massive stone walls of the chapter that incorporated the other end of "our" arch.

Our dog Cao was the cause of yet another kind of cross-cultural encounter. One morning, following a loud knocking at the door to the apartment, a representative of our landlord the Sheikh delivered a message: "Your dog has defiled our neighborhood! He has been running loose all over the rooftops of Jerusalem! The Sheikh demands the attendance of Mr. and Mrs. Forster in his apartment at six this evening!" Indeed, Cao had escaped our surveillance and had a glorious time bouncing from bubble to bubble across the neighborhood roofs, leaving his calling card in several places. We spent the rest of the day agonizing over the encounter we faced downstairs.

When we entered the Sheikh's domain, we found ourselves in a long corridor with chairs lined up on against the walls, stern-looking men on one side and stern women on the other. The Sheikh was seated at the end and Cliff and I were ushered to chairs on his right and left. Stern, yes, upset, yes, but our hosts proceeded with the formalities of Arab hospitality before getting to the matter at hand. They began with flowery greetings and inquiries about our health and what brought us to this city. Cliff was well versed in such formalities, having had years of practice dealing with the social protocols of Japan. After he told of his years as the son of the head of the Red Cross in the Philippines, his internment in a civilian prisoner of war camp during World War II, and his subsequent determination to follow a career where dialogue might replace warfare, the tension of the meeting melted. The Sheikh stood up and invited us into his living room, called for coffee and sweets to be served, asked a son to bring out their scrapbooks, and entertained us with old photos. Members of the family clustered around, telling their bits of the story, their journey from Central Asia to Jerusalem. Two hours later we parted with friendly smiles, clasped hands, and a gentle plea to please keep our dog off the rooftops.

Just a few weeks before we left for home leave in 1973, Cliff planned a schedule of interviews for an American journalist who had written many thoughtful and compassionate stories from the capital cities of the Middle East. But Georgie Anne Geyer had never been to Israel. She had established close friendships with a number of Palestinian leaders and was outraged by the recent killing of one of these leaders in Beirut. The Palestinian spokesman had been target of an Israeli commando raid into Lebanon, the kind of quick strike that was so often Israel's response to an incident caused by Palestinian guerillas crossing into Israel. The Israelis had hit their target in downtown Beirut and vanished as quickly as they came, leaving one casualty.

An Israeli soldier had been killed in this raid, as well. He was the son of friends of ours—residents of a kibbutz in the Negev—and had been chosen for this raid because of his scholarly interest in Arabian culture and because of his fluency in Arabic. This young man had been known for his understanding of the Arab point of view and had worked to improve the lot of Arabs living in Israel.

Cliff sent Gigi Geyer to Kibbutz Shoval to interview the parents of the dead soldier. She found no bitterness there. She found a quiet and firm strength, a pride that went to the marrow of the bones, and a deep sorrow lamenting the fact that energies and lives were diverted into war. "Our son was a very good man. He would never kill anyone. He was a man of the land and a man of peace trying to build a new society in this community where he was born and grew up. He didn't want to be a soldier. But when he was called to serve he knew he had to go. There was no choice."

The journalist said this was the most troubling interview she ever conducted. She had just visited the parents of the dead Palestinian. Their words were almost identical to those of the Israeli parents. The insistent

futility of the conflict, the kinship of the antagonists, the tragic flaw in
the "land of milk and honey…"

Cliff summed up his Israeli experience to Lew:

It was, overall, the kind of experience that you never forget
because it's so intense and you meet so many outstanding people on both sides of the issues, whether you agree or disagree
with what they're doing and saying. Most of them, including
the media people and many of the scholars, feel the way we do
about current Israeli policy. Certainly the opportunity to be
there when Golda was running things was a special experience.

What has happened since then, I think, has been a disaster.
I was appalled by the changes in Israel with the settlements in
the West bank and the rigidity of Israel's new leadership after
Golda. I felt their policies were going to boomerang on them,
and I think they have.

Indeed, our two years in Israel were a heady mixture of history and
story—with the immediacy of seemingly unsolvable political dilemmas
always lurking around the edges. And in 2009 those dilemmas still remain to be solved.

29

WASHINGTON ENCORE

I N JUNE OF 1973 WE were in Paris on our way to America for two months, leaving our Tel Aviv home intact and expecting to return to Israel for a second tour. The phone call from Bill Payeff, Cliff's good friend and former colleague in the East Asia Division of USIA, changed our plans. "I'm going to head up the Near East and North Africa division and want you as my deputy," Bill announced. So instead of continuing our Middle East adventure, we moved back into our home in the Washington suburbs.

Israel was part of Cliff's area of responsibility, and we all were drawn in as the history of that country continued to unfold. On October 6, the Yom Kippur War broke out, and as Cliff later put it to Lew, "All hell broke lose." When Syria struck Israel on that day, the surprise was reminiscent of Pearl Harbor. Israel's neighbors knew what anyone with experience in the area knew—that the nation's full attention would be focused on family and soul on the Day of Atonement.

Cliff recalled:

They were all observing Yom Kippur, and the Syrians just came across their northern borders, as did the Egyptians with their tanks in the south. We immediately set up a Middle East task force. The Voice of America radio broadcasts played a terribly important role during that time and we were working to make sure that U.S. reaction, official and unofficial, was getting through to both sides. Particularly to the Arab states, since we felt it was important for them to know just where we stood. VOA was also an important channel to let the Soviets know where we stood, since they were actively supporting Syria. Kissinger, when he sent in the cargo flights to Israel, couldn't get any support at first from European allies. The planes had to come through the Azores to refuel en route. It was a dicey time and USIA's support in getting the message through to the different parties became very important.

So we went through that conflict with the task force, working with our State Department colleagues. I think we had on that task force, as on the Vietnam task force later, a very special kind of professional cooperation between the State and USIA officers. There was a lot of respect for the expertise that we could provide, the importance of the Voice in getting the word through, and an acceptance and understanding of what information tools we could use during this crisis to support our policy actions.

The Arabs never forgave us for that intensive supply effort to the Israelis. We probably saved the Israeli nation at that time. You couldn't just let Israel go under. The Egyptians were moving in across the desert until Sharon pushed their tanks back into Egypt.

While Cliff was dealing with the extra demands that the war in Israel put on his office, the rest of the family tracked these events from home and school. We had a houseguest at the time of the Yom Kippur War, an American Jewish girl who had been one of Cindy's best friends at school in Israel. Debra was attending college in Pennsylvania and was with us for the weekend. We all gathered around the TV and watched film clips of bombing raids and tank columns pushing through the Sinai desert landscapes where Tom and Cindy had taken a side trip up the *wadis* (dry river beds) with Dr. Bailey in his search for Bedouin poetry.

Most bizarrely, the cameras captured Israeli and Syrian troops shooting it out under the chairs of the ski lift on Mount Hermon—naturally, both sides wanted to gain control of the Golan Heights. Debra watched the films with even more personal concern than we did. Her parents were in northern Israel where her father taught at Haifa University, and her brother was still at the American School in Kfar Shmaryahu. We all were acutely aware that young people we knew—kids who'd sat in desks next to Deb and Cindy, my former students—were carrying guns and riding tanks.

As news trickled in from Israel, we felt the weight of the war ever more keenly. The husband of Cindy's favorite teacher—the one who conducted classes in the bomb shelter—was killed in a tank that was exploded by a grenade during the first days of the war. The paratrooper son of our favorite political cartoonist was shot down. In a nation as small and as close-knit as Israel, every casualty was a searing personal loss for every citizen.

Yet, two months later, the Shalgis of Kfar Giladi on the Lebanon border, Eva Weintraub our USIS librarian, and even the recently widowed history teacher had the spirit to write notes to us at Christmastime, evoking the message of peace that Christmas symbolized. They lamented their losses, but they all expressed hope and confidence in the future. The bereaved cartoonist sent us a drawing and wishes for good cheer in 1974. The human spirit is indeed remarkable in lands like Israel and her neighbors, where war has been a way of life for generations.

Within our own two generations, four Forsters were in school in four different places. Tom was a sophomore at Reed College in Oregon and Cindy, brimming over with knowledge and ideas gleaned during those two Israel years, was impatient to finish high school and move on to a wider world of university scholarship. She was completing requirements for her junior and senior year combined at Walt Whitman High School in Bethesda. Doug was at the neighborhood junior high.

I was teaching history to grades five through nine at the Washington International School (WIS). That school, the vision of Dorothy Goodman, taught children bilingually from nursery school until high school, a choice of Spanish/English or French/English, and I had been hired to help develop a truly international history curriculum throughout the grades. Dorry's mantra was "a monolingual child is a handicapped child," and she saw her school as "the pilot school for the planet."

At the top two grades, to be added in the coming years, she would adopt a new curriculum that had been created to serve a global population—the International Baccalaureate Diploma Program (IB). This curriculum had been designed by an international team of educators to serve children on the move, those whose parents worked outside their home country, as well as children who stayed home but would be educated as global citizens. After two years in this program, students would take external examinations accepted worldwide for entrance to the most competitive universities, at advanced standing in the U.S. The IB was to capture my energies and passions and become the center of my professional life well past normal retirement age. And after he retired, Cliff took up the IB cause as his own, seeing it as an extension, offered from childhood on up, of the mission which he had set for himself when he selected his own career path.

At WIS I worked with students from over seventy nations and teachers from more than thirty. I helped develop the multiyear history curriculum and it was wonderful to have students coming back each year to explore the next epoch in the story of mankind. "You all remember," I could say to the seventh graders, "how we learned last year about the beginnings of Confucianism and Tao. Now we'll see how these philosophies influenced Chinese society in the coming centuries." In 1975 I would become head of the upper school and was in that position for the two years before we were reassigned back to Tokyo. It was with great pride that I helped to prepare students in the first WIS graduating class to achieve their IB credentials.

As I took on more responsibility at WIS, Cliff would again be dealing with political and military crisis. He and Bill were first and foremost Asia specialists and were pleased when their team was asked by USIA to move in June of 1974 from the Near East and North Africa division to their former niche in the East Asia division, Bill as head and Cliff as his deputy. Vietnam was at the top of the agenda and Cliff and Bill made frequent trips to visit the field posts, each time spending several days in Saigon. Cliff recalled being more and more depressed by each succeeding visit to Vietnam.

During the last days of U.S. presence in Saigon, Bill and Cliff went through the agony of long nights sitting by the telephone in the office, waiting for news of besieged friends and colleagues. At the end was the chaotic retreat and evacuation from the American Embassy. Bill had served in Indochina as had many of the men working in that office, and Cliff had become well acquainted with the Vietnamese as well as American USIS employees. One USIS American was married to a Vietnamese woman and his small home overflowed with several dozen refugee relatives. Everyone was scanning evacuation lists for familiar names, examining photos for familiar faces, waiting for the telephone call or a cable that would bring some order out of the chaos, some hope to those who had been separated from families. As Cliff told Lew,

> When the fall of Vietnam came it was a trauma for all of us. I guess I was the last one to have a conversation from the task-force center in State with the PAO in Saigon the night just before Saigon's fall. He was trying desperately to get our people out of the USIS building over to the embassy as a collection point.

Unlike our Israeli friends, who could exercise the healing power of writing Christmas messages to friends abroad and who could rebuild their lives in their own stubborn ways, those left behind in Vietnam were sealed off and put through a regimented program of reorientation according to the dictates of Hanoi.

But during this time there were positive developments in U.S. relations with the People's Republic of China.

> We were able to get USIS established in China for the first time during this period and that was primarily due to George Bush, who'd been named head of the U.S. Liaison Office in China and wanted to see us about establishing USIS in Beijing. Ambassador Bush was just great. He came down to our office and put his feet up, was very informal and relaxed, and made it clear that he wanted to have us in there. When he called on us, he wanted some advice on cycling—what kind of bicycle

to get. So I found myself talking about the bicycle that might be a good bet for China, and recommended a three-speed Raleigh. He wrote later from Beijing, thanking me although he finally got a Chinese bicycle to take the tough terrain. He was very convivial, very cooperative, and it was a good relationship from the beginning once we got the post established. USIS was back in the PRC capitol for the first time since the communist takeover. Eventually we were able to get the Fulbright program under way again, but that took more time and we had to proceed slowly.

Doug, like his sister, was hungry for more than the neighborhood school could offer. He missed the multinational interaction and stimulating conversations that make an international-school experience so rich. After he met some of my eighth-grade students at WIS he made up his mind. Even though it meant that he—whose academic record had been spotty—would suffer the burden of having Mom as school head, he wanted to join those students next year, as long as it wouldn't mean going back a grade. To solve his problem of not meeting standards for French, he made plans to spend part of the summer in France.

Cliff, by nature and as a result of his career, had infected us all with the bug of internationalism. Tom also was seeking new horizons. When he saw a flier on a Reed College bulletin board promoting an archaeological dig in Guatemala for the summer of 1975, he asked for our support in enabling him to go. With State University of New York sponsorship, he pointed out, he could even earn college credits. Having used the same academic carrot to convince my parents to fund my way to Europe in 1948, how could I (and Cliff) say no?

That summer, four out of the five of us were in different countries. Doug at age fourteen traveled solo to France to live with a farm family northeast of Paris for two weeks, then to participate in a French sailing camp on the Brittany coast for another two. Not only did he get his French up to the WIS standard, he was launched into an obsessive avocation that would keep him sailing through college and moving up from small to larger boat ownership as a member and avid racer out of the San Francisco Yacht Club after graduation from university. When he returned home at summer's end, he and his dad went sailing in their modest craft on Chesapeake Bay. Doug would shout commands at times of crisis—like when a freighter was bearing down on them in the main shipping channel and their motor had died—in French, which was not one of his dad's tongues.

Cindy, not to be outdone by her brothers' quest for adventure, and seeking to learn more about the country whose kings and queens had fascinated her since her early teens, headed to Oxford for a summer course in archaeology, followed by field work at the site of an ancient submerged ship.

When Tom traveled from Oregon to Guatemala I joined him for part of the trip; we met in Mexico and traveled by bus to central Guatemala. When he headed for his dig I took a side trip to see the Mayan monuments at Tikal before flying home. Each year of the history course I was teaching we touched upon developments across the globe, including Latin America. This was an area about which I knew almost nothing, and I rationalized that visiting Mexico's museums and Guatemala's villages and monuments would help me become a better teacher.

The dig was actually a disappointment to Tom—poorly organized and poorly managed—and he opted not to participate, but he took advantage of the proximity of an excellent Spanish language school in Antigua and the opportunity to explore the Mayan hinterlands. He stayed on through the fall and emerged from the experience with new skills and the appreciation of a new corner of the world.

Cliff and Cao stayed home, keeping each other company and checking the mailbox for news from abroad. During the winter it would be my turn to stay home, while Cliff made his regular inspection tours to Asia.

After one of those trips he came back with the tale of another of his interesting encounters. It took place on a flight between Singapore and Manila. He regularly used the quiet time while traveling to compile his notes, jotting down details from the last post visited before taking up the affairs of the next one. On this flight he was catching up on conversations and observations from Brunei, Indonesia, and Singapore before the plane landed in Manila.

His concentration was interrupted when his seatmate announced in Japanese to someone standing next to him, *"Are wa, Palawan desu."* (That's

Palawan.) Cliff looked out the window and without hesitation turned and said, in Japanese, *"Iie, Mindanao desu."* (No, it's Mindanao.) Then he saw that his travel companion was surrounded by a crowd of fellow Japanese, all staring out the window at the island in question, and at this gaijin who presumed to question their knowledge, and in Japanese. "How do you know?" he was asked.

"Palawan is long and thin, like a pencil, and Mindanao is round and fat."

They wanted to know how he knew so much about the Philippines and he told them he grew up there, had lived for two years on Mindanao, and as a boy traveled all over the country. The next question asked where he had been during the war.

"Gentlemen, I was under your benevolent custody, as a prisoner of war in Manila." Their response to Cliff's revelation was a chorus of sighs and exclamations about how horrible that must have been and how sorry they were that he suffered. He countered with comments to the effect that it had been wartime and everyone involved was following orders according to what they believed to be necessary, and that under the circumstances it could have been worse.

Now it was his turn to ask where they had been during the war. They were an air-force group who had been in the battle for Singapore and then the conquest of the Philippines. Like many old soldiers, they were taking a nostalgic tour of the battlefields where they had served and lost many of their colleagues. What part of Japan had they come from, Cliff wanted to know. "Hiroshima." And they pulled out photos of their young wives and children who had died in the atomic blast. It was his turn this time—to express horror, sympathy, and sorrow at the savagery of war.

Soon they were approaching the Manila airport. As the passengers debarked on the tarmac, the Japanese veterans pulled Cliff aside, asked him to pose with them in front of the plane for a group photo, Cliff in the center and all with their arms around each other.

The USIS officer from the embassy who had come out on the tarmac to greet Cliff (a courtesy afforded to diplomats in those days of gentler airport security) sputtered "What the hell...?" Cliff waved to his colleague and said, "This will just take a moment; I'll explain later."

The following summer, I was able to accompany Cliff on one of his Southeast Asian rounds. We were particularly looking forward to a return to Burma, the first time for me since we left in 1960. Ambassador David Osborne, whom we knew from when we had all been together in Japan, invited us to be his houseguests at the embassy residence. "Plan your trip so you'll be here on the fourth of July," he wrote. "Send me a list of Burmese you knew and would like to see again and we'll invite them to our reception." Normally, because of Burma's restrictive military government, civilians without official titles would not be able to attend a party at the U.S. Embassy without endangering themselves. However, a national-day reception would be viewed as neutral territory.

In the Rangoon we saw on this trip time seemed to have stood still. Unlike the other capitols of Asia, which boasted sparkling new high-rises and were hubs of commercial and cultural activity, this one was shabby and subdued. Driving through monsoon-soaked streets, we thought we caught a glimpse of our 1950s Chevrolet—banged up and rusting but still running. The friends we met again were also "still running," and though their lives were now restricted they were the same smiling serene people we had so enjoyed knowing during our two years among them.

A year later, in the summer of 1977, we would move back to Asia, and would continue to have experiences where past and present intertwined. During his third tour in Japan, Cliff was assigned to Tokyo to take over management of the entire USIS operation, as Minister-Counselor for Public Affairs. He would be a member of the "country team" of Ambassador Mike Mansfield. He would also begin his in-depth research into the life of General Masaharu Homma.

30

"TAP 'ER LIGHT"

RETURNING TO TOKYO WOULD BE a homecoming for Cliff and me. We had made a heavy investment in Japan: the psychic stress and rewards of language study; the eleven years we had previously spent among the Japanese people, learning about their history and culture; the attachments of friendship; the time spent building the programs and styles of operating that we felt were appropriate for Japan. Here was the opportunity for Cliff to give greater guidance to USIS Japan and to direct it from a position of "the buck stops here" responsibility. And here again was a chance to be in one of the world's liveliest and most intelligent cities.

In addition, as he told Lew Schmidt, Cliff would be on the team of an ambassador whom he admired and thoroughly enjoyed working with.

In 1977, Mike Mansfield became our ambassador to Japan and I received my assignment to be his public affairs officer in Tokyo. I'd always been a great admirer of Senator Mansfield and it was a real pleasure to meet him for the first time. The next four years with this ambassador, like the earlier Kennedy

period with Ed Murrow, were very special years. He was a marvelous man to work for, and he was always very interested in
USIS and our role in Japan. He knew how important we could
be to what he was trying to achieve and we worked with him
on his whole effort to try and de-escalate some of the economic
issues and tensions that were just beginning to build up over
the trade imbalance.

Most of that period, the embassy was involved primarily with our trade relations with Japan and, since there was so
much rhetoric on both sides, we had an important job to do.
The ambassador visited every prefecture, relying on USIS officers who accompanied him on all these trips. He recognized
the value of what we were doing and when Simul International,
a prominent Japanese firm, wanted to publish a collection of his
speeches in Japan, we worked with them on the project with
the ambassador's approval. For each speech, Simul included a
commentary by a well-known Japanese. It was extremely well
done and the ambassador was very pleased, as were we. Of
course Simul was overjoyed when that book became a real seller.

Ambassador Mansfield's press conferences were always on
the record. And at the end of each session, he would say, "Well,
boys, tap 'er light." The first person to come to me and ask
about this was the *New York Times* correspondent. Mansfield
smoked a pipe; "When the ambassador says 'tap 'er light,' I assume it's his pipe," the correspondent commented. "Yes, I guess
it is," I replied. Shortly after that, at a Japanese press conference,
the ambassador said the same thing. Several Japanese journalists came up to me afterward. "What is 'tap 'er light'?" they
asked.

I went to the ambassador when he was alone in his office
on a Saturday morning and asked for an explanation. He said,
"Well, Cliff, when I was a young fellow, I used to work in the
copper mines in eastern Montana. As you pound that stick of
dynamite into the shaft walls to release the copper vein, you'd
holler down the line, 'Tap 'er light. Tap 'er light—or you'll
blow us all up—and that's what we've got to do here in Japan.

We've got to keep these economic issues from becoming political issues by tapping 'er light. We don't want to tap her too
strong. Let's see if we can't do the job without raising the decibel count."

And he really worked at that. We all did. It was a combined
effort to keep the dialogue going, working with congressional
people coming through to try to avoid emotional diatribes. And
with the Japanese, to try to make them aware of what they
were up against with American public opinion and the mood of
Congress up on the Hill if they didn't open up on the trade side.
The problem was really on both sides.

Again and again, Ambassador Mansfield would say to audiences and
individuals alike, whether in Japan or in the U. S., that the relationship
between Japan and the United States "is the most important in the world,
bar none!" During his long tenure in Tokyo, bridging both Democratic
and Republican administrations, he worked in his quiet but forceful way
to keep that relationship healthy.

When Cliff, Doug, and I returned to Tokyo in the summer of 1977,
we'd been stripped of our family roots. Though many miles of ocean
and vast land expanses had previously separated us from our families
in a geographical sense, our parents had always been at the other end
of the telephone and telegraph lines; and though the price of a stamp
had escalated, regular postal service was a bargain we could depend
upon. We could bounce our ideas and experiences and dreams across
the ocean to them, and back to us came their wisdom and loving
concern.

No more. While we were still in Israel, my mother was killed in her
bed by carbon monoxide leaking into her apartment from the garage
below. My stepmother had died the summer before, following a short but
conclusive battle with cancer. My father died following an operation in
the winter after we returned from Israel. We were at least glad that the
children had stayed alone with him when we went back briefly to Tel
Aviv in 1973 to pack our household belongings. This gave them a precious chance to get to know the rich humanist heart and mind that lay
under the rather forbidding—to a child—manner of the scholarly lawyer

from Grand Rapids, Michigan. Tom, Cindy, and Doug knew they were wealthy indeed in terms of grandparents.

My mother had come to visit us often when we were in the U.S. and twice in Japan; the children knew the bounty of that spirited lady and felt her involvement in their lives. My stepmother, Rose, with an inherited Irish sense of the absurd and French sense of the pragmatic, was an extra pillar of strength following the divorce of my parents when I was ten; my children had a taste of what I cherished when we visited her in Michigan and Ohio. And though Cliff's father had died long before they were born, Cliff passed on the legacy of a mischievous idealist who had left Liverpool on his own at age fourteen, working his way across the Atlantic in a journey that led to being minister of a church in Northern California, to refugee relief work in France during World War I, to the grounding of a humanitarian tradition as manager of the Philippine Red Cross for eighteen years.

Cliff's mother had survived the San Francisco earthquake, internment by the Japanese in the Philippines, the loss of her beloved husband shortly after the war, and a stroke in 1974. At the time of the stroke, doctors said that for a lady in her mid-eighties they couldn't offer much hope. Nonsense! Cliff's sister and the friend who shared the house wouldn't accept such an attitude, and never would Gladys Forster admit defeat. She recovered and continued to reign over our lives as a benevolent Queen Mother. She radiated girlish joy and shared her rich memories and current commentaries with us all. She kept the tiny Montague, California, post office in business, sending out her love to each one of us. For Cindy, some historical reminiscence. For Tom, a bit of philosophy. For Cliff, an evaluation of the latest political dilemma. But Gladys' time came, too, and we sat around her bed in an Oregon hospital for several wrenching days in July of 1977. Her final love letter to her children, grandchildren, and great-grandchildren, the letter to be opened when she died, admonished us all: "Remember, my name is 'Glad.'" She urged us to celebrate her life by buying a bottle of champagne and drinking a toast in her name.

Having accomplished that bittersweet task, we arrived in Tokyo and realized that, with my sister and her husband and their two children still teaching and living at Nishimachi School, we had more members of our family together in Tokyo than we would have any place else. So this was coming home in many ways. Many of the people whom we had known the longest were now living here—or had never left. Like Bill and Mary Jane Sherman, many were also back for a repeat assignment to the embassy. Bill was now deputy chief of mission (DCM), the second in command after the ambassador. Tom and Maggie McVeigh still oversaw the monthly play-reading group that brought Broadway into our living rooms on a rotating basis, and their beachside guest house was still available for us to use as a home away from home on weekends.

"There are more of my best friends in this room than I would find in my home town of Louisville, Kentucky!" Mary Jane remarked when we were at a ladies' luncheon given by an American who had been in Tokyo twenty-five years. I felt the same way. It was good to pick up where we left off in 1970. I was teaching again at Nishimachi. We invited Japanese newspapermen and university professors to our home in Azabu. Many of these were friends whom we had entertained in our Shinagawa house. The difference was that the reporters were now editors and assistant professors were now respected scholars. Also, the house we now lived in had about four times as much space as we'd had in Shinagawa. This meant we would frequently find ourselves hosting enormous receptions, which served an important role in conducting Cliff's official business. But we missed the intimate exchanges we had at the smaller parties that limited space forced upon us in the 1960s.

The Azabu house, an embassy-owned residence, looked enormous and forbidding from the outside. White stucco walls faced the street. In spring, the austerity was softened by banks of blooming azaleas. When Cindy came to visit, she dubbed our residence "the Azalea fortress." To carry the fortress image even further, we found ourselves under the watchful eyes of round-the-clock, blue-uniformed guards, opening and closing the gate, saluting as we came and went. Smiling. Watching. Waiting. One guard was the author of a popular comic strip and spent his spare hours drawing.

Why did we need a guard service? Because our neighbor was the Chinese Embassy, a multistoried red-tiled building, considerably more forbidding than our house. Every now and then Japanese right-wing groups would stage a protest against the communist government of

China. When Chinese fishing boats appeared in coastal waters claimed by Japan, when Chinese officials came to Japan on a state visit, whenever there was an issue to shout about, the demonstrators mounted loudspeakers and broadcast their displeasure. Several times they tried to storm the Chinese Embassy to deliver their messages in person, but each time they were stopped—usually in front of our gate—by a wall of Japanese riot police who wore helmets with transparent face masks and carried shields and clubs. Our blue-clad guard's function seemed to be simply to stand by, at attention, observing.

Cliff grumbled, "When I was sixteen, I was shut in behind gates with Japanese guards. I really didn't expect to have Japanese guards at my gate forty-five years later!"

At least we could have complete confidence in the security of our neighborhood. Small chance of someone entering to rob us while we were away from *this* house for the weekend. At night, we had to stop and be waved through police barriers even to get into the neighborhood.

The embassy office building also had an impregnable façade. The new building had gone up ten stories and down three into the plot of land that formerly had held a charming two-story chancery built in the 1920s. Back then, the entire American diplomatic mission worked and resided in the compound, at a much more leisurely pace than that of the complex and often frenetic diplomacy of the seventies. The property a few blocks away that had housed the Annex since the war—a far larger building than the original embassy—was sold, bringing in enough money to finance a handsome new building where the entire staff could again function under one roof.

USIS (soon to be temporarily renamed ICA, "International Communication Agency") was on the second floor. Modern, efficient, spacious, and attractively furnished, the building lacked the charm and grace of its predecessor but suited the nature of its business, and people worked comfortably within its walls. Cliff's office was on the corner overlooking the entrance. Tired of sitting all day shuffling paper, he had a stand-up desk put by the window. There he could compose office memorandums on his feet and sneak a glance now and then at the outside world. If he wasn't out in the Tokyo traffic, at least he could see it.

Only three Forsters were living in Tokyo. Cindy was in her second year at Brown University and Tom was back at Reed College. Both would come to visit during their Christmas holidays but stayed in the U.S. during the summer to work at summer jobs. Even Cao had stayed behind. We knew that exercising those long dog legs would not be easy in metropolitan Tokyo and thus reluctantly left him with friends who knew and enjoyed him. Doug was now a sophomore at the American International School in Japan (ASIJ) and commuted to that suburban campus daily via a walk to the local subway station, a subway ride, a change to a train at the Shinjuku transportation hub, another change to a local trolley, and finally a dash across an open field. Not as convenient as Nishimachi, which was in our neighborhood (and only went through grade nine), but ASIJ had long been one of the exemplary schools for expatriate youngsters and the high-school students enjoyed their freedom to travel out of the city. Doug was pleased to be in an international school again and to reunite with some of his former pals.

Tom, his girlfriend Julie, and Cliff's sister Gerry all came to spend Christmas with us in 1977. We shared a poignant experience when we visited the country village of Mashiko, home of the master folk artist Shoji Hamada, whom Cliff and I had met in 1964 during the first U.S.-Japan Cultural Conference in Washington and the weekend in Colonial Williamsburg. Julie was a potter, teaching ceramics at Reed College in Portland, Oregon. She knew a great deal about Japanese design and techniques in clay and was eager to meet this "living national treasure."

Hamada was now in his late eighties, and very frail. When we called ahead, we were told he might or might not be able to visit with us; the family took one day at a time. Accompanied by my sister and her husband, we made the four-hour drive in the Hawkins' large van, allowing us plenty of space to carry back pottery from the many kilns that had sprung up around Mashiko after Hamada established his home and studio there as a young man. The town had become a mecca for pottery aficionados.

We finally arrived in Mashiko with its handsome old farm homes and attractive shops, and pulled into Hamada's compound. When we asked in the museum if Hamada-san could receive us, the woman told us she was very sorry, but he wasn't well today, and the family had

decided a visit would be too taxing. But, please, would we make ourselves at home and enjoy the museum—which showcased the arts and
crafts that Hamada had gathered during his travels around the world—
and the outbuildings.

We were disappointed, but not surprised. After exploring the compound, we had a quick picnic and climbed back into the van. As we were
about to leave, a car pulled into the parking area, driven by a middle-
aged man who hurried around to help an old man in the passenger's seat.
With great deal of effort, the old man stood, holding onto the door of the
car. Cliff was the first to realize what was happening and rushed out of
the van to clasp the old man's hand.

"Hamada-san!"

The driver—Hamada's son—explained that Hamada had wanted to
greet the American visitors. The thin, frail potter looked closely at Cliff,
then burst into a smile of recognition. Cliff reminded him of the 1964
conference and the trip to Williamsburg. "Oh, yes. I remember. That
was a *good* trip!"

Cliff then introduced Julie as the visiting potter from Oregon, one
of his great admirers. Hamada-san acknowledged Julie, clasped both her
hands, then seemed to fade away into a private reverie. "We worry about
him," said his son. "It is hard to persuade him even to eat."

We thanked the son profusely and helped him tuck his father back
in the car. We were probably the last foreign visitors to see this living
national treasure, who had done so much to revitalize Japanese folk crafts
in the twentieth century, and to raise those crafts to the status of arts. He
died a few days after the New Year.

Throughout his life, Cliff's past, present, and future had interwoven
in unexpected ways, and this was once again true during a several-week
period in February and March. Every year, USIS held a conference bringing together the Country Public Affairs Officers from the East Asia and
Pacific Region. The 1978 meeting took place in Manila, and I accompanied Cliff to his "hometown."

We arrived a day early. I decide to spend our first morning soaking in
the sun by the hotel pool—a welcome relief from a chilly Tokyo—while
Cliff went to meet with his friend Bill Lane, publisher of *Sunset* magazine and former Ambassador-at-Large in the Pacific. On the way to the

meeting, he stopped to pay his respects at the old Red Cross building, where the terrible massacre had taken place in 1945. The original
structure had been rebuilt, but debris remained, and Cliff picked up
a piece of stucco, remembering the way his father had jumped up on
the scaffolding during the construction of his labor of love. He was
carrying this souvenir with him as he continued on to his meeting.
Crossing one of Manila's notoriously complex intersections, he was
struck by a truck.

Rather than attending a conference with his peers, Cliff spent two
weeks in a Manila hospital bed with a view of the site where he had
been interned by the Japanese as teenaged prisoner of war. Throughout
the accident and transfer to two hospitals, he held onto the chunk of
stucco from his father's beloved Red Cross building, which remains in
our home today. Shortly after our return to Japan, we traveled together
to visit American Centers in coastal cities on the Sea of Japan. As the
officer in charge of all USIS operations in Japan, Cliff was pleased once
again to make regular visits to centers in the prefectural hinterland.
He always felt that some of the most important work was done in the
smaller cities.

This was the trip when we made our excursion to Sado Island—
in part to celebrate Cliff's return to good health—and encountered the
monument to General Homma. From then on, Cliff's interest in Homma
grew, and he took advantage of his final years in Japan to seek out more
background on the conquering general so despised by the American internees during the war, the general whose condemnation and execution
his father—certainly one who had every reason to be bitter and want
vengeance—had questioned.

I, in the meantime, was back at Nishimachi but out of the classroom
this time, helping Tane Matsukata map plans for growth and stability in
the newly created position of vice principal. Among other strategies, we
saw the need for and benefit of an alumni database and magazine, and
I began designing and editing the first issues of the *Nishimachi Internationalist*.

One morning I received an excited call from the Japanese receptionist
downstairs. "There is a *big* man here who wants to see you." I reached the
front hall to find my former student Zdenek Hrdlicka, who picked me

up and twirled me around as a gesture of greeting. His father, the former Czech ambassador, had been in disgrace with the Soviet controlled government after publicly opposing the stifling of Czech freedom. Zdenek kept a low profile during his college days in Prague, married a diplomat's daughter who spoke French as well as English, and together they had established a trilingual interpreting agency.

Zdenek had received the first issue of the *Internationalist,* knew I was now in Tokyo, and secured for himself an assignment as interpreter for a group of Czech labor leaders coming to visit Japan. With a couple hours off-duty, Zdenek had managed to elude his group and visit his former school. We were able to keep him on campus long enough for him to meet with the junior-high students and tell them what it was like living in a communist society, and how members of his family managed to work their ways around the restrictions for a semblance of normalcy. Cliff and I would hear the rest of his story much later, when we visited the Hrdlickas in free Prague the summer after the "Velvet Revolution" of December, 1989.

For any teacher, being contacted by former students is one of the great rewards of the profession, and this is especially so when one's students are scattered across the globe. Many Nishimachi alumni began communicating regularly with the school—and with each other—once the magazine was established. Other graduates, both Japanese and expatriate, had remained in or returned to Tokyo. Some, as they married and had children, had begun sending the next generation to the school.

Planning for a desperately needed physical expansion of the school on a finite city lot was more of a challenge. But we had help when a world-class expert in the use of space came to Tokyo. We had visited Lawrence Halprin at his studio in San Francisco, where he showed us drawings of his past and current projects and described the design process he used to revitalize cityscapes across the U.S.—bringing the entire community together into workshops where they articulated dreams of how this space could enhance their lives. Cliff felt the process would be of interest to architects in Japan and invited Larry to come as a USIS exchange grantee.

At the end of Larry's visit, we invited him to our home for a quiet family meal. I told him about Nishimachi's need to make better use of its limited space and asked for advice on how we might use his "creative community" design strategy. With his inspiration we came up with a two-day planning festival, with all the stakeholders taking part.

The first afternoon and evening, the faculty and staff met in groups, first by specific interest levels, then across these boundaries. Each interest group drafted an outline of what their most urgent space needs were, in order of priority, and each composite team looked at what was needed for the school as a whole. The next day we added students, trustees, and parent activists to the discussion. Everyone brainstormed to produce lists reviewing the school's history, what was good and bad at present, and what would be needed in the future. The planning festival ended with a pep rally on the makeshift basketball court where each group hoisted posters illustrating their conclusions. The trustees responded with a commitment to formalize, fund, and finalize major building projects over the coming years, allowing Nishimachi to grow and fulfill its mission.

Throughout our time in Tokyo, Cliff and I often attended Japanese-sponsored events that provided surprising glimpses into U.S.-Japan relations. One of these, in the summer of 1978, was the opening of an exhibition at Mitsukoshi, a major Tokyo department store, featuring thirty-one survivors from a shipment of 12,739 "dolls of friendship" that arrived in Yokohama in 1927. Donated by different individuals or organizations, each of the blue-eyed "messengers of goodwill" carried a "passport," complete with a visa issued by the Japanese Consul General in New York. We learned the full story as we walked through the exhibit; the ship carrying the dolls was met in Yokohama by a procession of kimono-clad little girls, who presented the ship's officers with bouquets and received dolls in return. The remaining dolls were sent all over Japan; many were put in places of honor in primary schools and kindergartens. A song was written to celebrate the occasion—"My Blue-Eyed Doll"—and became Japan's popular hit of the year.

As relations deteriorated between the U.S. and Japan, things symbolizing America became suspect. When war broke out between the two countries, the blue-eyed dolls were rounded up by local military groups and destroyed. Some were publicly "executed" in schoolyards as an object lesson to the children.

In Tokyo, Ambassador Mike Mansfield and his deputy Bill Sherman presented Cliff an award honoring his thirty-year tenure in the Foreign Service.

A few mothers and teachers refused to play the game, hiding the dolls under the eaves of their houses or burying them at the bottom of storage chests. One school principal consigned her doll to a friend for safekeeping, warning the friend in a letter to "hide this prisoner."

In 1972, a grandmother named Ayako Ishimaru learned that one of the dolls had been put on display in a school in the northern part of Japan. She was very moved by the doll's survival through the twists and turns of politics and tried to contact the Rochester, New York, man who had sent the doll in 1927. He was dead, but this was the start of a crusade for Mrs. Ishimaru. She found in her own prefecture three of the original one hundred dolls that had been sent there and sponsored a ceremony of "consolation" in their honor. The publicity about her ceremony brought to light other dolls and the collection of thirty-one was presented to the public on the thirty-third anniversary of the end of the Pacific War. The wife of the Foreign Minister, Mrs. Sonoda, attended the opening and recalled that one of these dolls had been in her school.

Some dolls still had their passports and tags identifying donors like the San Mateo, California, Blue Jay Club. "Special Passport No. 2,945" was "issued át the request of the Committee on World Friendship Among Children." It bore a visa "seen and certified to be good for a goodwill trip to Japan," signed by Consul General Saito and stamped with the official consulate seal. Next to one doll was her passport, opened to show the message written in English on one page and Japanese on the following page:

To Boys and Girls in Japan

This passport introduces to you *Margaret Fox,* a loyal and law abiding Citizen of the U.S.A. who goes to visit Japan as a Messenger of Friendship and to see the Hina Matsuri, March 3, 1927.

This messenger represents the Boys and Girls of America and carries their Greetings and a Message of Goodwill.

Please take care of *Margaret* while in Japan and give her any help and protection that may be needed. She will obey all laws and customs of your country.

> With all good wishes,
> "Uncle Sam"

The woman who guided us through the Mitsukoshi exhibit had been one of the little girls who met the ship in Yokohama. She pointed to herself in the picture from a newspaper story describing the ceremony. As we moved from one doll to another around the room, several Japanese women were muffling sobs and drying tears. I, too, felt choked up. What an experience these dolls represented. And what volumes that experience said about the ups and downs of international relations.

Yes, indeed. Tap 'er light!

31

"WE HAVE FRIENDS ALL
OVER THE WORLD"

I N NOVEMBER OF 1978, CLIFF and I visited China, and once again
Cliff experienced echoes of his past. His first memories as a child
were those of the summer spent in Peking (as it was called then)
when he was four. He had passed through Shanghai every few years when
the family went on home leave from Manila. His last visit had been as a
teenager in 1939, when he and Gerry traveled to California without their
parents, and their father cautioned them not to "cause any international
incidents."

This time, in 1978, China was beginning to emerge from the trauma
of the Cultural Revolution, gingerly welcoming visitors from the West,
and edging towards the establishment of full diplomatic relations with
the United States for the first time since 1949. Signs in the airport, in
hotels and tourist stores, and at the train-station exit into Hong Kong all
proclaimed, "We have friends all over the world."

To achieve a tourist visa, still hard to come by, we had to join a tour.
Turned down in May, in August we received a letter from Luxingshe, the
China International Travel Service in Beijing, granting us a twelve-day stay.

After study, we agree that your couple will enter Peking on Nov. 3, visit Xian, Shanghai, Hangchow and exit China via Shumchun... Please advise us before September 8 your personal particulars and your specific requests and interests in visits in China.

The letter was all we needed to get our visa from the Chinese Embassy next door to our Tokyo residence. The counsel, Mr. Li, noted that we were neighbors and hoped that we would enjoy our visit to his country.

We were met at the Beijing airport by Ms. Chang Rung Hsia, our guide from the travel service who would escort us around the capitol and accompany us throughout our trip. In each subsequent city a local guide would join us. Our "group," much to our delight, turned out to be a tour for two. We were glad to be in the hands of this friendly twenty-four-year-old. Just one year out of the Foreign Language School of Beijing, she spoke superb English. She also enjoyed Cliff's sense of humor and was fascinated that he had been in Peking as a child. She took on his search for childhood memories as a personal treasure hunt, to be added to the already programmed Imperial Palace, Temple of Heaven, Great Wall, Beijing #41 Middle School, Commune, Industrial Workers Neighborhood, and Friendship Store. Marble Boat? No problem. White Dagoba? Yes, indeed. Nine Dragon Screen near a lake? Hmmm. That was more difficult. Peking Union Medical College? This was where the Forsters had been given an apartment in 1938, and Ms. Chang had no idea where it might be.

In our hotel, we leaned out over our sixth-floor balcony to catch the sounds and sights of China's capitol at night. We were in the heart of a city of eight million (twelve million if you included the suburbs) and there was an eerie quiet and darkness. The only signs of life were a dim glow of light and the tinkle of bicycle bells breaking through the silence. A strong odor of coal gas hung over the night. We recalled satellite pictures of urban areas at night that had been shown in a lecture by a Japanese space scientist. The megalopolis of the Eastern U.S. and that of Japan showed up, etched in light, as if one had drawn a map. The photos of China at night were dark; it looked as though no one was there.

Our first visit was to the #41 Middle School, which was enclosed in a walled compound built by the British in 1912. We were received in the conference room by two women; Teacher Chen took notes of all that was said and Vice Principal Chiang did the talking. "Before Liberation," she told us, "our school had about three hundred students. Today we have 1,800 students and 160 teachers." As a teacher I was interested in learning how schools worked in China and we had put a school visit on our pre-tour request list.

Chiang went on to explain the grade system in the school, the courses taught, the schedule over the course of the year. "Four to six weeks are spent in agriculture or industry or military training. Every year the students go to the country, so they can spend some time with the workers and peasants." The students also worked in the school factory. "We make products used in the Number 103 truck. So when the students see a truck in the street, they are very happy and think: 'It is my truck!'"

Chiang then took us on a tour of the campus. As we walked across the large sports ground, she apologized for the unsightliness of a makeshift arrangement of a woven mat supported on a crude scaffolding, then explained that it covered the entrance to the tunnel the children were making. When the tunnel was completed in another year or so, they would be able to move their entire school underground in case of enemy air attack.

When we went into classrooms, everyone applauded, we applauded in response, and then the students went back to their work. Two portraits hung in each classroom: one of the late Chairman Mao and the other of the current Chairman Hua. In the third-year English class, the lesson for the day was a story about "imperialist bandits" and the risk taken by a young girl in carrying a message behind enemy lines. The students' English sounded good and the teacher had excellent intonation. The teacher gave special emphasis to the punch line of the lesson. "A communist is *never* afraid to die for his country. Now repeat that, children: A communist is *never* afraid to die!."

Cliff was reunited with the Marble Boat in the Summer Palace of the Imperial family and saw the White Dagoba in Beihai Park north of the Forbidden City. Miss Chang found out from elderly Chinese strollers on Sunday where to locate the Nine Dragon Screen on the other side of the park. When we were out walking on our own after a particularly filling Chinese lunch, Cliff discovered the old Peking Union Medical College, now the Capitol Hospital. He was rediscovering the scenes etched into his childhood memories.

We asked Miss Chang if it would be possible to arrange a visit to Mao's tomb. That was not on our official agenda but she agreed to try.

Our request granted, we were squeezed into the front section of a line of several thousand people, five abreast, extending like a Great Wall across Tiananmen Square. We moved slowly towards the mausoleum entrance. In the first big hall was a giant white seated Mao, reminiscent of Lincoln in his Memorial at Washington. The line split, went into a smaller hall, joined, split again, and finally entered the hall where Mao's body lay draped with a red flag and exposed under a transparent case. No one spoke from the time the line entered the building. The only sounds were the shuffling of the many, many slowly moving feet and the sobs of mourners. It was a deeply moving experience. The emperor was dead, but the emperor lived on. The modern-day pyramid had been built by super-human efforts in eight months after Mao died. Visiting officials and local citizens had all pitched in to put a stone in place, to have a hand in building the memorial to the fallen hero. The memorial was a pilgrimage site and Mao was still very much a beloved hero in November of 1978.

In Shanghai, roles reversed and Cliff became the guide for Ms. Chang and the young man who was our local escort. We were housed in one of the noble old hotels of the East: The Cathay, now the Peace Hotel. This had been headquarters for Cliff's family whenever they visited Shanghai. If they were traveling by ship, as was usually the case, they came ashore to eat in the Cathay dining room on the eighth floor and enjoy the sweeping view of the Huangpu River. The suite assigned to us was the ultimate in elegance: three rooms (bedroom, living room, dining room) and two bathrooms wrapped around the corner on the seventh floor. The rooms were paneled in dark carved wood. The ceilings were decorated with floral panels. There was a fireplace in the living room. The thick carpets and heavy furniture of the imperialist era were still there, a taste of past capitalistic grandeur. But the new regime had managed to remove most of the style and glamour from the rest of the building. The halls were dark and dreary. Utilitarian counters provided keys, stamps, books, and a few souvenirs for sale. As we walked towards the elevators we were faced by a sign a meter high, illuminated in neon: "WE HAVE FRIENDS ALL OVER THE WORLD."

When our two guides took us on a boat ride along the riverfront, Cliff started pointing out the landmarks he remembered, the commercial and financial towers that had run business and amassed fortunes throughout Asia. The guides were fascinated. They knew nothing of the past history of these preliberation bastions of capitalism and eagerly took notes on the Clifton Forster tour of the city.

From Shanghai we flew into Xian in a two-engine Fokker-Friendship airplane that was aged and Spartan. We were the only foreign passengers; the others were mostly military. The front seats had been reserved for us, and hanging down from the window was a notebook inviting our "criticisms and suggestions." We used the three and a half hours to read. Cliff and I were reviewing the 1978 *National Geographic* article on the Xian imperial tomb excavations and rereading chapters on the Tang Dynasty in history books we had brought along with us. Miss Chang was reading Edgar Snow's account of the months he spent with the Chinese Communist Army in 1936, *Red Star over China.* "We Chinese really like this book," she volunteered. "But it is hard to find."

We visited the anticipated historical sites, both ancient and modern, and were given an unanticipated treat when we attended a puppet show in a small theater with a dirt floor, featuring a selection from China's favorite epic, *Monkey: A Journey to the West.* This fictionalized tale of a Tang Dynasty monk who journeyed to India in search of Buddhist learning had been banned during the Cultural Revolution, deemed too bourgeois, too frivolous, for the new Chinese citizen. But in 1978 new winds were blowing in China and *Monkey* was rehabilitated. In Xian a puppet troupe was formed under the leadership of two old masters who had been living in exile. The audience consisted of children and elders, the grandparents who had secretly kept the story alive by telling it to the youngsters. They were enthralled by the magic of the tale come to life, and so were we. I told Miss Chang that I wished I had photographs of the puppets, to share some of this magic with my students back at Nishimachi School.

The next night, we were invited to a banquet by the local Responsible Person for the China International Travel Service. The banquet hall turned out to be a screened-off corner of the dining room in the hotel where we stayed. The guest list was our pair of guides, ourselves, and the Responsible Person who was a tough old soldier, general in rank, veteran of the Long March with Mao. He took Cliff on in a current march of vitriol, hammering him on all the wrongs of American foreign policy over the last several decades. While plying him with fiery Chinese wine, he probed Cliff's background with searching questions. It was a tense "feast."

Suddenly our host changed his expression and demeanor: He smiled affably, then profusely thanked Cliff for his father's wartime contributions through the Red Cross "to the Chinese People." We had made no mention of the Red Cross or the family's wartime experiences, but the old soldier had obviously done his homework on Clifton B. Forster. Smiling even more affably, he told us that a car was waiting outside to take us to the puppet theater, where we would be met by the leaders and taken backstage to watch from the wings. "This time, Mrs. Forster should take some photographs during the intermission to show her students in Japan," he said.

We left China by train, crossing the southern border into Hong Kong. We hailed a taxi to take us from the train station to the Peninsula Hotel. The driver looked at the heavy coats we carried, warmth unnecessary in the mild autumn of Hong Kong. "You been to Peking?" Cliff said that indeed we had and asked if he, the driver, had been back to visit China. "No! No! I ran away. From Canton. Everyone wearing the same blue there: men, women. No freedom. Two worlds: China and Hong Kong. But now Hua. Better than Mao."

Indeed the China we had just visited was another world. One which somehow combined continuity and radical change. Ringing in our ears was the song of the New China, the phrases that we had heard or read again and again during our twelve days:

"On behalf of the workers I welcome you to the commune (factory, museum, school, industrial settlement, hospital)."

"Now I will give you a briefing about our commune (factory, museum, school, industrial settlement, hospital)."

"We welcome our Foreign Friends and hope you will come again. Please give our regards to the American People."

"After Liberation…"

"Since the Gang of Four…"

"Long Live the great unity of the people of the whole world!"

"According to Chairman Mao…"

"According to Chairman Hua…"

"The Responsible Person…"

"Modernize by 1985!"

"Move forward rapidly to the year 2000!"

"Please give us your suggestions and criticisms."

"We have friends all over the world!"

The liturgy of the revolution was limited. But in November of 1978 it had a friendly tone. The stridency of the forties, fifties, and sixties had been muted.

32

THE GENERAL'S DAUGHTER

B Y EARLY 1979, U.S.-JAPAN TRADE imbalance had continued to
grow, and so had the tensions between the two countries. Japan
made high-quality cars and television sets that the American consumer wanted to buy. Japanese market research and sales promotion were
highly sophisticated and effective. Japanese car manufacturers altered their
product to fit the market; U.S. cars, on the other hand, came to Japan—
where people drive on the left side of the road—with the steering wheel on
the left. American businessmen considered the Japanese market too restrictive, complaining that they weren't allowed to sell a fair share of the oranges
or beef that the Japanese consumer wanted. As negotiations for quotas went
on in Tokyo and Washington, each government appointed senior negotiators to oversee the talks. In the background was an implied threat that
Congress, sensitive to cries of unfair Japanese competition from its con-
stituents, would impose tariffs on Japanese goods unless more American
products could be sold in Japan. As Washington felt pushed by constitu-
ents, the Japanese government had the same pressures bearing down on its
parliamentarians. Both governments acted with an eye on future elections.

During the 1979 spring, weeks before the leaders of the industrialized world were due to meet together for the first time in Tokyo, the

negotiations over trade issues reached a new level of tension. "We mustn't let economic differences become political ones," was heard frequently from thoughtful people on both sides. "The relationship between our two countries is too special, too important to both peoples, to let disagreement over trade escalate into angry accusations."

"I feel rather *hara-hara*"—fluttery in the stomach—"about all this," said a Japanese professor of international relations.

"It is the perceptions more than the realities that really count," said a Japanese newspaper editor. "Not what the statesmen and diplomats say to each other, but what the farmer and office worker see and hear on the television screen."

"He doesn't like us very much, does he?" was Cliff's Japanese secretary's reaction to a harangue by an American politician against Japanese products being "dumped" in American markets. Portions of the speech were broadcast on the evening news of the Japanese government network. The speaker had volunteered to lead American workers "to the docks of Yokohama" to block Japanese export shipments if necessary.

Prime Minister Ohira went to Washington to meet with President Carter. It was agreed to shelve the trade issues for the moment. The two leaders focused their discussion on the areas where Japan and the United States could—and for their mutual benefit should—cooperate.

Energy was top priority. Both societies depended on vast quantities of energy to turn the wheels of daily existence and business. They agreed to pool their talents and seek new alternatives to oil. The whole scope of international relations, from the fragile peace in the Middle East to the new role being played by China, were on the agenda for summit discussion. What would be the responsibilities and attitudes of these two major industrial nations towards the world balance of power in the coming years? What could they do together to alleviate the problems of the developing nations?

Educational and cultural exchanges were of particular interest to Cliff. Continuing to study and appreciate each other would help maintain a friendly dialogue. At the time of Ohira's visit, Japan announced financial support for new exhibition halls for the Japanese art collections of the Smithsonian in Washington and the Metropolitan Museum in New York. During the previous months Cliff, as Chairman of the Fulbright Commission in Japan, was deeply involved in negotiating a new operating agreement that brought the Japanese government into the Fulbright program on a cost-sharing basis. This meant a doubling of funds available to send American Fulbright scholars to Japan and Japanese to the U.S., to teach and to study. Because of inflation, that meant not a doubling of exchange scholars but the ability to maintain the existing program. Three years earlier, the U.S.-Japan Friendship Commission had been created by an act of Congress to provide grants to a wide range of artists and institutions that worked towards expanding Japanese-American contacts. The annual meeting of Japanese and American journalists, writers, professors, and government officials had continued since the Kennedy presidency.

Out of these meetings and their subcommittees, in addition to the earlier exchanges of television programs, new initiatives came into play. Curriculum units on Japan were written for the public school systems of North Carolina and Pennsylvania, American high-school teachers visited Japan, and many other projects reached down to the grass roots in each country. During the 1979 season of tense trade talks in Washington and Ohira's visit, the New York Japan Society sponsored a series of activities in cities across the United States. Under the umbrella title of "Japan Today," the people of Denver, Atlanta, San Francisco, and elsewhere saw contemporary Japanese films and met some of the top sociologists, political scientists, and artists whose careers centered on comparative study of American and Japanese affairs. Other Americans gained insights on contemporary Japan through traveling exhibits.

In Japan, USIS-sponsored visitors lectured at cultural centers in Tokyo and around the country about topics ranging from politics to space programs to literature, later meeting at one of our homes for informal discussions. At one luncheon at our house for American poet Theodore Weiss and his wife—they jointly edited the *Quarterly Review of Poetry,* published in Princeton—we invited several Japanese poets, and a warm and friendly discussion flowed around the table, shared delight in a shared line of work. After lunch someone suggested that the poets recite a few lines each. Yoshimasa Gozo sat on the floor and intoned excerpts from his long poem about a courtesan of the Edo period. Weiss responded with a verse written while living in London. Other poems were recited, each in the original language. No translation was offered and none was needed. The music of the language and the mood of expression carried the message and made this an afternoon of successful communication.

During this period, Cliff began to deepen his research of General Masaharu Homma. One of the members of Homma's defense team during his trial
for war crimes in Manila was now practicing law in Tokyo, a fellow member
of the McVeigh's monthly play-reading group, and Cliff talked to him about
the trial. George Furness told Cliff how troubled he had been by the one-sided
proceedings and how he had come to have great respect for the general during
the trial. George said the prosecution was made up of senior military officers,
who obviously had indications from MacArthur's staff that the Japanese generals were to pay the price for their wartime leadership of America's greatest
military disaster. Yamashita, who commanded forces in the Philippines after
Homma was recalled to Tokyo and sidelined, was tried and sentenced to execution by the same military tribunal. A defense team was hastily assembled
from among junior officers who happened to have law degrees, their leader
a young major who had gone directly from university into military service.
George put Cliff in touch with Major John Skeen, now living in Baltimore,
whom Cliff would later meet later and whose correspondence with his wife
during the trial was passed on to Cliff after Skeen's death.

Cliff started conversations about Homma with some of the Japanese
members of the USIS staff. One, Takuchi Ito, offered to help him find
background information on the years before the invasion of the Philippines. Ito-san discovered that Homma's daughter was living in Kamakura, a short train ride south of Tokyo, and offered to seek an appointment
to meet her and to serve as interpreter.

Hisako Inomata was reluctant to be interviewed about her late father,
especially by Americans, but consented to meet with Cliff and Takuchi
Ito in Kamakura in January, 1980. In a phone call with Ito-san before
they met she said to him (as written in his notes for Cliff):

> I feel assured to have heard that Mr. Forster is interested in
> describing human aspects of my father, going (but not necessar-
> ily restricted) to his days preceding the Philippines. A number
> of television stations have approached me with a request for an
> interview, but I have declined all of them, for their primary
> interests have always been my father's last days. His days in the
> Philippines represent really a small part of his whole being. I
> am pleased to hear that Mr. Forster's interest goes beyond the

war. I do recall a few episodes about our family from when I
was a child. These accounts were retold a number of times by
Mother in the later years of my life. I hope they might help
shed light on Mr. Forster's approach. I will be glad to mention
these to him when we meet.

In the early years my father served as chief information officer
of the General Staff, and as such he did his best to be of help to
the media. Now that I understand that Mr. Forster was in a similar position at the American Embassy, I will be happy to meet him.

*Tokyo USIS staff member Takuchi Ito introduced Cliff to the daughter of
Masaharu Homma, leading Cliff to a new perspective of the general and his legacy.*

The meeting was arranged to take place February 4th in a steak house called Kamakura-yama, on a wooded hill in the western part of the ancient city. Mrs. Inomata asked if Mr. Forster "could sit tailor style on tatami mats" and Ito-san assured her that he could. The following are Ito-san's notes of their conversation.

I still remember tales about some of the days our family spent together on our way to London by boat (in 1930) when my father, then a colonel of the Army, was transferred to the Japanese Embassy in London as military attaché. I was two years old then. At each stopover on the voyage, Father would take us on an inland trip of the country we were in so that we all could see the people and the land firsthand. So we were able to visit the countryside lying beyond port cities in India, Singapore and some of the Middle East countries.

Earlier in 1918 Father had an opportunity to visit the frontline in Europe as an observer from the Allied Forces and witnessed for the first time tanks in actual combat. It is an irony of history that Douglas MacArthur was also present at the scene. That occasion was enough for Father to get interested in modern tank warfare, a subject on which he lectured in his later years at the Army War College.

Even during the days when he was assigned to the frontline in China, my father was a voracious reader as he had always been, and used to buy books from Europe and America via Maruzen bookstore in Tokyo. As these books were delivered to our house, Mother would pack and ship them to his unit on the continent. Here I will show you a copy of one of those books, "Gone with the Wind," and right here you will see his scribbling saying he had "started reading on August 13 and finished on the day of the October offensive" in China. I am told that he liked the pungency of George Bernard Shaw's humor, and that his interests ranged from fiction to plays.

Father was a man of literary bent—quite an unusual attribute for a ranking officer of the army at the time. He had a number of units under his command of the 27th Division in

China publish a literary journal which solicited essays, short
stories, and poems from troops and officers. Through these activities his units came to be known as a "cultural corps." When
he led the troops in the Philippines, Father had arranged for a
tour by Japanese writers and novelists, among whom were Hidemi Kon and Yojiro Ishizaka.

Father loved to play tennis and to listen to *rakugo* storytelling. While serving in China and later in Taiwan, he even wrote
a number of popular songs under improvised pseudonyms such
as "Ichiro Nanking" or "Taro Taiwan" for King Record Company. These qualities are quite uncharacteristic of high-ranking
army officers during those days, and I believe that they had
a lot to do with the general education he received in his boy-
hood. Unlike many senior officers, who first entered the Preparatory Military School at the age of eleven before going on to
the Military Academy, Father spent five years at a regular high
school which he finished at age sixteen, and was then admitted to the Academy. The five years of general education at high
school, I believe, went a long way to cultivating an outlook and
personality better balanced than those of the Preparatory Military School graduates, whose values and outlook were forged
through intensive military indoctrination to which they were
exposed at the most susceptible ages in their life, twelve to
sixteen.

On my father's conduct in the Philippines, I would simply say—without trying to defend or justify it—that so huge
crowds of people were forced to funnel through such narrow
routes with no planning at all that he actually had no grasp of
long-range implications of what was happening.

My father was given a place to die in a manner worthy of
a warrior. I feel that General MacArthur had appointed an excellent group of attorneys for my father in court. On the other
hand, however, I know about a Minnesota attorney who wrote
in effect that the tribunal was only a prearranged affair and that
the decision had been a foregone conclusion. In other words, he

thinks that what counted to the U.S. political-military establishment was the procedure rather than the substance.

Later in 1980, Mrs. Inomata made a visit to the site of her father's
execution and, on her return to Tokyo, granted an interview that was
published in the *Mainichi Daily News* issue of December 22nd.

On April 3, 1946, Lt. Gen. Masaharu Homma, former commander in chief of the Imperial Japanese Forces in the Philippines was led out to a spot in the grounds of the former Los
Baños internment camp, to face an execution squad of 13 American riflemen.

According to his daughter, Hisako Inomata, now 52, on information received from a Buddhist monk and an interpreter
who were present at her father's death by firing squad, Homma
chatted amiably with his executioners and delivered a 30-minute
sermon on the evils of war, which so moved the men that "when
my father told them he was now ready to die with dignity, the
soldiers couldn't bring themselves to pull the triggers," she says,
fighting back tears.

"He called to them three times, 'Please shoot! I am ready.' But
nobody moved. Eventually one of the men took aim. My father
prepared himself, and shouted 'Banzai for peace' in such a loud
voice the soldiers shuddered. At that time I was in Tokyo with
my mother, but I feel deeply I heard him shout at that moment.

"The soldier fired and my father fell. The Buddhist monk
turned him over and noted that a single bullet had penetrated
his heart. He died like a samurai, the only Japanese prisoner
permitted to be shot rather than hanged at the express orders of
General MacArthur, who had a lot of respect for my father. All
the other condemned men were hanged like criminals."

In an exclusive interview with the *Mainichi Daily News* at
her home in Kamakura, Mrs. Inomata revealed she had recently
returned from a trip to the Philippines where she erected a memorial on the spot where her father had died.

"It is sunny, warm," she says softly. "It lightens my heart to see the sunlight on the tombstone. My father would have been happy to see it, as he always told me, 'Hisako, don't feel dark and troubled. Don't cry.'"

"I am not trying to clear my father's name, for he was always innocent. I sincerely believe that. War trials are a farce. But that's over now. My memorial in the Philippines is a tribute to my father and the futility of war. I am sure he would have liked that."

It was impossible not to be moved by Homma's daughters words. The meeting with Hisako Inomata in Kamakura, conversations in Tokyo, and now this article were adding new dimensions to the image of the general that Cliff had held before. As he talked to Japanese scholars and read what he could find in English, he was belatedly following the advice offered by his father when Cliff, in 1945, had rejoiced over the condemnation of Homma, "Give this a lot of thought before you reach any final decisions of your own."

The quest for more information about the general's life and trial, and the germ of a story that Cliff felt he had to tell, would travel with him when he returned to Washington in the summer of 1981.

33

FROM THE DESK OF THE DIRECTOR

I N 1981, CLIFF WAS ASSIGNED to Washington once more, this time as
Director of USIA's Office of East Asia and Pacific Affairs. We had
ended what would be our final tour in Japan and these Washington
years would be the last ones with the agency. This time, as we settled
into our Bethesda home, bringing all our familiar furniture out of storage and resuming neighborhood conversations, our nest was an empty
one. And as each child branched out after undergraduate study, they
reached towards careers that would take them on paths quite different
from their parents' but also propelled by an international background.

Tom followed up his Reed degree in Philosophy by earning a master's
degree in landscape architecture at the University of Oregon. His focus
had been on preservation of the landscape in a global sense, sustainable
agriculture beginning with community organic gardens and expanding
into ever-widening networks to share skills and achievements on an international scale. He married Julie Reisner, the gifted ceramic artist we
had first met in Japan, and they created a home in Eugene with her studio next to the house.

Cindy, graduating Phi Beta Kappa with a degree in history from Brown, had moved with a friend to San Francisco seeking a job in the realm of social service. Her experience in Israel, especially the school-without-walls week spent studying the Israeli Arabs, had imbued her with a sense of concern for those who were marginalized in society. But as she explored the area where they lived in San Francisco's Mission District, she felt severely handicapped by not being able to speak Spanish. Her solution was to follow in big brother's footsteps and head to Guatemala for a summer of intensive Spanish learning. While there, she became so concerned about the history and current politics of that nation that she was determined to return to academe to learn more and be able to discuss what she was feeling as a scholar. While handling various jobs, she worked her way through first a master's then a Ph.D. in Latin American studies at Berkeley's University of California.

Meanwhile, Doug was working towards his degree in business (with a strong "minor" in sailing!) at the University of Oregon. I returned to Washington International School in an administrative role similar to the one I'd held at Nishimachi, and would shortly become head of the upper school once again.

Cliff had barely arranged the contents of his desk when he was summoned to serve as escort officer for a planeload of VIPs headed for China. Because the head of the delegation was U.S. Supreme Court Chief Justice Warren Burger, they were transported in "Air Force One"—the presidential plane—although technically the name was used only when the president was on board. Charles Wick, President Regan's close friend and the Director of USIA (a position that had been elevated to Cabinet status), was acting as the host for a cultural mission: the opening of an American art exhibition and the signing of a cultural agreement in Beijing. The first significant cultural exchange since diplomatic relations had been established between the U.S. and the Peoples' Republic, the show was a collection from the Boston Museum of Fine Arts, "Three Centuries of American Art." The other accompanying Very Important Persons were members of that museum's board of directors, each a distinguished citizen who expected treatment reflecting his or her stature. Chief Justice Burger was scheduled to cut the ribbon at the opening ceremony the afternoon following their arrival, and Charles Wick would sign the cultural agreement.

When the plane landed in Beijing John Thompson, the public affairs officer, was there to greet the visitors, and to take Cliff aside with an alarming message. "The show may not happen." All had been carefully reviewed, and approved, by representatives of the embassy and the Chinese government during its installation. But that day several high-ranking Chinese political officials had toured the exhibit and were shocked by the twentieth-century art. "Potentially too damaging to the moral character of the Chinese public. The twentieth century has to be removed," they said. The embassy took the position that it was all or nothing: "This is the exhibit we agreed to send, and we won't allow it to be edited and truncated."

John told Cliff that, as they spoke, intense negotiations were still going on between representatives of the two governments. "What's the chance of a positive outcome?" Cliff wanted to know. John said, "About fifty-fifty." The possibility of this voyage of thousands of miles by his planeload of VIPs being thwarted at its first port of call, and the inevitable explosion of tempers he would need to deal with, was not something Cliff wanted to share with Wick or the others. John said the negotiations would go on into the night.

"OK, we'll say nothing for now. When we're at breakfast tomorrow, you come into the dining room and give me a 'thumbs up' or 'thumbs down,' and I'll take it from there," Cliff told his friend and colleague.

The signal at breakfast was "thumbs up." What a relief! The embassy negotiators had prevailed and the exhibit as designed would be opened with due ceremony that afternoon—and with none of the distinguished visitors having been disturbed by the crisis.

As special envoys of President Reagan, Charles Wick, accompanied by Cliff and local USIA staff, made a formal call on Premier Deng Hsiao Ping in Beijing. Wick had a wry sense of humor and knew how to use it as a political tool. He noticed that Deng was chewing tobacco throughout their conversation, turning aside regularly to spit into a nearby spittoon. Wick interrupted the interpreter's recitation of the thoughts of China's supreme leader. "I have a question for the premier." Everyone waited eagerly for something of international significance. "Do you ever miss that thing?" he asked, nodding towards the spittoon. Everyone burst into laughter and U.S.-Chinese political tensions were relieved. In Shanghai, the delegation met with the all-powerful mayor of that city, who had been assigned to raise the contentious issue of the sovereignty of Taiwan. When the Mayor asked why the U.S. persisted in wrongly treating Taiwan as a nation separate from the People's Republic of China, Wick assumed a blank expression. "Taiwan? Taiwan? Where is that?" The interpreter could barely articulate his translation of the question, he was laughing so hard. It was impossible to restart the Taiwan discussion—again tension was deflated, and the discussion was tabled.

The entourage traveled on to Hong Kong, where the notables were visibly relieved to find the familiar comfort of western luxury hotels in contrast to the accommodations available at that time in China. The last stop was in Manila, where Cliff had scheduled a conference of all the public affairs officers in the Asia/Pacific region—similar to the one he'd been unable to attend several years earlier, in the wake of his accident—their first opportunity to meet with Director Wick. They were all entertained at Malacañan Palace by President Marcos and his wife. Imelda Marcos capped the evening's entertainment by serenading her guests with "California, Here I Come." Many were enchanted by the palatial treatment, but Cliff and his colleagues in the field were uneasy. The Marcos regime with all its excesses was in its waning days and the Foreign Service professionals were wary of being too cozy with the perpetrators.

I hadn't been able to travel on this particular mission, but when he returned Cliff entertained family and friends with tales about the ups and downs of shepherding a planeload of VIPs across cultural chasms in China and the Philippines. Later when I talked with John Thompson, who had sat through the Beijing night negotiations trying to salvage the Boston Museum show, he said, "Nancy, be glad you weren't along on this trip. Cliff was run ragged."

Recalling his time heading the Agency's area office in Washington, Cliff told Lew:

> It was an interesting time for us, in many ways, as area directors. A number of changes were instituted by Wick, like the WorldNet TV program. There was some question about

continuing the Fulbright program at one point, which the area directors resisted. We felt it would be a disaster if we were to reduce that program in any way. There was an effort to cut back on our posts, which we again resisted.

On a trip to China in 1982, Cliff met with the first group of Fulbright teachers in that country after the long period when China was closed to Americans. Living locally and working together with scholars in places far distant from Beijing—in terms of modernization as well as in geography—the Fulbrighters were a window on the world, a window with two-way views. Chinese were hungry to catch up with the outside world as brought into their neighborhoods by these men and women, and the Americans were just as eager to learn about China by being on the ground in this place formerly walled off by the "bamboo curtain."

I believe that after a while Wick began to realize he had a very impressive program out there in the field and excellent officers to work with. But it took a while for him to come to that realization, which is understandable, since he was coming in from an entirely different environment, the private sector, and USIS operations were new to him. After a while he wanted to attend all the conferences in the field "to be there with my PAOs."

The Director and I had our differences, but I think all the area directors at that time held firm on what they felt had to be done. He always challenged us. I certainly didn't agree with some of the things he was doing, and he knew it. So my last two years in USIA we were on the wrestling mat several times. Sometimes you were up. Sometimes you were down. He did bring in additional funding and we were grateful for that, although again we differed on the ways we felt it should be spent.

On the return from the 1981 trip to China for the Boston exhibition we were confronted with requests for major cuts in the program and it looked like we might lose some of our smaller posts. Holding these posts together, just making sure we kept our presence there, was one achievement I felt very

happy about. And our trip to China led to a number of important developments with the establishment of new posts such as
Shenyang and Chendu. We were doing a lot of work to open up
in China, meeting with Chinese officials constantly to imple-
ment the cultural agreement we'd signed earlier in Beijing.

It was a productive time and we were very fortunate to
have such an able staff in Beijing under John Thompson. I
should also mention the superb work of Virginia Loo Farris and
George Beasley who held down our China desk in the Area office. Like John, they spoke Mandarin fluently and had excellent
contacts with the Chinese. They were working long hours to
help set up the new posts and to launch our cultural program
in China. It was also helpful to have Arthur Hummel, a former
USIA officer who had been our PAO when I was in Burma, as
the U.S. ambassador in China during this time. Incidentally, we
were able to strengthen the Fulbright program in China and the
grantees did an outstanding job.

Those were some of the major accomplishments during a
period of relative calm in Asia. The situation was beginning
to deteriorate in the Philippines under Marcos and some of us
could see that coming. I personally felt we were getting too
close to Marcos and his administration. I expressed this view
to the director several times. Meanwhile, in Indochina, we followed the Cambodian situation with great concern. In Korea,
there was no real change except for student demonstrations that
resulted in the fire bombing of the Pusan Center.

That center was "manned" by a woman, one of three who had distinguished themselves in Korean language training and were assigned to
outlying Korean posts. The then U.S. ambassador and several other top
officials were horrified when they heard women were being sent to leadership positions in the male-oriented societies of Asia. Cliff went "to the
mat" on this one and, with the backing of government lawyers, said that
these women were fully qualified officers, the assignments were selected
on the basis of merit and training, and they must be allowed to proceed.
They went and served with distinction, as pioneers for the women officers

who came along later. One went on to become an ambassador to several very challenging sub-Saharan Africa nations.

As Cliff indicated in his comments to Lew, he was constantly battling to keep a vibrant USIS program in action, and to use all the tools developed by experienced professionals through the years to respond to new challenges. He would come home discouraged but had a great cure-all for stress. Building steps. Our house was at the top of a hill, and the back yard sloped into woods that screened us from neighbors below; they owned halfway up and we owned halfway down. After a particularly stressful week, Cliff would carve out steps into the hillside, leading into the woods. He'd had good intentions of working on his Homma project in his spare time, and he did make some progress, but he found that physical exertion was more what he needed. By the time this Washington assignment ended, our hillside was laced with flights of Forster-made steps.

As supervisor of all the public affairs officers in the East Asia region, Cliff did his best to keep them abreast of events back in the U.S. One way he did this was to institute what he called his "PAO Letter," a regular informal glimpse of the mood in Washington. His letter of November 15, 1982, was PAO Letter #19.

It is difficult to do justice in writing to the events of these last four days beginning with Veterans Day but I want to share some of the experience with you since it was a very special time. I have not known a time when I have been as moved by the outpouring of grief, pride, relief, affection, and comradeship between civilians of all ages. It was long overdue.

I am speaking of course of the recognition of those who fought and died in Vietnam and the coming together of veterans from all over the country. Beginning on the 11th at Arlington National Cemetery with the eloquent address of the Secretary of Defense and continuing to the climax event with the Eucharist at the National Cathedral yesterday, there was a strong sense of involvement with participants reaching out to each other. When I dropped by the Cathedral during the twenty-four-hour vigil last Saturday morning a legless veteran

in a wheelchair was reading the names for his half-hour segment, the tears streaming down his face. There were no dry
eyes that morning among the assembled. As for the parade, it
defied any kind of description. Having been in Washington for
the victory march of the troops down Constitution in 1945 led
by General Eisenhower and again later with Admiral Nimitz in
from the Pacific coming down Pennsylvania, I can only say that
Saturday's parade was equally if not more moving. Walking
along, not marching, were Special Forces' vets wearing their old
berets and camouflage gear, others in business suits, an Indian
contingent with their ceremonial headgear, General Westmo-
reland leading the parade in civvies, no medals, the veterans in
wheelchairs and on crutches behind him. Compared to all the
precision-marching and spit-and-polish of those earlier World
War II returning-home parades, there was a humanity about
this one with the onlookers reaching out to shake hands, merg-
ing with the veterans.

And, finally, the monument—that stark, low-profile wall
with its 57,939 names carved into the black marble. The *Washington Post* editorial of November 13 says it all in my view and I
wish to share it with you along with two other articles which I
found to be among the most impressive of the many appearing
over these last four days. It is a beautiful monument not only
in its simplicity but again for the way it reached out to so many
of the mourners and onlookers. Gold Star mothers mixed with
veterans to seek out names of loved ones and old buddies. I will
not, nor could I, adequately describe the drama this last weekend with veterans meeting up again before the wall, many of
them for the first time since the conflict. A memorial to the victims of war and yet so very alive in preserving the names and
evoking so much emotion among the still living.

While you will be reading and hearing a great deal about
those weekend events I do feel I owe it to you to share some of
the sadness and joy of the whole experience while it is still fresh.
There is a great story to tell about America here but I am afraid
it would be difficult for us to do it justice. A reverent silence

before the Monument, each with his or her own thoughts, perhaps is best after all.

When I once again became head of the upper school, grades six through twelve, at the Washington International School, I got more than I bargained for. Along with the satisfaction of being one of the helmsmen for this unique institution and the joy of working with the international body of students and faculty, I fell heir to rising labor unrest. With good reason, the teachers wanted to be paid salaries that came close to the market wages for private schools. I was caught in the middle—I fully appreciated a new generation of women who wanted their professionalism tangibly recognized, but as "management" I was on the opposite side of where my sympathies lay. The discontent wasn't quelled until well after my departure from the scene.

When a new opportunity arose, I found it difficult to pass up. Philip Bossert, the president of a small liberal arts college in Hawaii, had heard about the International Baccalaureate. He wondered if it could be introduced at Hawaii Loa College as a precollegiate academy, filling a need for a private secondary-school option on the windward side of Oahu. He was visiting Washington and scheduled a visit to WIS to see the program in action. I was his guide for the day and the outcome was an invitation to come to launch the IB on his campus.

Cliff was close to retirement age and welcomed the idea. "You've followed me around the world all these years, and now I'd be happy to follow you to Hawaii!" We accepted the invitation in January, but before setting out I would complete the 1982-1983 academic year at WIS and Cliff would follow through on his pet projects at the agency until June.

In his final comments to Lew, Cliff mentioned the strong team of officers who were working with him in the East Asia area office, naming one after another and describing their special strengths. These were named, but he also admired and cherished many others who shared the USIS experience over the course of his career. The list is long, enriched by those local employees who served for many years in their native countries and provided invaluable expertise and continuity. Each name invokes respect and affection.

So I felt that the area was in very good hands and it was time to say "sayonara" and head out to Hawaii with Nancy, who had just been offered a very special job to establish the International Baccalaureate Program in this state for the first time. After her accompanying me to exotic places, I figured it was her turn and I would follow her for a change and carry the bags.

Lew asked, "No regrets?"

I think there will always be some regrets, which I guess many of us have experienced. USIA was our "way of life" for so long and it was hard to break away, although I felt the time had come. There were exciting and challenging periods in those years of great change following the war, and we were fortunate to have worked with so many special people abroad, not only our own staffs but with the many contacts we made in the different countries where we were privileged to serve. It was a very special career.

And there are such good officers going out there now, all of them so well-trained and with linguistic ability. I think that if I had any problems with the organization in recent years, it has been a case of too much emphasis on the technology of its programming, not enough on personal relations. That sounds very simplistic, but you know what I mean. Earlier there was a tremendous enthusiasm and involvement, a real sense of mission that I sometimes find missing now. I think about the money that went into WorldNet, for example, and what they got out of it. If that had only gone into people, into programs really involving Americans in direct contact with our audiences overseas, certainly more of it into libraries—the kind of libraries you and I have been talking about—and more into center operations and exchanges, this would have made far more sense in my view.

Cliff, as area director, called a conference of the public affairs officers in the East Asia region, to convene in Honolulu in the spring of 1983.

It was here, in the presence of his respected colleagues and treasured friends, that he made the first public announcement of his intention to retire in June and move with me to Hawaii. They responded by buying a large hammock that Cliff was instructed to hang between a couple of palm trees at our retirement home. Dave Hitchcock, the Public Affairs Officer in Tokyo, sent a slightly more formal farewell in a June telegram from the American Embassy.

For EA/Director Cliff Forster from entire USIS/Japan Staff:

All of us are thinking of you today, as you close one chapter and prepare to open another in your distinguished career, which has contributed so much to USIA's programs and priorities over the years. Not only in Asia but also in the Middle East. What we most appreciate of course has been your dedicated and splendid service on behalf of U.S.-Japan relations for thirty years. At every level our agency has to offer its careerists—from Kobe, to Fukuoka and Tokyo; from Desk Officer to Area Deputy and finally, capping your career, to the position of Area Director.

It was not only your obvious ability that made so much difference. But also your infectious enthusiasm reaching every USIS element and post in Japan which saw you in action, heard your voice, and read your exhortations and numerous thoughtful analyses.

Japan remains for the U.S. a country and culture we have difficulty in communicating with. The famous and oft-referred-to "communications gap" may never be closed entirely. But we have increasingly succeeded in bridging that gap, anticipating likely areas needing special attention and suggesting imaginative ways of welcoming the most serious problems in public affairs and cultural understanding. No one in our memory can take more credit for these successes over the years than you can.

As you head—once again—to the Pacific, we know your eyes and thoughts, and always active mind and pen, will be focused on this part of the world and on the continuing search for better communication between East Asia and the United States.

To you and Nancy, we send our warmest best wishes. May the breezes of Hawaii blow gently on you both, not only to swing that new hammock, but to help propel you back out here soon and often!

Good luck Cliff and Banzai!
Hitchcock

Before we packed our bags and vacated the house, Doug made a farewell trip back to his birthplace in Washington. The sailing enthusiast had indulged his passion from his first days in college, as captain of the University of Oregon sailing team. He had further access to sailboats and earned spending money when he took a job at a marina on a local lake, and in 1982 he had taught sailing at the Annapolis Sailing School, only an hour away from us in Maryland. This time he came with a companion, Kerry Tolleth, whom he had met when she competed against him on the sailing team of Lewis and Clark College. The two of them rented a twenty-four-foot sailboat to take us on a weekend excursion exploring the inlets of Chesapeake Bay where Doug and his dad had first sailed together. Now the skills of the son had far surpassed those of the father, the sky was clear, and there was no need for shouted commands, in French or any other language.

For twenty-one years the house in D.C. had been the roots of our family tree. It held a lot of vivid memories—joy at the birth of Doug, sorrow at the death of President Kennedy, frustrations from work carved into steps on the hillside, lines proudly drawn on a wall in the basement marking the growth of each child, and many great parties. But, much as we enjoyed living in Washington's metropolitan area and treasured our many friends there, we didn't grieve over our departure. We were moving to Hawaii!

34

THE EMERITUS YEARS

O UR NEW HOUSE IN HAWAII more than compensated for the one
we left behind in Maryland. Reached by a steep winding road,
its three levels perched at about 1,800 feet on a ridge that overlooked a green valley to the next ridge in one direction, and over the
back of Diamond Head and to Pacific Ocean sunsets on the other. High
ceilings and wraparound windows with sliding doors leading out onto
a lanai took full advantage of the wonderful view. The house itself was
modest, but had ample space for the two of us and the many guests who
visited us in Hawaii, especially during snowy winter months. All four
bedrooms were often filled with family and friends and Cliff and I each
had our own workspace on the lower level.

During his twenty-one years of "retirement," Cliff did a lot more
than swing in that hammock. From the beginning in Hawaii, he was
immersed in international dialogues, first with the Pacific Forum, which
was to achieve great respect as a conduit for discussion and policy for-
mulation among leaders throughout the Pacific and back in Washington,
and later as Director of Honolulu's Pacific and Asian Affairs Council,
which offered informative programs for both youth and adult members

of the community. He also spent many hours supporting my work with the International Baccalaureate Diploma Program and traveling with me to IB conferences in Europe, Asia, and the United States. And he finally had time to devote to his manuscript on General Homma, doing research and drafting chapters that intertwined his own experiences with his encounters with the General's story.

I spent three years at Hawaii Loa College, the first one planning and the second and third launching the first two classes of IB students. The work was challenging, recruiting students to spend their last two years of high school on a college campus where they would follow a rigorous program almost no one in Hawaii had ever heard about. I also pursued the special goal of bringing students from China to do the program, waiving tuition and finding homes where they could live.

In September of 1985, two young women came to Honolulu from Beijing, the first students from the Peoples' Republic to study at the high-school level in the U.S. They had completed China's ten years of preuniversity schooling, and two years at Beijing Teachers' College studying to be English teachers. If they were successful in achieving the IB diploma after two years with us, their college would award them its four-year degree.

Chen Meng moved in with us and became our Chinese foster daughter; our nest was no longer empty. It was a steep—and fun—learning curve for all of us. She had been a junior Red Guard in the waning days of the Cultural Revolution, but at heart she was a typical teenager wanting to escape her shell. Her hatching included coping with totally new vocabulary in biology and studying modern world history from a very different perspective than she had learned in China.

One evening as I was preparing dinner she asked Cliff to help her understand the history assignment for that day, analysis of *The Communist Manifesto* by Karl Marx. She wasn't sure about some of the English words and was confused about the meaning. Cliff guided her through the document, explaining point by point. "Uhh!" she finally exclaimed. "Mr. Forster, that's junk!" The idea that the family was subservient to the state grossly offended her, the daughter of a very close-knit and proud family. I, from my perch in the kitchen a half-level up from the living room, chuckled inwardly. I loved the irony of an ex-Red Guard seeking illumination on communist doctrine from a retired U.S. diplomat!

Chen Meng and her fellow student, Yue Ping, had each been allowed to leave China with a mere $32 in currency. To earn spending money they both worked at the school, and Chen Meng's mother sent her monthly packages with lovingly hand-sewn clothes, toothpaste, and film—all of which were easily affordable in China on the parents' combined salaries as skilled chemists in a Beijing factory. Those packages were always a source of wonder to our mailman, fat and cushioned and wrapped with neatly stitched white-cotton fabric rather than brown paper. The padding used to protect the contents was sanitary napkins.

One Saturday returning home after grocery shopping, I spotted a handmade sign. "There's a garage sale up the street," I told Chen Meng. "Let's stop and see what they have."

"But, Mrs. Forster," she commented, "you already have a garage!" She was a fast learner, and soon was happily supplementing her mother's homemade clothes at weekend sales.

Cliff, in the meantime was trying his wings in his first job as a civilian, working at the Pacific Forum as the assistant to a retired admiral who had a reputation for running a tight ship as a submarine commander. Lloyd "Joe" Vasey's mission was to create a respected center for research and dialogue in the middle of the Pacific—goals very similar to those Cliff had formulated during his Foreign Service career. As I headed over the mountains to my job on the windward side of Oahu in the mornings, he went an office in downtown Honolulu.

One of Cliff's projects was to create an opportunity for dialogue between parliamentarians from countries in Asia, the U.S., and Canada. This idea grew out of his 1971 project for the State Department's Senior Seminar, when he had traveled to strategic studies institutes in Europe and met scholars and writers who were anxious to meet and exchange ideas with their colleagues in Japan. Under Cliff's guidance, the Pacific Forum hosted the first of what would be several meetings, across borders and cultures, among people who debated policies and made laws. They came together in the gentle climate of Hawaii at the confluence of East and West in the Pacific, a place where people from very different backgrounds have melded into a congenial society. This enhanced the grace of the dialogue.

When he wasn't working on projects for Joe Vasey, Cliff was sorting through the records of his research about General Homma, his meeting

Retired in Hawaii, Cliff began writing the story of his captor, General Homma.

with the General's daughter, and conversations with members of the defense team at Homma's military trial. He began drafting the story that he felt should be told.

Emerging was a portrait of a Japanese military man who had considerable experience abroad, spoke English, and had read widely in Western history and literature. Born on Sado Island in 1888, a graduate of Imperial Japanese Army Academy and Japan's Army Staff College, Homma had been assigned to the Japanese Embassy in London in April of 1918, and was attached to the British Expeditionary Force in Europe from November 1918 until the following November. At that same time, Douglas MacArthur was also on the Western Front and Homma remarked to his defense lawyers during his trial that he had great admiration for the American general and regretted they had not met during World War I.

Homma had been a resident officer in India in 1922 under an officer-exchange program between the British and Japanese Armies. In 1926 he became a member of the faculty at the Army Staff College, and in 1927 was assigned as aide-de-camp to his Imperial Highness Prince Chichibu (the emperor's brother). In 1930 Homma was once again assigned to Europe, first to England as army attaché, then for two years in Geneva, mainly at the Japanese legation to the League of Nations. He was appointed chief of the public affairs/press section in the army ministry in 1932 and once again, in 1936, made an official visit to Europe. He was rising in rank and by 1938 became commanding general of the 27th Infantry Division in North China.

Elevated to commanding general of the 14th Army in 1941, Homma was ordered to lead the invasion of the Philippines from Taiwan following the Pearl Harbor attack, and to defeat the American and Filipino forces in Manila within fifty days. His failure to do so, coupled with suspicions about his former familiarity with the West among his more rabidly nationalistic colleagues, led to his recall to Tokyo, at the time the young Cliff Forster was under Japan's benevolent custody.

Homma was replaced by a general deemed to be more aggressive and who was lionized for Japan's victories in Malaysia and Singapore, General Tomoyuki Yamashita. Divested of significant responsibility, Homma retired in August of 1942 and returned to his home on Sado Island. At the end of the war he returned to Tokyo, where he was arrested by U.S. military officers and taken to Manila for his trial as a war criminal.

Drafting his Homma manuscript, Cliff wrote:

> For General Homma, the fall of Manila had been an empty victory. MacArthur had eluded his grasp by the strategic move of his forces into Bataan and his headquarters to Corregidor. The initial stages of Homma's campaign were highly successful and Homma's forces occupied Manila within thirty days. MacArthur's withdrawal of his forces into Bataan, however, required Homma to fight on for another four months, much to the dissatisfaction of Homma and of General Headquarters in Tokyo. The surrender

of one of America's most esteemed generals would have been a great psychological victory for the Japanese and MacArthur's ability to elude capture by breaking through Japanese lines to reach Australia from Corregidor only compounded the Japanese dissatisfaction.

The failure to win an early victory and obtain MacArthur's surrender was to cost Homma dearly. He had won the enmity of Prime Minister Hideki Tojo and the Army Chief of Staff, General Hajime Sugiyama, who were critical of his inability to cut off MacArthur's retreat into Bataan, which had resulted in a long drawn-out campaign. In June of 1942, Homma was relieved of his command by General Headquarters, given menial tasks in Tokyo, and soon put on reserve status.

Homma had also won the bitter enmity of MacArthur, whose forces he had defeated on the field of battle, a defeat MacArthur was never to forget. Nor was he to forget the atrocities committed by Homma's forces during the "Death March" following the Bataan surrender, when Americans and Filipinos in weakened condition were cut down in large numbers while forced to walk many miles north to their prison camps. Homma is often refereed to as "the Butcher of Bataan" by many Americans who remember the Death March.

Just before leaving the Philippines for Tokyo in the summer of 1942, Homma told a well-known Japanese writer, Hidemi Kon, of his high regard for MacArthur.

"He is a fine general versed in the arts of pen and sword. I think of him as a good soldier and a good political administrator. I am quite satisfied to have fought against him for my honor."

The feeling was not reciprocal and in February of 1946, Homma was found guilty of war crimes by a U.S. military tribunal established by Macarthur in Manila. No evidence was produced during the trial that he had been aware of the Bataan atrocities or had given orders to commit them. He did admit "moral responsibility" and asserted that he "should have known" of the acts of cruelty.

This set a new precedent for military trials and was contested in the dissenting opinions of Justices Murphy and Rutledge when the Homma sentence was appealed to the U.S. Supreme Court. While the majority opinion held that the Court was powerless to intervene since the Army had the legal authority, Murphy and Rutledge maintained that Homma's trial, as in the case of the earlier trial of General Tomoyuki Yamashita, had violated due process under the Fifth Amendment and was therefore unconstitutional.

Homma's execution took place the following April in the foothills of Mount Makiling near the town of Los Baños southeast of Manila. The U.S. military witness to the execution, Colonel Thomas Jenkins, stated in his final report to the Commanding General, United States Army Forces, Western Pacific:

"Masaharu Homma was shot to death by musketry at 0100. He had no statement to make; faced toward Japan; gave a 'Banzai' for the Emperor and another for Japan. He was calm, collected and showed no sign of emotion."

Cliff was stimulated by what he had learned and was now writing down. He found himself evaluating the experience of the Japanese General in a new light, which forced him to reexamine the impressions of his youth and to consider the relationships and insights he had developed during our many years in Japan. Ever gregarious, Cliff was eager to share his work with his friends, and the Homma story became dinner-table conversation when we entertained and when we dined out. Many who listened were fascinated and encouraged him to carry on. When we visited California, however, those who had been his companions in internment camp reacted with dismay. "Why would you want to tell the story of the Butcher of Bataan?" they asked. Undaunted, Cliff continued to write.

In 1985, Hawaii Loa College was struggling financially. The faculty, while personally gracious to me and supportive of my students, was unhappy that the fragile budget was saddled with a new, noncollegiate program that would take several years to pay for itself. They voted to terminate the IB at the end of the academic year. That vote sent me shopping for a new IB home, and I was lucky to meet Lester Cingcade, the new headmaster at the Mid-Pacific Institute, a private school with boarding and day students in grades seven through twelve. Cingcade sought ways to strengthen the academic program of this century-old institution, which had originally taught farming and woodworking skills to boys and housekeeping to girls. He also wanted to build upon the potential as a boarding school to become more international, and decided the IB was a perfect match for his goals. We made plans to move the program to Mid-Pacific in the fall.

I also made plans to attend the annual conference for IB schools, taking place that year in Washington D.C. Cliff accompanied me, and arranged ahead of time to spend a day in Baltimore with John Skeen, the army major who had been a reluctant leader of Homma's defense team. Sadly, Mrs. Skeen called the day before the appointment to say her husband was ill. Skeen died before that meeting could take place, but his family, through the years, had heard his account of the Homma trial and knew his disappointment in its outcome and the admiration he developed for the strength of his client. They were delighted that Cliff was interested in the story; they too felt it should be told. Mrs. Skeen sent Cliff copies of the letters that the major had written her from the Philippines, as well as other correspondence relating to the trial. These letters further illuminated the person of Masaharu Homma and provided insight into the dynamics of his trial and sentence. Cliff and I read them with fascination—and awe.

John Skeen was based at Angeles in the Philippines as an infantry major when he received orders to proceed to Manila for the trial of General Homma. He had graduated from law school and passed his Maryland bar exams just before the war, in October of 1941. In December of 1945 he expected to be shipped home within two weeks. Instead, he wrote his wife, he had to postpone his return "to try some damn Japanese general." He knew nothing about Homma and cared less. War was over. The other lawyers felt the same way. Skeen had been selected as chief counsel only because of his rank, Major, rather than his qualifications as a trial lawyer.

At 11:45 p.m. on Saturday December 15, 1945 he wrote to Dorothy Skeen:

My sweetest darling,

Before I start to cry I want to tell you I *love* you more than anyone in the world. You are wonderful and I need you, need you tonight. I have had too much to drink, but I have been drowning my sorrows. Something happened to me today that shouldn't happen to a dog. Within one minute I became essentially screwed and famous. I told you last night I was going to Manila to check on my new job. I was really slapped in the face. I am now Chief Defense Counsel for General Homma and will be until after the trial, which will probably extend to 60 days after 5 January. The worst has happened. After four years, the Army has decided I was once a lawyer.

I am one of the most famous guys in this town right now. When I walked into JAGD section of WESPAC the Colonel nearly jumped over the desk to greet me. The heat was on and General Donovan wanted to arraign Homma on Tuesday morning. After arguing with the General, we will have the arraignment on Wednesday morning. I have never worked harder in my life than I did today. I spent the entire day running from colonel to generals trying to find out the score. Tomorrow I gather together my two captains and two lieutenant assistants for a planning of the strategy etc. We have an office in the high commissioner's building across the hall from General Homma's cell...

After a few days I will recover from the shock of being essential and will give the SOB everything possible in the way of defense. I haven't talked to him yet, but expect to officially announce my services tomorrow sometime. They tell me he speaks fluent English which will help a great deal...

I will keep you posted on the happenings, but in the meantime read the papers about how our friend Masaharu Homma ex-Lt. General is making out. If he doesn't do well, you know whose fault it is, but really I shall do my very best.

I love you more than ever.

All my love.
Jack

The following day, Sunday, Skeen started reviewing papers from the Yamashita Trial, which had just ended, to learn what he was up against. He also met Homma. As he wrote Dorothy,

> This is a tough way to learn the practice of law after four years of being away from it and so little actual practice before I came into the army... The prosecution has been working for many months with the war crimes commission and apparently they know all the ropes. I know we will do a good job for the old man, even though I am afraid it is hopeless with public opinion in its present state. He is a most appreciative and pathetic figure, but I believe will make a favorable impression before a commission.

At eight p.m. on Thursday, December 20th, Skeen wrote,

> I am beginning to get straightened out and things should run a bit smoother. Yesterday, as you probably read in the papers, we got a slap from the commission. I asked for one month to prepare. The prosecution admitted that it would take longer than the two weeks they asked, but the commission arbitrarily set the date for trial as 3 Jan. It is almost a physical impossibility to get the work done in that time and it certainly cannot be done properly and to the best advantage of the accused. Lady, this whole procedure is a most tremendous farce. I am ashamed that the American people permit such a shameful thing as this to occur. Not that war criminals don't deserve to hang, but the colossal hypocrisy of these trials is disgraceful. It is claimed that a fair trial is being accorded, but the whole affair is the nearest thing to the Gestapo that our nation has ever devised. Everyone concerned in the trial, i.e. commission, prosecution and defense, is under Gen'l MacArthur. When the trial is over it is Gen'l MacArthur who reviews the proceedings and approves the sentence. The final straw is that the accused is a man who defeated our gen'l in battle. In the face of present world public opinion no man could receive a fair trial under this setup. The result is inevitable.

The trial concluded in early February with the conviction of General Homma and his sentence to be executed. On February 9th, the condemned general wrote a letter to his defense team:

Major John H. Skeen, Jr.
Captain George W. Ott
Captain Frank R. Coder, Jr.
Captain George A. Furness
1st Lieutenant Robert L. Pelz
1st Lieutenant Leonard Wetanpsky

I found myself utterly impotent to express adequately the profound gratitude I feel at my heart for the hard and tremendous fight you all put up for my defense. It is indeed a tough work, for everything is against me and all the circumstances are most unfavorable.

However, you all stood by justice and tried your very best, leaving no stone unturned to give me a fair trial which I know is denied to me from the outset.

You are quite justified to have prejudice against me as the commander of hostile forces and I was pictured an entirely wrong man thanks to the propaganda, long before you knew me.

Nevertheless, you showed me nothing but empathetic understanding and consideration, and presented in the most efficacious manner to the court my version upon the case, letting it see the other side of the picture.

I realize now that I should have killed myself many months ago, if I had known it should come to this. Only I could not think that the commander-in-chief can be punished by death for his moral responsibility.

I am well aware what the verdict would be and I have had no illusion on this point from the beginning. There is no greater love than to die for your friends.

Many officers and men died in Bataan and elsewhere in the Philippines, having fought under my command. It is not without significance for me to join them. When I come to think that I am the man wholly misunderstood by the world, I feel sad, but it cannot be helped.

God in Heaven will judge me and historians in the future will judge me rightly. My countrymen know why I am to die and none of them believe my guilt. That is enough for me. I thank you all again. Please accept my heartfelt gratitude and appreciation to the impartial stand you have taken so bravely. I respect Americans all the more for your sake.

I wish you all very happiness and good health.

> Your grateful servant,
> Masaharu Homma

The defense team responded to Homma's letter on February 11th:

Dear General Homma,

Your letter of February 9th deeply touched us all. We felt that it was typical of the kindness you have shown us ever since the first day we met you almost two months ago. We are glad to know that you think we have done well, even though it may not have been enough.

We cannot agree that you should have killed yourself long ago. Rather we think you showed rare courage after you were relieved of your command and when you testified before officers of the army you had defeated. We feel that you owed it to yourself, your family, your country and the world to tell your story, your side of what happened. If the finding of the commission is what you expect, we believe that it is the verdict of today and will not be the verdict of history. Apparently the war still goes on, but some day men's passions will have cooled and truth will be sought and respected.

We are very proud of having defended you, not only as officers of our army but also as members of another great profession, lawyers, whose duty it is to defend those whom they believe guiltless. When we first met you we knew you only as the man about whom we had read in the newspapers. Now we

know another man, a sensitive and courageous man, a great
general and gentleman, the man for whom so many friends and
comrades testified and the man your wife described so bravely
and truthfully on the witness stand. We have come to hold you
in great honor and respect.

Sincerely,

Major John H. Skeen, Jr., et al

Major General Basilio J. Valdes of the Philippine Army was an ob-
server at the trial. In May he wrote to Arthur Eby, the Secretary of the
Barristers' Club of Baltimore, to communicate the high esteem he felt for
Skeen and to praise his defense of General Homma.

The job had been imposed on him. As a good soldier, he
obeyed orders. He studied the case thoroughly and presented
a brilliant defense. He was severely handicapped though, because Homma was convicted by public opinion both American
and Filipino long before the trial began. I have a great respect
for him as a lawyer. Never, during the course of the trial, did
he interpose silly and unnecessary objections to prolong the
proceedings. It was the unanimous opinion of the five generals composing the military commission that Major Skeen did a
magnificent work in a very difficult situation.

A very different opinion of the trial and the role of John Skeen was
voiced by a retired colonel, William Beck, from Phoenix, Arizona. Copies of the following letter, written while the trial was underway, were sent
to General MacArthur and to the Manila press.

Major Skeen:

I fully believe that I express the sentiments of 99% of all
right-minded Americans and 100% of all Filipino people when
I say to you that when you were detailed by higher military authority to act as counsel for the Japanese general, Homma, you
were expected to do just that, and to go no further than to see
that the defendant's legal rights were conserved at the military

court before which this Asiatic beast is being tried for his unspeakable crimes against American boys in uniform and hapless Filipinos.

But on the contrary, you lean backward, and go entirely out of your way to bring about a defeat of the ends of justice by an employment of all the infamous shyster tactics of a "lower-east-side-Shnitkin."

...Newspaper columns and editorials show an outspoken criticism of your questionable ethics of court procedure. As a lawyer you should be spit upon and scorned by every good citizen...

Just what will be thought of you by the survivors of the "Death March of Bataan," and by the bereaved relatives whose loved ones were wantonly murdered or fell and died in that march, as you, a responsible—and supposedly respectable—commissioned officer in the pay of the United States attempt to win freedom for this notorious war criminal—who every American and Filipino know is guilty as hell—is something to conjure with...

Ye Gods, and seven devils from Hell! How about the tears of countless mothers whose boys, from no fault of their own, and without their consent were snatched from loved ones to be thrown into the bloody holocaust of war, and as prisoners of war were tortured and killed by yellow bellied savages...

> Very truly,
> Wm. F. Beck

Three and a half years after the General's trial and execution, Fujiko Homma wrote the following letter to Major Skeen:

> No. 10 Oharamachi
> Bunkyo-ku, Tokyo, Japan
> 19 September, 1949

My Dear John H. Skeen:

Please forgive me that I have not written you after departed with you. I was delighted to send this letter to you, entrusting with Mr. Furness.

How have you been getting along? I can recall clearly and well about you and your great actions.

I appreciate very much your kindness towards us and I and my children do feel the eternal thanking and the highest respect to you as well as my late husband told you in his letter.

I was ill in bed for a month after I came back from Manila, and I heard of my husband's death in the bed, but I became well soon. I am very well, now.

My first son, Masahiko, demobilized from Siberia ten days ago after the elapse of seven years. I have three children now, and I am very happy. To my fortune he has not changed to the Communist.

We decided to carry on a garden-husbandry (the high grade) or the chicken-farm in the nearest future. This plan is for reconstructing of my family life. He is a graduate of the Tokyo Agricultural University and I am also interested in the country life.

My daughter, Hisako, is now attending the International College of the Sacred Heart and her subject is English language. She learned the shorthand in this summer vacation and she training this technique while she attend this college. After her graduation she wants to study at the States.

I have a ray of hope which is to look after my children's growth, though there are many hardships in front of me.

Japan is entering to the cool autumn day by day. This season is the most pleasant season in Japan. Many beautiful autumnal flowers, especially chrysanthemum, bloom beautifully. We will have many harvest in this season, for instance rice, bean, chestnuts, grape, persimmon and so forth.

I would like to send the letter to you from now on, so please inform your address.

Then, I will pray for you and your family health.

Cordially yours,
Fujiko Homma

P.S. I have received husband's final record through Mr. Furness from General MacArthur in April.

As I reread these letters in 2009, I am deeply moved, as was Cliff when he first received them. Despite a full-time day job, Cliff spent evening and weekend hours at his downstairs desk, laboriously typing his manuscript with two fingers on an ancient upright typewriter. When his family finally persuaded him to modernize, he reluctantly turned to a Tandy computer, protesting that the best journalists all used the hunt-and-peck system on typewriters.

His new day job was at the Pacific and Asian Affairs Council, Honolulu's equivalent of the World Affairs Council in San Francisco and other cities. These organizations sponsor political speakers and grassroots dialogues on current issues, informing a wide cross-section of citizens and working with students in schools to increase their international awareness. The former executive director had been recruited by Hawaii's governor to establish and run a foreign affairs section out of his office and Cliff was asked to take her place. Here his and my careers were even more fully aligned, as the council moved its office into a building on the Mid-Pacific Institute campus and we escorted its students to statewide student conferences and an annual Model United Nations.

Following the end of the Gulf War in February 1991, students at an IB school in Jordan had organized a peace conference, bringing together students from other IB schools to discuss ways to prevent future war. "We have just known the fear of being caught in the middle of a war zone and experienced rockets flying across our country to Israel," they told their principal, who was originally from Palestine, "and we don't want this to happen again." Impressed by their initiative, and the logic of students in the worldwide network of IB schools coming together to discuss issues from their different perspectives, we organized a follow-up conference at the Mid-Pacific Institute.

For our June '93 conference, the students chose the theme "Sequel to Rio: A New World Harmony," hearkening back the pioneering 1992 United Nations meeting in Brazil that focused the world's attention on challenges to the environment. Environment was defined in its broadest sense, encompassing culture, economics, politics and nationalism, and education. The student delegates lived together in the school dorms and experienced a demanding agenda of working and plenary sessions, interspersed with trips to museums and cultural centers, Pearl Harbor and the U.S. Military Command, working farms, and local attractions like Diamond Head Crater and Sea Life Park. A week of meetings on Oahu was followed by a work week on the island of Kauai, which had recently been ravaged by a hurricane. In an article for the August, 1993, issue of *IB World* I wrote:

> From the moment the first foreign students began arriving and moving into the school dorms, there was an exciting interaction between the students of various nationalities... Students from lands where there is ethnic strife (the former Yugoslavia and East Africa, for example) were impressed by the racial and cultural harmony they saw in Hawaii. Presentations by several of our guest speakers pointing to the frustrations and failures of this society to satisfy the needs of Hawaiians made for a realistic view of problems but did not detract from the sense that these problems are being addressed in Hawaii with considerably more success than elsewhere.
>
> The students not only learned from each other and with each other, but were given a "sense of place" here in Hawaii and an opportunity to hear different views about global as well as local environmental issues. We had an impressive array of scholars, artists, and professionals who rallied to accept invitations to participate.

Memories of achievements during our years with USIS and Cliff's ready-made skills were pivotal in the planning and execution of the student conference. *The Honolulu Advertiser* for Sunday, June 20th headlined an article: "Earth's children: Their harmony offers lessons."

The contrast was striking.

In Vienna, leaders of the world's countries fought down and dirty at the United Nations Conference on Human Rights over whether all humans are entitled to a certain level of safety and dignity.

At the same time, here in our Island state often touted for its racial harmony (albeit sometimes to romantic extremes), nearly 90 youths from 17 nations sat peacefully with one another this week to reach accord on how to ensure the future of our planet.

The following year I was eligible for a sabbatical leave. I had been tiptoeing into the world of the internet and was intrigued by the possibilities it offered for communication among students and teachers of IB schools. My project would be to visit colleagues in different parts of the world, to explore together how we might converse and educate with this incredible new resource. It was also a great excuse for Cliff and me to enjoy the pleasures of travel and visit some of the schools that had sent delegates to Honolulu. We packed our bags and set off on a voyage to four continents and nine countries, from Beijing to Italy to New Zealand to Mexico. Seeds were planted, and within a few years the IB was officially studying ways to use the new technology for management, instruction, and nurturing international-mindedness.

The following summer, while we were visiting our children and grandchildren in California and Oregon, seeds of another kind were planted in our minds. Our offspring were all on the West Coast, and Hawaii was a long and costly plane ride away. "Why is it," our three-year-old granddaughter asked, looking up at us with tears in her big brown eyes, "that you only come for a few days and then we don't see you until Christmas?"

We decided it was time to move to California, as soon as I completed the necessary "pay back" year following my sabbatical. We wanted to see more of our four grandchildren—along with their parents—while they were still young, and at age sixty-six it was time for me to exit the classroom.

When we left Hawaii in 1995 we had been there twelve years, the longest we had ever lived in one place. Again we were leaving a home that held many wonderful memories, as well as that gorgeous Diamond Head and Pacific Ocean view. And again, we packed all our worldly goods, including Cliff's extensive reference library on the Pacific war and the tea chests with those bulging envelopes of papers and photos marked "to be sorted later," plus my boxes and boxes of teaching materials. Fortunately the house we had already bought in California had many feet of bookshelves, built-in file cabinets, an upstairs alcove where the chests fit perfectly, and room in the basement garage to store those boxes. And our living room with a cathedral ceiling opened onto a spacious deck with a marvelous view across an inlet of San Francisco Bay to the region's highest mountain. Instead of ocean sunsets we could watch the sun sink behind Mount Tamalpais.

When we moved into our home in Tiburon, Doug's family lived about fifteen minutes away in Mill Valley. He was working with Old Navy in San Francisco and his wife Kerry had her hands full with two preschoolers, daughter Taylor age four and son Wyn nearly two. The parents were pleased to have on-call babysitters nearby and we looked forward to the times we could have one or both of that young pair all to ourselves. Doug, who had seen his own grandparents only sporadically over the years, was delighted that his children were not so deprived.

Our other offspring were not as easily accessible, but at least we were all on the same landmass and in the same time zone. Tom and his new wife, Sarah, had bought a twenty-eight acre farm on Orcas Island in Washington's Puget Sound and with their small daughter, Makala, were living a rustic life in a yurt while building their house with timber from their farm as support pillars and flooring and straw bales for the walls. We joined their neighbors and other eager workers who pitched in to put up the walls over several summer weekends. Fliers left around the island and on the ferries that connected the islands to the mainland promised baby sitting and gourmet organic luncheons to all comers. Foundations were being laid for a model organic farm that would become an educational institution, a gathering place for like-minded people.

Cindy had established herself as a professor in southern California, teaching courses on Latin America at Scripps College. Her students came from the several schools in the consortium of Claremont colleges that share classes and professors. Her graduate research had been in and about Guatemala, and when classes were not in session she returned, and still does return, to Guatemala to continue her research and be with her friends there.

I was now out of the classroom but, it developed, not out of the IB. The organization's regional office in New York was coping with a rapidly expanding program, and needed volunteers with IB experience and free time to help with that expansion. This was an opportunity to work with some wonderful colleagues and to visit a wide array of secondary schools in Canada and the U.S. As before, Cliff was an enthusiastic supporter of the program and my roles with it. In 2000, I was asked to become executive director of the California International Baccalaureate Organization (CIBO). I launched the CIBO office from my desk in our second-floor loft, where it operated for the next five years.

When we weren't on the road, Cliff resumed work on his manuscript. But he was finding it more and more challenging and was easily diverted. He found it much more fun to write the likes of the long letter about growing up in Manila that he sent to Dick Moore after Barbara died, or to go for a hike on the mountain or head for the village below our house to have a latte and conversation at Jeannie's Java Shop in the Boardwalk shopping center.

When family and friends urged him, nagged him, to get on with the project, he balked. "There's just so much more to tell," he would protest. He felt the project was bigger than he'd bargained for. "This needs more scholarly research, cross verification of facts and allegations." If not the manuscript, we urged, then write down the marvelous stories you've told us, tell about your own life.

In September of 2006, the manuscript lay in his files, incomplete.

In October of 2004, five Forsters gathered at Point Lobos, California, to celebrate the life of Cliff's sister Gerry.

35

L'ENVOI

ON SUNDAY EVENING SEPTEMBER 9TH, 2006, Cliff finished reading a news magazine, gathered up assorted papers (including a story grandson Wyn had been working on for his eighth-grade English class while visiting us earlier in the day), and started upstairs. He lost his balance and fell backwards, hitting his head. He never regained consciousness and died ten days later.

Throughout his life—as he progressed from binational teenager, to prisoner of war, to sailor in the U.S. Navy, to university student, to career Foreign Service officer, and finally to productive retiree—Clifton Forster traveled the same highways and byways. The moral compass for this journey was set in his Manila childhood. Whether formally at work or exploring on his own, Cliff drew inspiration from encounters along the way, savored life's challenges, and never failed to seize an opportunity to participate in the dialogues of the day—across frontiers as well as in the company of intimate friends and family.

As for so many of his generation, World War II was a searing and formative interlude. Becoming an enemy alien in the country of his birth was an experience Cliff and his fellow internees learned to live with at the time and carried thereafter as part of their lifetime intellectual and emotional baggage. Even now, approaching the second decade of the twenty-first century, the survivors of Santo Tomas and Los Baños—and six decades later their numbers are declining—gather every February to celebrate the dates the camps were liberated. Many wrote books about their experiences; many others reserved discussion of those difficult times for the friends who were there. Cliff loved to tell tales of internment, the upbeat ones that had a spot of humor. It speaks to his character that he spent the majority of his professional years getting to know and working with the citizens of Japan, and attempted to understand and tell the story of the general whose military triumph had turned his world upside down.

Cliff is gone, but his stories live on in our memories. Many of the stories were never written down, but he left surprising treasures in that tea chest, enough to weave together an account of his encounters and insights, to go back and accompany him along his journey crossing frontiers both cultural and political.

The internationalism that was a constant through Cliff's life has passed on to the next generation, and the next. Our farmer son branched out from his island community to become involved in sustainable-agriculture initiatives on a national and global scale, meeting with decision-makers in Washington D.C. and extending his work onto a world stage in Rio, Johannesburg, Rome, and most recently at the United Nations in New York. Our professor daughter has written, in Spanish, a history of the indigenous and marginalized people of Guatemala as her gift to those friends who shared their stories for her research. Our sailor son, who spent many years visiting factories in Asia, Latin America, and the Middle East as a representative of Old Navy, owned a business in California in partnership with a factory owner in Turkey and continues to work with colleagues in Asia. Our oldest grandchild Nathan majored in international relations in college and currently is in Paraguay working with farmers as a Peace Corps volunteer. His sister returned to the United Nations for the fourth time this year leading a delegation of students from Orcas Island to participate in the Sustainable Agriculture and Rural Development meetings held there for two weeks every May.

The news of Cliff's passing stirred many fond memories among family members of course, but also a legion of friends and former colleagues. At the memorial service held in November at St. Stephen's Church in Belvedere, near the shores of San Francisco Bay, I was surprised and touched by the many familiar faces filling the pews, from so many eras of Cliff's life. Classmates and fellow internees from the Philippines. Dick Moore and Hal Mason, fellow summer lumberjacks who had earned their Stanford spending money in the Northern California redwoods. Numerous Foreign Service friends including Harry Kendall, Dave Hitchcock, and Bill Lane—former Ambassador to Australia and publisher of *Sunset,* whom Cliff had gone to meet on that fateful day in Manila when he was hit by the truck.

Gerry's son Charles, age sixty-five, attended with his wife, his sons, and two grandsons. Friends we had made during our eleven years in Marin County gathered to celebrate Cliff's life, as did a contingent of teachers from Southern California with whom I had worked while director of CIBO. They adored Cliff and later created a CIBO award for IB students, the "Cliff and Nancy Forster Lifelong Learning Scholarship."

Although unable to attend the memorial service, Takuchi Ito, who had so eagerly accompanied Cliff in his Homma treasure hunt, wrote to the family from Tokyo:

> Together with those former Japanese colleagues of mine who had the privilege of working for the late Mr. Clifton Forster at different times from the 1950s through the 1970s at the U.S. Embassy in Tokyo, I would like to offer my deep condolences to you on his untimely passing.
>
> As I recall Forster-san, if I may call him so out of my affectionate respect for him, he was above all a man of embracing personal warmth. Wherever he was, for instance, in our office environment, Forster-san's presence alone had the effect of making people around him feel at ease, even at those moments that were tense and stressful, which was the norm of our days at the office.
>
> In dealing with us Japanese coworkers, Forster-san was a passionate leader who expected every one of us to do his/her

best toward our common cause: building U.S.-Japan relations on a more stable and durable basis—at a time in the postwar history when the Japanese were finally ready, during the 1970s, to look for their place in the world community. And we did our best to live up to his expectations. But once he was back to his private self, Cliff Forster-san was always filled with avuncular warmth as he dealt with us Japanese members of his staff.

After he had retired from the Foreign Service, Forster-san revisited Japan a number of times. On one such occasion, I was asked (myself being a retiree by then) to go to Kamakura with him to meet a close relative of an imperial Japanese army general who had passed away a few decades earlier in the Philippines. On our way back to Tokyo by train, Forster-san reminisced just momentarily, it seemed to me, about an episode dating back to his mid-teen years when he and his parents were forced to spend in Manila in the early 1940s in captivity by the imperial Japanese army. He was on this subject for no more than ten seconds or so. In what was unsaid—and has remained so ever since—I could see again the kind of genuinely warmhearted, compassionate person that Forster-san was, and it is how he will live forever in our memory. He was forgiving—always.

Lastly, during his official life spent in Japan he had won a great many true friends and admirers among academicians, journalists, artists, and private citizens. In the early 1970s it so happened that a prominent Japanese political scientist was invited by *Foreign Affairs* magazine to do an article on Japanese politics within the framework of U.S.-Japan relations. The first person the Japanese author chose to meet and ask for personal advice about the precise structure of his article, as he was getting ready to put his thought on paper, turned out to be no one but Forster-san. The author had called on Forster-san a number of times until he put the finishing touches to his article. There and then, I saw two minds bound together in true rapport and trust in each other's wisdom, impartial judgment, and personal integrity. I feel privileged to have cherished this episode to this day, and I will keep it to myself for years to come.

With my sincerest thankfulness and Sayonara to Forster-san.
Takuchi Ito (USIS Tokyo, 1953–1984)

Mark Peattie, who had gone from his USIS career—for which he had
been trained as a Japanese language officer—into one as a professor of
Japanese history, spoke at the service at St. Stephen's.

My name is Mark Peattie and I speak of Cliff Forster as a
longtime friend and as a colleague in the United States Foreign
Service.

I first met Cliff in the late 1950s during my assignment as
a field officer with the U.S. Information Service in northern Japan. At the time, he was a regional officer with the same service
in central Japan. Later, when I was assigned to our field post in
Kyoto, I served under him when he was the field program supervisor in Tokyo.

In those days, the Information Service was engaged in what
is now called public diplomacy—explaining American values
and purposes to foreign audiences, in our case to those in Japan.
While today's headlines trumpet an American war on terror, in
that time we were engaged in a contest between ideas—democratic versus totalitarian. It was waged in the Japanese press, on
television, on lecture platforms, in university seminars, on the
shelves of bookstores and libraries, in the reading rooms of our
American cultural centers, and in all those places where, in a
democracy, ideas can and should be weighed, tested, and sorted
out for public enlightenment and judgment.

For any American to participate in it effectively, it was a
contest which required a particular set of qualities. By heritage,
training, experience, and inclination Clifton Forster had all of
them.

The contest required American professionalism, intelligence,
and resolve. A courageous and public-spirited father, a youth
spent in the Philippines, two years in a Japanese prison camp,
several years in Naval Intelligence, and wide reading and training at Yale provided all these qualities in full. Those qualities

in turn undergirded his devotion to America's finest principles
and his confidence in our mission to explain the United States
to our Japanese friends.

The competition in ideas called for sensitivity and understanding. Cliff saw, and made the rest of us see, that in the
turbulence of colliding ideas our enemy was a corrosive ideology,
not those persons who were beguiled by it. Yet Cliff knew that
neither side had a monopoly on truth and that in the babble of
disagreement, in order to make yourself heard, you had to listen. Cliff knew how to listen.

The American effort required enthusiasm. Not mindless
cheerleading for a set of bureaucratically designed policies, but
a genuine spirit of optimism, initiative, and resilience born of a
belief that America, for all its faults, stood for hope, generosity,
and fair play. This spirit was innate in Cliff, whose zest, humor,
and fundamental decency were central to our sense of professional camaraderie.

The contest needed wisdom, patience, and perspective.
While some in our service saw our field posts—the American
Cultural Centers—as ready ammunition to be expended if need
be in the heat of ideological battle, Cliff believed that their value, created slowly in small ways over time, was their acceptance
by Japanese communities as important local institutions. He
believed that this acceptance was precious currency to be spent
wisely and carefully.

The contest required trust by those who listened to us.
Such trust could only be earned by confidence in the integrity,
understanding, and openheartedness of the Americans who
worked among them. Clifton was the gold standard of public
service in this regard. Those of us who served in the field after
he had left Japan reaped the rich harvest of good will that he
had sown years before.

I have spoken too long and yet have said not enough. Perhaps it is sufficient to assert that Clifton Forster was respected,
cherished, and now is mourned by his colleagues. No finer gentleman ever served this republic.

Tom also spoke at the memorial service, sharing his personal "Reflections on Dad's Life."

How does a son tell the tale of a father to a gathering such as this? Can a son know himself without knowing his father? I know and knew my father through his telling of the life he made with Mom, and the lives of his heroes. I last sat here in this church with Mom the first time she came to a Sunday service after Dad's death. We heard a sermon on heroes that Jim Ward gave, and listened to how, in the circle of humans telling stories, heroes are made, history enacted, identity conferred, truth told and challenged. My childhood was filled with stories—magical, bigger-than-life stories of daring and humorous exploits, mischievous and heroic tales—told in circles of relatives, family friends, and fellow travelers and tellers of stories.

As I grew older the stories got more serious—from famine and earthquakes, to wartime incarceration in the Philippines, to political drama and even dangerous moments in Asia. Mixed in with stories of tragic history were always the humane and the comic stories. For years, our dinner tables and evenings with family friends were filled with the funny and the outrageous as well as the grave and pending—the stories of the present reality. For quite a few years in Tokyo, Dad and Mom participated in a play-reading club of fellow Foreign Service and other gaijin longtimers in postwar Japan. We children did our own enactments, and one of our recent joys has been watching enactments that grandchildren have performed for their grandparents.

As a marauding young teenager in Japan and with my accomplices for good and evil, sister Cindy and brother Doug, we created our own stories, often with close families such as the Moores and Nichols, in fabled locations like Akamon among the forests and temples of Nikko and in shared beach vacations on the Japan coast. Life, in being retold, became drama, and the retelling of our dramas was constant—"remember the time when Tom rolled out of the car as a baby?" For us kids, as perhaps all kids, repeatedly force-fed story-food can induce nausea and other strange reactions, but children have children and learn that such reaction is part of the story, too.

A major thread through narratives that swirled in and around our family life was an extolling of service to human dignity and justice. Dad's commitment to the Foreign Service during the Cold War years and Mom's teaching world history in international schools riveted this legacy of service into our family psyche. Dad's own life story was riveted by his father's service as a Red Cross official in Asia. With the handing down of these storylines, we kids had our own rebellions and reconstructions to work through. It was hard not to question the truth in the telling, coming of age in the years of Woodstock and the peace and feminist movements of the late sixties and seventies.

Through the lengthening of my own life story, I see now that the greatest gift Dad bequeathed was a drive to seek the stories of people and cultures—not just in a superficial way, but to really know and appreciate history, religion, language, and politics. Together Mom and Dad celebrated learning to live amongst individuals from cultures divided by language and history, finding common ground through friendship and shared experience. I see this gift passed to Cindy and Doug. I see it in Nathan, Taylor Anne, Makala, and Wyn, and in so many extended family and friends, including those of you gathered here to honor Clifton Forster, a man who loved people and loved life.

But back to what it was like to have a dad like Cliff. Stepping into his moccasins was not easy. As you know, he grew up in the golden twilight of American empire on Manila Bay in the 1930s. Dad was sixteen when that familiar world collapsed with the Japanese invasion of the Philippines in 1942. One of the stories of survival in the prison of Santa Tomas was through dramatic performance and theater. After the trauma of a sudden and forever changed world, marked by hostile and dangerous conditions in Santa Tomas, someone else might have retreated into a safe domestic career in the U.S. But no, Dad was driven to serve a world in need of rebuilding and new understanding to prevent repetition of global conflict and war.

So he became a student and friend of the culture that was his family's captor, Japan. His devotion to rebuilding Japanese-U.S. relations spanned more than three decades. He was mid-wife to sister cities, a cultural affairs officer not afraid to push what Washington thought appropriate. He sought out cultural adventures like early electronic jazz, rock musicals like *Hair,* and other avant-guard cultural exchange projects. They all became stories of our life in Japan—and my, did he record, collect, and archive, using whatever technology the times made available.

For much of the last twenty years Dad assembled amazing archives of all the stories he and Mom lived over half a century together and stories of their parents and earlier generations. Of course, the way that stories of origins and adventure, history and politics are told reflect the teller's values. As the tellers' son, I admit I struggled with some of the values that shaped the stories and their morals. But the important thing I learned is that my own identity took shape in relation to the content of the rich texts of both Dad's and Mom's lives.

As you all know, Dad could connect with people so well. He could also be somewhat disconnected by the very power of his own story. Yet in the twenty years after retirement, Cliff enjoyed connecting with and watching the professions of his children and the personalities of his grandchildren evolve, even participating in a discussion on globalization and empire led by his grandson Nathan on our Orcas Island farm. Dad had what we called "Cliffisms," his own maddeningly endearing ways, like his stubborn insistence on reading every guidebook ever printed, or his long ritualistic healthy breakfast preparations.

I cannot end this reflection on Dad's life without extolling the character and strength of his wife, our mother, Nancy. Partners for fifty-seven years, Dad was not Dad without Mom. Theirs was a union of purpose and service, a model for so many, bearing witness with humor, and through the telling and retelling of stories, to a vision of a world with dignity and understanding that is nothing if not inspirational. Mom is without doubt the central backbone that held everything together for Dad and for our family. Her strength was Dad's strength, and their strength together carried them through so much life.

Dad abruptly fell from his still very active life, on the verge of a new adventure with Mom and their friends the Peatties to the eastern Mediterranean and Turkey. He so loved living for the next adventure, so loved life's small daily joys, that I imagine the way he left so abruptly might be what he would have chosen, if not the timing. His final act became a gift to his family, bringing our family closer together, and now you, his larger family and good friends. He would love to have exactly this gathering here happen, and encourage the telling of stories. Dad would love to be here in the flesh with all of us, and we can rest assured that he hears and feels our love today.

During the brief period Charles Forster and his family spent together in their Oakland home following repatriation from Japanese custody, Cliff and his father found a slice of a large redwood burl and inscribed on it verses from a poem by Rudyard Kipling. Once completed, their handiwork hung above their fireplace. When that house was sold, the burl became Cliff's family treasure, and still hangs in the final home we shared together.

Fires

Men make them fires on the hearth
Each under his roof-tree,
And the Four Winds that rule the earth
They blow the smoke to me.

With every shift of every wind
The homesick memories come,
From every quarter of mankind
Where I have made me a home.

Across the high hills and the sea
And all the changeful skies,
The Four Winds blow the smoke to me
Till the tears are in my eyes.

Oh, you Four Winds that blow so strong
And know that this is true,
Stoop for a little and carry my song
To all the men I knew!

ACKNOWLEDGEMENTS

I AM GRATEFUL TO THE MANY people who helped me tell the story of Cliff Forster's encounters.

Lydia Bird, editor *par excellence*, nurtured me through valuable additions, deletions, and clarifications as we worked together over many productive months. She helped turn a compilation of records and memories into a coherent narrative, then shepherded me through the complex process of book production.

Hiromichi Ito not only introduced Cliff to the general's daughter and served as a valuable assistant in the early days of his research on Masaharu Homma, but also reviewed the Homma chapters and helped locate photos for this book.

Hisako Inomata, despite her reluctance to offer interviews, graciously agreed to meet and share recollections of her father with Cliff.

The family of Major John Skeen generously provided copies of crucial correspondence pertaining to the trial of General Homma.

Masayuki Ito of the Hatano Gyosei Service Center in the Sado City Office kindly gave his time to research and send me photos of the Homma monument.

Lewis Schmidt, at the behest of the U.S. Information Agency, traveled from Washington to Honolulu to record Cliff's Foreign Service story for diplomatic archives.

Eva Weintraub read the chapter on Israel and made important suggestions.

Cliff's two good friends from internment days—Jackie Flannery Kathe and Marge Hoffman Tileston—read chapters on that experience, and Marge shared her diary-burning story and the letter Cliff wrote her grandparents.

Dick Moore, after the death of his wife Barbara, urged Cliff to write down childhood memories, thus preserving the stories in Cliff's voice.

Shigeo Imamura extended the hand of friendship when we arrived in Matsuyama and gave us important insights from the point of view of a Japanese citizen born in the United States and trained to revere and fight bravely for his ancestral homeland.

Charles Howard passed on valuable papers saved by his mother, Gerry. Additionally, he meticulously reviewed and commented on the first proof of the manuscript, contributing important insights and corrections."

Greg Fields captured the spirit of *Encounters* in his cover design and produced the informative interior maps.

Son Tom and granddaughter Makala worked with me to select appropriate photos from the family archives.

Lou Gopal, producer of the 2006 documentary *Victims of Circumstance* about the civilian internment experience in the Philippines, provided still photos from his collection.

Daphne Phillips devoted her professional skills to putting the photos, many of them old and in poor condition, into publishable form.

A devoted corps of professional colleagues accompanied Cliff, actively engaging in international dialogues to achieve mutual respect and understanding—and they had a lot of fun together in the process.

Mark Peattie read an early draft of the manuscript and provided valued support, support bolstered by other distinguished internationalists who read and commented.

John Hall quickly answered the distress call every time I encountered difficulties with my computer, thus enabling me to continue writing.

Friends of many nationalities, in each of the places we lived, enhanced the adventures that make up this book.

Last, but far from least, my children Tom, Cindy, and Doug, as well
as many other family members and friends, patiently listened to Cliff's
stories, urged him to write them down, then encouraged me as I took
over where he left off.

Tiburon, California
September, 2009

NANCY KEENEY FORTSER shared the adventures and absorbed the stories of Clifton Forster for nearly six decades. Together, they journeyed across cultural frontiers from California to the Philippines, Japan, Burma, Washington, D.C., Israel, Hawaii, and back to California. During those years, Forster developed her own career as an educator in international schools and an administrator, inspector, and director in the International Baccalaureate (IB) program. She lives in Tiburon, California.